MAGIC
AND
FATE

MAGIC

AND

FATE

*Being the Not Quite Believable
Adventures of Sissie Slipper*

Rachel Billington

MACMILLAN

First published 1996 by Macmillan

an imprint of Macmillan General Books
25 Eccleston Place London SW1W 9NF
and Basingstoke

Associated companies throughout the world

ISBN 0-333-63234-6

'Rainforest' by Judith Wright (first published
by Angus and Robertson, Sydney) is quoted
with the permission of the author (page 179).

1 3 5 7 9 8 6 4 2

A CIP catalogue record for this book is available from
the British Library

Typeset by CentraCet Limited, Cambridge
Printed by Mackays of Chatham PLC, Chatham, Kent

To Suzy

Chapter One

In which Sissie, Super-model, finds that Pride comes before a Fall and Sven swears that Vengeance follows Death.

THE LIGHTS GLARED, flared, dazzled. Head up, chin down, glide along the mirror image. Widen eyes, headlamps beaming forward, part lips, white teeth gleaming, swivel hips and swing legs, soon to be sweeping round at the point of the pier where the sea thunders, the roar of the crowd, waves breaking dangerously. *It's going well.*

The point is reached, the silver figure poised, slender arms slightly raised, dripping silver beads from armpit to elbow, head capped with a swathing of purple shimmer, unwinding down the shoulder-blades in fin-like points of metallic glitter. High heels of glass, six inches high, lifting the tube legs so that they seemed not to touch the reflective smoothness beneath. Magnificent! *Extraordinaire*! Glorious! A triumph!

I'm glorious, a triumph. Sissie knew it, felt the thrill of it at the turn, poised like a silver fish, tail out of water, crystal drops spinning out round her, sparking off the eyes of her admiring audience. All eyes on her. Focus, cynosure. Three years for this. Three cheers for Sissie.

Behind the lights, behind the crowd, Rudolf peered, cutting a path of darkness and anxiety. Arms crossed, brow low, silver hair the only thing that gleamed, even though his suit was pinstriped with silky pink. He tapped one foot. A beat. He had chosen no music. The clothes were enough, he had said in interviews, to Sven, to colleagues, friends, his mother. 'La musique? C'est vraiment

1

nécessaire?' But now he taps his foot. The crowd is baying as the model poises, a silver purple comet above the earthliness. The crowd is making the music of applause, appreciation, awe and admiration. Rudolf's foot stills and his brow raises. With one hand he smooths down his jacket and with the other he raises the points of his silver hair till they stand up like well-beaten meringue. *It is perfection*. For a second his eye is off the catwalk.

One glass heel, returning from its pirouette at the end of the pier, shivers on the edge of the mirror, hardly caught, merely brushing thinly across the surface. Sissie feels it, moves her arm a little wider to right the balance, remembers that strength comes from the centre and holds her abdominals tight and hard. The shoe is round now to take over the glide from its partner, back along the Milky Way, unrolling in front of her to the music of the stars. Headlamps forward, lips parted, swivel hips, swing legs . . . Out, out into outer space the heel spins, chips off the planet into an orbit above the crowd, disappearing into darkness. A glass projectile, six inches long, glittering as it goes like an icicle, a stalactite. Abdominals are no use now. Sissie falls, crashes noisily off the slippery edge of her path, arms knocked, legs knocked, body whacked by her scintillating tail as she cartwheels over the side. Finally her face gets a crack.

But models are made of the sternest stuff. Sissie feels no pain, not even, yet, the anguish of humiliation. She just wants to get back up there and finish the job. *I've got to get up*. The crowds have withdrawn, the tide turned, the waves breaking backwards with a squashing, whispering noise, so she has space as she clambers back on, and she has the sense to remove the good, well-behaved shoe. Let the remains of the other cling to her foot, for all she cares.

She's made a bit of ground in her fall but there's still three-quarters to cover. Eyes wide, chin down, legs six inches shorter but she's walked in bare feet before. Swing along, Sissie, beautiful, magnificent Sissie.

Rudolf is frozen. In his hand he holds the glass heel which shot towards him, its master, so that he could hardly avoid catching it. It feels like an icicle in his heart, a cold wound that has stunned him into immobility. Worse, far worse, is to follow. He looks up, attention caught by renewing of flashlight's glare. He cannot believe she is coming down towards him. Why did she not fall into a black hole, dive out of the light in all her glory, his glory, and disappear? At very least, why did no one shroud her in darkness and remove her from his stage? But here she is, hips swivelling, head up, a travesty, a mockery of all he had created, blood, scarlet, oozing into droplets through her metallic clothing.

Sissie, feeling the sea returning again with a whoosh and the flashlights popping, rises above the pain, which is now beginning to drag at her knees and elbows and across one thigh, and bares her teeth in a terrific no-holds-barred smile.

A ghastly shiver takes Rudolf's pink pinstriped body and the icicle in his heart, melting slightly, leaks out through his eyes. *Xciy ggryt njuut logftt?* Which, in an obscure East European language, means, 'Has it all come to this?' For Sissie's smile, so well intended, so brave, so English indeed in its attempt to discount the reality, has revealed the mouth of a witch, a black hole where a front tooth should be, a hag, an old crone with, perhaps, a touch of the vampire where a trickle of blood shows up dark against the whiteness of the still pure incisors.

It was when the crowd began to laugh that Rudolf clutched his chest as if the glass heel which, incidentally, he still held, had pierced his heart. At just this moment, Sven appeared at his side, his large blondness all dressed in white as if for a wedding. He was in time to see Sissie making her exit, giving a last flirtatious swirl of blood and tatters, smiling her ghastly smile to ribald whistles and cheers which she, brave dupe, thought adulation.

Sven, usually the man of action in an artistic partnership which had been through its ups and downs but was thought at last to be heading for the big up, hesitated. Maybe he estimated the time for action past. He stood at Rudolf's side, staring outwards but close enough to hear what was the great man's final word: '*Kill*', or something like it, since before he could elucidate the syllable into command, explanation or expletive, Sven felt a curious sliding sensation at his side and, turning quickly, saw that Rudolf's mouth had fallen open, that he was sliding downwards. Just in time, Sven caught him under the elbows, held him up with his superb muscles, and then, spotting an unoccupied chair, eased him into it. As he did so, there was a sharp tinkle as the glass heel fell from Rudolf's unclenched hand and dropped to the floor.

Death was not outside Sven's experience. So many of his friends had died from Aids that at night he dreamt of thirteenth-century Europe when bubonic plague was raging. He was surprised to wake up between clean sheets instead of a rat-infested straw-filled mattress. Sometimes he was surprised to wake up at all.

Yet holding up the lifeless form of his beloved Rudolf – even the meringues on his head were drooping – was a step into a new profundity of outrage. Rudolf had survived so much, living through a different war as a child. He had his own nightmares unspoken, a history where even Sven did not venture. 'Paris is my garden of paradise,' he used to say in one of the seven or eight obscure languages that he patronized. In Paris he had triumphed, in Paris he had failed, overcome failure, one heart attack, and was about to triumph again.

At this very moment he should be receiving the homage due to a great designer, an unrivalled master, a superb moulder, a garment sculptor, a presenter of the human body with the drama of genius. Instead he sat on one of his own gold chairs, hired at such expense, with the word 'kill' lingering on his lips and the ribald laughter of his uncouth guests crashing about his ears.

Sven was filled with black and terribly Nordic anger. Huge already, he swelled up and almost out of his suit. 'The maestro is gone!' His voice, once, though briefly, trained for operatic purposes, bellowed through the high-pitched twitterings and gigglings, the whispering of paper-pushing journalists, the clicking and popping and jumping and even running of over-active photographers. They were still enjoying themselves.

The maddened voice reached even Sissie where she stood solitary among the racks of exquisite clothes. At the end of the racks was a mirror, large, ornately framed in gold, a little foxed with age, the sort of mirror that you would expect to see in a ballroom on a film set for *War and Peace* or *Gone with the Wind*. But now it leant casually against the wall, like the whole room, disordered, glamorous, unexpected. Sissie knew the mirror well. It was a famous mirror, a talisman for Rudolf over the thirty-odd years of his career. The walls it had leant against hardly bore thinking of, but once only it had hung and that was when he had shown in the Marquesa della Fiori's Villa Principia in Rome and six servants had hung it from a golden chain. Later, the holes made by the six nails necessary to sustain its weight had caused the ancient wall to crumble and the Marquesa, ever fickle and notoriously mean, had sent the bill for its repair to Rudolf. It had been calculated on the basis of restoring an ancient monument, as Rudolf pointed out philosophically. At the peak of his success, he paid with generous protestation of sorrow but the mirror never hung again.

Each time Sissie looked in the mirror, she saw a noble line of models, her predecessors and her rivals. The foxy patches gave a life of its own to the mirror, which made it difficult to be certain how truthful was the reflection. The mirror kept the models on their toes, Rudolf admitted privately to Sven. They could not know if they had yet found perfection: they needed him to tell them. Yet, ever hopeful, they still looked.

'What is it? What is it?' Sissie cried, as she came off the catwalk. And her dresser, a young Greek girl struck dumb with shock, took her to the mirror. So there she stands, staring at an image that all the foxing in the world cannot make anything but horrendous. The gap-toothed smile is worst of all, of course, but even such a sudden ageing by fifty years might not have been so convincing without the transformation of magic clothing into rags and glowing tubular limbs into the bloody skin and bones of a battered old hag.

Into her concentrated gaze of despair there intruded Sven's bellow of pain. Words did not carry but the pain did. *Sven has always hated me. Sven will kill me.* Thus, unconsciously, Sissie echoed Rudolf's last word. Never in the years that followed did it cross Sven's mind as odd that someone as pacific as Rudolf should have chosen such an untypical final emotion and that maybe it had been a quite different word in one of the five or more languages he didn't understand, 'kiel' perhaps, or 'keil' or 'keel' or 'cyl'. It was possible, after all, that he had not even finished the word and it would have become 'kilt' or 'kilted' or any other non-murderous variation.

Naturally Sven's bellow not only silenced the crowd but also drew them to where he stood, a large avenging angel above Rudolf, who was slumped as far as the gilt chair allowed, in his deathly

5

elegance and, if you overlooked the pinstriped suit, not unlike Christ deposed from His cross. In a moment the flashlights were heartily at work. Too late, Sven realized his mistake. Even in death Rudolf was not to avoid humiliation. Important clients, it is hardly worth noting, had speedily left the macabre scene for something more up-beat.

'What a way to go!' exclaimed one excited paparazzo, as if in admiration. Amazed at the panache of these cold-hearted vultures, Sven's gaze swung blearily from face to face. His anger had exploded in that one counter-productive bellow and now he was becoming entombed in grief. Gathering what willpower remained, he turned to a dresser, an assistant, the media-relations director who, now that it was too late, stood around their master's chair. At least, most stood: the Greek dresser crawled under the chair whence she retrieved the guilty glass heel. She already held the whole shoe and the broken shoe, collected, presumably, from where Sissie had abandoned them.

Turning to these colleagues, Sven said with an effort, 'Ambulance?'

'A medic is already on his way,' pronounced a young man with an American accent and an air of efficiency.

'A medic,' repeated Sven wonderingly. In his mind he saw a tall, pale-faced man wearing a black Homburg, a long black overcoat and carrying a black leather bag. This was the kind of solemnity to pronounce death on his dear genius.

Meanwhile the salon was clearing of people. Someone snapped off the catwalk spots so that only four uplighters remained, stationed in each corner of the room like sentinels, lighting nothing but a cracked ceiling and a corner of not very elegant plaster moulding. At the same time, a team of highly energetic boys began to stack and remove the rows of gilt chairs, destined shortly for another show. 'Life must go on,' proclaimed their every bend and lift and stack and carry. No one had the strength to object, although the young American did wave away their leader when he appeared with a piece of paper, perhaps a bill to be signed.

Sissie prised herself from the mirror. Shrugging herself out of the remains of her once scintillating costume, she examined her battered body. For someone who had known bodily perfection all her life, it was a nasty shock. Really, just about unbelievable. What she needed, of course, was a nice sensible person to point out that cuts mended and bruises faded and, if she paid out some of her savings, she could end up with frontal teeth no less pearly than those she possessed before – and more lasting. Film stars, she might have been told further, chose to knock out their natural ivory for the perfection of artifice. Not everyone springs delectable from their mother's womb. Bleaching, cosmetic fillings, porcelain veneers, implants and creative bridges are all within the modern woman's grasp.

Sissie was alone, all attention gathered round the lifeless form of Rudolf. Even now her fellow models were striding and whirling at the next show for she had been the last to appear, the grand climax, the bride. Her only companions were the ranks of glorious clothes, hanging round her in their empty splendour.

'Oh! Ah! Oh!' Sissie wailed at last, moaned and cried. Tears came to join the blood from her mouth. Crouching, slick and pink and slender in her body-stocking, she was more like a huge hairless stick insect than a human being. Everything hurt now, not just the sight of things. Rising a little, she snatched a whiff of pastel chiffon from a hanger and wound it round her face. Comforted by the feel of it – a designer crêpe bandage worth thousands – she tore down another and another. This mauve and lemon blouse would do for her knee, this lilac with lime for her thigh. The blood seeping through the thin material made a pretty shape as if a scarlet butterfly had landed on a vase of sweet peas.

This profligate behaviour had not even the excuse of Rudolf's passing away, the value of his designs dying with him, as it were, for Sissie did not realize he was dead. Her actions were entirely self-centred. So absorbed was she in her bandaging, that it came as a shocking surprise when her solitude was shattered by two men and a woman bursting from between a white fake-ermine cape and a long pink satin tunic with silver buttons. (Sissie had modelled both earlier.)

The leader of the group, spotting the girl – not hard to miss with her sweet-pea chiffon decorated with bloody butterflies – leapt towards her, spouting efficient French commands over his shoulder.

7

The man behind opened a bag he carried and in a trice Sissie was recumbent on the floor with the three crouched round her, testing her every this and that.

Unsure whether she wanted to be the centre of so much medical attention, however well meaning, Sissie struggled to sit up. 'I'm not dying, you know.'

'Qu'est-ce qu'elle a dit?' The doctor, hand on Sissie's pulse, looked up enquiringly.

'She said she's not dying.' The girl, speaking in English, gave Sissie a frown. She should not be a spoilsport when surrounded by so much special talent.

'Je ne suis pas en train de mourir!' yelled Sissie, letting the chiffon drop from her mouth. 'What I need is a dentist.'

'Mais, oui . . .' began the girl, looking at her mouth with revulsion. And this was the last attention Sissie was to get for, as if by suction, the whole medical team suddenly disappeared from her side into the true deathly presence of Rudolf.

'Voilà!' Sissie heard the cry, as if in triumph. 'Voilà, le cadavre!' She had become so thoroughly off-stage that no one cared a jot about her any more. Death comes in many shapes. Recognizing this situation, as if she had seen it waiting all along, Sissie rose from the floor. She must take herself away but first she must know whom death had visited.

Still not certain of her invisibility, she crept and sidled through the same doorway that, not so long ago, had seen the magnificence of her arrival on the runway, her disdainful triumph and too soon after her ridiculous retreat.

This time no one watched her come in. Four deep, they gathered around the body of the fallen maestro. Too late for medical attention, too late for anything but lamentation, which was beginning to get into swing.

'Dead,' whispered Sissie to herself, hugging the dark overhang of the catwalk. 'Rudolf dead?' Like everyone, she knew he had not been well, the heart attack five years ago, an operation, various unspecified problems perhaps linked to a fondness for cocaine when his career had hit the doldrums. But dead? Impossible for Sissie to link her own falling down with this unimaginable tragedy. Rudolf had been everything to her, he had created her. He had turned her into a young goddess. She was the queen of the catwalk. People came to shows because she was as much part of the display as the glorious garments. Her face and/or body filled magazines all over the world, slim nose, silver blue eyes, smooth high brow, sculptured mouth, translucent skin, long neck, black shiny hair, delicately moulded shoulders, collar-bones, high rounded breasts, dark pink nipples, ribcage just visible, navel round and neat, hips sloping gently, thighs smooth and shapely, knees elegant, legs and feet long and graceful. Even her toes were perfect, each nail symmetrically oval, the joints as pretty as the joints in her hands which, of all her features, were probably the best.

Sissie groaned. When Rudolf had discovered her, she had been a hand artist, called in by commercial producers to open packets of cornflakes, turn the knobs on dishwashers, wield the tin-opener or lay out the catfood dish. He had transformed her into the glory girl.

Edging along the side of the catwalk, Sissie came from floor level to behold exactly what was happening. Most of the photographers had already dashed away, holding their cameras defiantly aloft. They must catch their deadlines without delay, reveal to the world the macabre death of Rudolf at the climax of victory. It was not for them to write the headlines or even the story, but their cameras were vivacious witnesses to all the delights of tragedy. Off they slid, skating down the runway, fleety, flinty messengers of death.

This left the medics in charge. The rubber-soled doctor, with his sharp French commands, despite being half the size of Sven in his white suit, had all the energy of someone with a job to do, not much time and no interest in haute couture. Death was old hat to him. Rudolf's death was routine old hat, although the photographers had been a nuisance. If they had not skated off when they did, he would have clapped his hands at them until they rose, like vultures from the carcass, and dispersed into thin air.

'Tenez!' he ordered now, and 'Apportez!' A stretcher appeared out of nowhere, Rudolf placed upon it in a trice, Sven, like a colourless, deflated balloon, sagging over him.

Sissie wished to get nearer, to talk to Sven, find out exactly what had happened. But the speed of events and the consciousness of her disagreeable appearance (it would be a long time before she could get over the feeling that beauteousness is next to godliness and its opposite a sin best hidden) made her hang back until it was too late. In a matter of seconds the cadaver on its bier, hardly visible for the entourage that surrounded it, had exited.

Only the golden chair remained, a throne without a king.

Trailing clouds of bloody gossamer, Sissie made her way towards it and sat down. Rudolf was dead. She pronounced the words to herself but they did not sink into her brain. Neither did she link his death with her own downfall except with a vague sense that tragedy had struck all round.

Not everyone had left the scene. Behind her she could hear the dressers whispering to the security staff as they pushed the clothes along their rails. These clothes were worth hundreds of thousands, the beading, the draping, the delicately printed colours, some hand-painted on silk as fine as a dawn cobweb. Normally there would be bossy people to wrap them up and treat them as carefully as any living creature but now there were only underlings, hushed by death and reduced to shunting Rudolf's greatest creations backwards and forwards along their tracks like goods trains in a siding. 'Comment ça s'est passé?' said one. 'Qui sait comment ça s'est passé?' responded another. Perhaps they were worried about their jobs! *There is nothing for me here.* Sissie stood up, took a tottering, venturesome step towards the door.

The streets of Paris were warm, wet and very clean. In the dusk of middle evening – it was about nine o'clock – the smooth surface of the road and pavements shone as if they had been polished. There were few people around and Sissie, wrapped in a long, silvery grey mackintosh, felt ghost-like, invisible. As she neared her apartment in the Rue Jacob, she began to doubt the dramatic happenings of the evening. Seb, she hoped, would throw a brighter light on it all.

Chapter Two

In which Sebastien proves himself too Poetic to be much Comfort.

SEBASTIEN WAS writing a poem in praise of Sissie's beauty while shaving his chin. It was the chin's smooth curves as the white foam fell from it that reminded him of the perfection of her knees and which had led him to contemplate further areas of that matchless creation.

'The cream that tastes of snow . . .'

'La neige rappelle de la crème . . .'

Sebastien, who had a French mother and an English father, toyed with his two languages as a way of avoiding responsibility. He contemplated the hand that held the razor, likening the fingers to the branches of a tree, the wrist and forearm to the trunk. Tiresome though these conceits might seem, they reflected Sebastien's admiration of the Jesuit poet Gerard Manley Hopkins, whose meticulous noting of nature, whether clouds, trees or grasses, he was hoping to apply to the human body. Abandoning his own poetic attempts, he bounded, naked, to where Hopkins's notebooks lay open on the studio floor.

All was mist and flue of white cloud, which grew thicker as day went on and like a junket lay scattered on the lakes . . .

This was Swiss mountain scenery but Sebastien preferred Hopkins's description of the English countryside, particularly his seascapes.

I looked down from the cliffs at the sea breaking on the rocks at high water of a spring tide – first, say, it is an install of green marble knotted with ragged white, then fields of white lather, the comb of the wave richly clustered and crisped in breaking . . .

Sebastien hugged himself, suffering from cold and excitement. Sissie! Leaping up from the floor, he remembered promises given. Whatever was the time? He was supposed to have shopped, producing the best that St-Germain-des-Prés could offer including pâté de foie to celebrate Sissie's triumph on the great Rudolf's catwalk. All this he had promised, not once but several times. And he had done nothing. And now it was too late.

Disillusioned with himself, Sebastien wrapped the bedcover around his body and poured himself a glass of flat champagne.

The moment Sissie opened the door, she knew there would be no comfort from Sebastien. He loved her as a beautiful object. His tastes were romantic, adulatory, immature. But, then, so were hers. She wanted to be told that she was more beautiful than Botticelli's *Venus*, than Raphael's *Madonna*, than Leonardo da Vinci's *Mona Lisa* or even Picasso's *Head of a Woman* made from painted iron, sheet metal, springs and found object (colander). His aesthetic appreciation had sustained her belief in herself as she struggled sweatily into body-stockings still smelling of the previous occupant and pushed her itching scalp into yet another too tight wig, which felt as if it were infested with lice. It was not all glory on the catwalk.

But Sebastian of the languid limbs, at least as graceful as her own, who never joined the vulgar crowd who gazed at her – except once when some ancient marchesa friend of his family's had announced her intended presence (in the event she never appeared) – Sebastien, with all his brilliance and education, had picked her as the perfection of young womanhood. This placed her, in her own opinion which was, after all, what counted, high above other successful models. They, too, might hold the crowds for their few seconds of glory and command megabucks for the length of their necks and the swing of their hips, but she, alone, had history behind her. Sebastien stamped her with the imprimatur of past greatness.

Sebastien had decided to use the further half-hour that he had before Sissie's return by creatively negating his failure in the culinary area. Thus he had programmed a little balletic sequence, which he hoped Sissie would join and forget or forgive the lack of bread and pâté. He had enhanced his dress, or undress, for the occasion, winding a turban of one of Sissie's scarves round his head and two strings of pearls round his neck. As soon as he heard Sissie's key in the lock, he bounded like a young Diaghilev and took up a pose in front of the door. One arm pointed upwards, as it were to the gods, and the other stretched out in joyous welcome to his returning nymph.

But now he was faced with a spectacle of nightmare, out of horror, out of ghoul. Sissie had not even remembered to keep her mouth shut so that her black and bloody hole was horribly obvious.

'Oh, Seb!' she cried, knowing in the pit of her that it was all, all, a mistake. He would not console or cuddle her. His white, shocked face, his arm turned from welcoming to fending off, told her this. But still she couldn't stop herself and cried, 'Oh, Seb!' and, 'Look what's happened to me!' and, 'It hurts so much.'

And Sebastien laughed, a good-sized bellow. 'Ha, ha! Make-up credited to Count Dracula. A good joke, Sissie, but too vile to be convincing.'

'I fell,' Sissie reproached him, although she knew he knew, really. 'My shoe broke and Rudolf died. Tomorrow it will be in all the papers and then you'll be sorry.'

Sissie stopped. She heard the petulance in her voice, but where was the tragedy? Rudolf dead. Her fashion father. No joke, this. Only an echo that she could not admit. 'Well, can I come in? Sit down – even have a drink of water? You stand there like a cross between an avenging angel and the Statue of Liberty.'

This made Sebastien move aside enough for Sissie to push past a bronze horse (the apartment was filled with modelled horses) and lower herself with utmost care onto a low couch. The echo, growing, somebody dead, pursued her and with it that dreadful sense of *déjà vu*, which makes the hour turn rancid in the mouth. 'Anyway, I'm sick of it all!' sighed Sissie. 'All that posing and poncing.'

Sebastien now began to recover a little and took a tentative step towards human sympathy. 'Have this glass of champagne. It's deliciously warm and flat. You're probably still in shock. Just try and relax and then tell me all about it. Incidentally, you're bleeding on the sofa.'

The echo was receding. She was in shock, that was all. She should not be angry with Sebastien, for his limits were no narrower than her own. They had chosen each other for their strengths not their weaknesses.

'I'm going for a bath.' Outside the bathroom, the pale leaves of a Virginia creeper hung across the window like a curtain. The room was lined with mirrors reflecting, usually, the perfect beauty of its human occupants. But now Sissie kept her eyes on the window, admiring the shape of the leaves lit from behind by a street lamp, lit from the inside by the one light she had switched on. Slowly she eased herself into the hot water, almost enjoying the sharp pain as it caught her cuts and abrasions. Tendrils of blood, shaped not unlike the creeper, made wavering patterns in the water before diffusing into a general pinkness. As the steam rose and turned the mirrors a misty, milky white, Sissie thought, It's lucky I broke no bones. Although my ribs feel bad. Perhaps I've broken my ribs. Then she thought, Seb and I have had enough of each other. Then she thought, I really, truly, deeply do not want to be a model any more.

It was enough. When Seb came in, carrying between his forefinger and thumb a scoop of caviare, laid on a square of toasted biscuit – a peace-offering found in the kitchen cupboard – Sissie's eyes were closed. Popping the caviare into his own mouth, he stood watching her. Now that her personality was closed off from him, he could stare at her with a just acceptable level of disgust. She had slid so far down in the water that her chin had been washed clean but her eyes ran black with mascara. Her body, veiled as if in gauze by the rose-coloured water and the pearly, moisture-laden air in the bathroom, nevertheless showed signs of the battering she had received from the sharp edge of the catwalk. Blue, green, purple along the ribs and the thighs, dark violet on her knees, deep crimson mottled along one arm. After all, Sebastien found he was not disgusted. She reminded him of the palette of a master.

Sissie opened her eyes. 'No,' she said wearily, seeing him

standing close over her. 'Not now, thank you.' Not ever, she said to herself.

Sebastien wondered whether it was worth pretending that she had misunderstood his attitude in the darkening room. 'I was bringing you a bite of caviare,' he said, in injured tones.

'Well, where is it?'

'Don't be so pedantic. I can always get you another.'

'Why don't you?' Sissie's voice was blatantly hostile. She had woken to a shocking pain in her ribs – in fact, pains in many places – but that wasn't the main point. 'Don't you even want to know what happened?' she called after Sebastien's retreating back, and then groaned.

He didn't. They both knew that – at least, not the true, nasty, untidy, unhappy story. Rudolf has died. *Rudolf has died*. The worst thing, Sissie thought as Sebastien turned round with a blank face of unconvincing attention, is that I cannot understand that. I certainly cannot feel it. I feel the pain round my ribs far more sharply. 'Rudolf's dead,' she said aloud.

'What?' Sebastien was trying to avoid a growing sense of inadequacy and guilt.

'I never thought Rudolf would die. I suppose your first death is sure to be the most unbelievable.'

'My first death was a boy at school.' Sebastien came back to Sissie. There was a generality in her approach, which made him feel more cheerful and able to contribute. 'He was seventeen and he hanged himself on an oak tree on the far boundary of the first-team cricket pitch.'

'You seem to know a lot about him.'

'Actually, I found him.'

Sissie stared. Why was he telling her such a thing when she was suffering so much? This was her moment of tragedy, not his. Sissie imagined what it would be like to have a mature man as a lover, someone who was prepared to make her the centre of attention or, at least, pretend to.

The water stirred and sluiced as Sissie sighed and then rose slowly. Of course Sebastien had receded now that she needed help in stepping out of the bath and towelling herself dry. Perhaps she should go for an X-ray. The idea did not appeal. Those green-clad medics, crouching round her like flies round a corpse – except that it had been the wrong body, not a corpse at all. How quickly they had risen from her and settled on Rudolf instead.

Limping through the flat, shoulders hunched, hands cupping elbows, towel lightly draped, Sissie began to cry, tears dripping and dropping as they might off a not very energetically plumbed fountain. Sebastien saw her from the kitchen and felt distracted enough to eat, yet again, the caviare on toast he'd made for her. Although she was no longer bloody, the bent, shuffling walk made her aged, a parody of age, she who had become famous for her sublime youthfulness.

'O! What a fall was there!' Sebastien muttered to himself as the last egg of caviare slid deliciously down his throat. For a subliminal second he saw the boy's body hanging, like a sack, from the tree.

A little later in the evening Sissie made a decision. 'I shall go to England to get my mouth fixed.'

Sebastien was crouched on the bed beside her, gazing at a picture of a horse's head created out of fur. Since it was a skewbald horse it must have taken someone a lot of time and trouble. 'I wonder,' he mused, 'if I lived here for years and years whether I would get used to the horror of that horse or even, perhaps, become fond of it. Learning to love the thing you hate.'

Sissie did not answer. Empty of food, because she dared put nothing into her broken mouth, except pain-killers, she did not feel like a discussion on the principle of aesthetics. Besides, there was nothing more to be thought or said about this fur stallion, beloved by the owner of the apartment (not her), which had presided over so much of their lovemaking. Sebastien could only have raised the subject to avoid commenting on her departure for England.

Sebastien turned the right way round and, picking up a book, began to read.

'I probably shan't return,' said Sissie, speaking out of the dimness of encroaching sleep.

'Darling, darling, darling Sissie.' Sebastien put down his book and, at last, with great gentleness, tried to hold Sissie in his long arms. Too late.

'Ouch. Aagh.' She slid from him irritably, taking her bruised body as far away to the other side of the bed as she could manage.

'Then I'll read to you instead.

"A beetling baldbright cloud thorough England
Riding: there did storms not mingle? and
Hailropes hustle and grind their
Heavengravel? wolfsnow, worlds of it, wind there?"'

Chapter Three

In which two sisters study photographs of Sissie's and Janice finds much to admire while Mary gets into a rage.

PHOTOGRAPHS OF SISSIE lay all over the table – some had even dropped off onto the floor. Sissie's face so heavily made up that she was hardly recognizable, Sissie's face naked and vulnerable as a young child's, Sissie's face, pink, golden, greenish, topped by huge straw hats, tight cloches, a swimming hat adorned with flower petals at the centre of which a bright eye gleamed.

Two middle-aged women, one smartly turned out in yellow and white, the other drab as a hen pheasant, pulled the photographs this way and that. Actually, they were less interested in the images of Sissie's face than those which at least incorporated her body.

'That's my favourite!' exclaimed the woman in yellow and white greedily. 'Just look at her shoulder, so straight and true, and the line of her neck and her lovely bust under that wisp of chiffon. You look, Mary.' Janice pushed the poster-sized photograph over to her sister.

'It is nice,' agreed Mary, listlessly. 'Her legs are so long and straight I don't know where she got them from.' She put down the photograph. 'Can I have a cup of tea now?'

'In a minute. Now, don't you admire this one? She's on the catwalk, you see, or what they call the slipway in New York. Those shorts with the beading on are worth ten thousand pounds. Can you believe that? And there's another – hold on a minute, I'll see if I can find it – where she's wearing a bikini – a tiny bikini, mind you, hardly enough material to make a napkin – which is worth even more. Here it is. All in the cutting, of course. That's what Sissie told me.'

18

Mary looked obediently but it was obvious her heart wasn't in it. Everything about her suggested that lack of energy and enthusiasm on the wane was a habitual state for her, not merely brought on by too many photographs of a young and outstandingly beautiful woman. 'I'll plug in the kettle, at least.'

'No. Don't you do that.' Janice abandoned the photographs reluctantly. 'You know what you're like with kettles. Forgetting to put water in and burning out the bottom.'

'That was only once, Jan.' A defensive note sharpened the lassitude. 'I do live here on my own, you know.'

'What you do on your own is your business. But while I'm here I want to see we both finish the afternoon alive.'

'Oh, Janice.' Mary went back to the table and, as if to placate the other, began once again to sift through the photographs. Around her head pale lozenges of light danced prettily. They were coming through the lace curtains which guarded the four little windows round the room. This was a caravan, a space just comfortable for one. Left to herself, Mary showed more interest in the photographs, most of which had been cut out from magazines or newspapers.

'I like this one!' she exclaimed with quite a bit of energy as Janice advanced with tea-things on a tray. 'I prefer romantic ones, you see, when there isn't all that flesh.'

'Perhaps that's only natural.' Janice put down the tray right on top of the photograph Mary had chosen. 'Given your history, I suppose flesh,' she emphasized the word rather horribly, 'is not likely to be your cup of tea.'

Neither woman smiled as, exactly on cue, the kettle whistled noisily. However, the cups of tea changed the atmosphere for the better.

'It's a lovely spring we're having,' said Mary, watching the light, slanting lower now and bouncing off table and floor.

'You certainly see enough of it here,' Janice replied, good-humouredly enough. 'Not a bit of paving or a streetlamp in sight. I don't know how you stand the loneliness.'

'I like the sea and the sky and the views of the fields and headlands.'

'I know. I know. I know you're happy here. I'm glad of it.' There was a short pause before Janice put down her tea-cup and began clearing away the cuttings. 'Perhaps you'd rather I didn't bring you all these pictures of Sissie next time I visit. I'm just so proud of her and I want to share her success with you. After all . . .' Her voice tailed away for a moment. 'It seemed only right, considering.'

'Thank you, Jan. She's a beautiful girl. She does you credit.' Mary lifted the tray slightly and extracted the photograph she had admired. It was a double-page spread in colour. Sissie, dressed like a medieval princess in flowing velvet gown, cloak and tight jewelled cap, was gracefully leaning forward to feed two peacocks. 'I shall pin it up on my wall.'

'If you can find space.' But Janice was clearly pleased. 'She's at the very top of her profession. So young too. It makes everything worthwhile. Rob and I are agreed on that. I expect you feel it too.' But she had made the mistake of being too hopeful.

Mary folded up the photograph, and opening a drawer, tucked it away with empty cotton reels, safety pins, pencil stubs and other bits and pieces.

Janice sighed but instead of commenting began to clear away the rest of the photographs. 'Six months, then?' she said.

'Six months,' echoed Mary, keeping her eyes downcast.

'And you're all right for money?'

'All right for money.'

'Well, then.'

It was clearly the end of the visit but Janice seemed reluctant to go. 'I wish I could do more for you, Mary,' she murmured, in a less confident voice than before.

'You've done more than anyone else.' Mary seemed to be stating a fact without any emotion.

'You are my sister.' Janice moved restlessly round the little room and then suddenly stopped, facing away, and spoke. 'Lately, I've sometimes wondered if we did the right thing.'

'It was the best way.' Mary's dull voice made it clear she was not prepared to think about whatever Janice was suggesting.

'I don't know. I keep reading things about the dangers of concealing the truth . . .'

'If you ever tell her, I'll kill you.' Mary's voice, cutting across Janice's hesitancy, was so fierce and loud that Janice shrank back as far as she was able, which was not very far.

'I didn't mean to upset you, Mary.' Now there was a defensiveness in her voice and even an edge of fear. 'I'm probably just being too sensitive. Silly, after all these years. It's for you to decide. She's your daughter.'

If Janice had thought her last words would placate her sister, she was quite wrong. Mary's voice was even fiercer and shriller than before. 'She's your daughter! You're her mother! And if you ever come here saying things like that again, I'll move like I did before but I'll make sure you can't find me this time. She's your daughter and that's the beginning and the end of it!' Breathless, Mary sat down heavily on the chair and after a second put her head down on the table where the photographs of Sissie had so recently lain.

'Oh dear. Well. Of course. I'm sorry. I'd better be going.' Janice picked up her bags and jacket in a distracted way. 'I'll just go now. Rob will be back with the car or, if he isn't quite, he will in a moment or two. I can wait outside. Do me good to get a bit of fresh air before the journey. Look at your lovely view.' She went to her sister, wanted to kiss her or touch her but Mary stayed, head flat on the table, implacable.

'Won't you even say goodbye, then?' No answer. 'I can't go without you saying goodbye. I couldn't sleep tonight. I'd imagine such things. If I promise that I'll never ever tell Sissie the truth of what happened, will you say goodbye then?' No response. 'I do promise anyway. Mary? Please. I'm begging.'

'Goodbye.' The words were a mumble but not pronounced in those terrible tones. It was just about enough for Janice, who touched her sister's shoulder and went to the little door of the caravan. 'I'll see you in six months, then.'

The door opened and closed with no reaction from the woman at the table. Soon the sun sank below the level of the windows so that she was shrouded in a soft dusk. Eventually she raised herself from the table and the chair and, going across to the window facing west, drew back the lace curtain. She had looked at the same view in the same concentrated way several times a day for the three years since she had been at the caravan site. As usual, she felt the strained muscles of her body soften, the lines in her face smooth out, the noisy tangle in her brain quieten.

The sun was just setting into the sea, casting a rosy glow upwards into the pansy-coloured sky and downwards into the deeper blue-green of the water. The headland was a light spring green where the grass rolled backwards from its height and a deep golden as it turned the corner of the bay and dropped down steeply into the water. Smooth green grass filled up the rest of her picture, unbroken by trees, hedges or, on this evening, by the herds of sheep that sometimes grazed there. A thin white line, which marked the coastal path, ran just behind the edge of the grass but no one walked on it. It was too late, too near darkness for that.

'I love it,' Mary murmured to herself. Without such a view, she would not have felt it worth staying in the world.

The sunset glow was leaving the sea now and floating upwards from the horizon, the brilliance of the colours thinning and becoming overlaid by the thick darkness of night. Mary loved these last minutes of light most of all and often would walk out through it, feeling as if she had stepped into a canvas. But on this evening, after the visit from her sister, she felt too fragile to move, safer here at her window, looking, waiting, until it was blackness all around. Then she would draw the curtain, see the caravan was locked securely, fill her kettle and light her stove.

Mary watched her beloved shapes gently disappearing into night and, perhaps because her visitor had made her more sensitive, she found the lines of headland and horizon and humped hills transforming themselves into the flanks and hindquarters of a large, quietly sleeping cat. When she had first come to the caravan, Janice and Rob had tried to give her a dog. They said it wasn't safe for her, a woman on her own, in such a desolate place and with such odd neighbours, if anyone at all.

The last thing Mary had wanted was a dog, with all its noisy demands, but now the idea of a cat took hold of her in a way nothing had for years. She pictured it curled up on a blanket on her little bunk, kneading the wool with its claws, purring. The next morning she would go to the farm over the hill, which was sure to have too many cats. A kitten would be playful and not yet properly independent so she would ask for a stray.

Slowly, carefully, Mary drew the curtain across the darkness. It was over twenty years since she had felt any pleasure in the thought of the following day.

*

'She's no better, I'd say.' Janice and Rob drove away from the sunset in Rob's fairly new BMW.

'You always say that.' Rob took his wife's hand to soften the criticism. 'I've told you for years she won't get better.'

'Well, she's worse.'

'Worse. That's not good.' He waited for her to say more.

'I told her I was worried about Sissie not knowing the truth and she absolutely flew at me. It reminded me of when she used to have those terrible rages.'

'That was a long time ago.' Rob looked across his wife. They had left behind the wildness of the Dorset coast now and were stopped at traffic lights in the main street of a small town. Rob had seen a pub, old-fashioned and friendly-looking. 'We could stop here for something to eat.'

'No. No. If you don't mind, I'd rather press on and get home.'

Rob drove on. 'I warned you what her reaction would be.'

'I forget how close to the edge she is.'

'You don't forget. You just can't bear to accept it.'

'Sisters are like that, they remember their childhood. She was such a jolly little girl. Robust. I was the sensitive one. I still can't believe anyone can change so completely.'

'She won't be that cheerful little girl again.'

'I don't know.'

'She won't be, Janice, and there's nothing you can do about it. You've done more than most sisters would to help her. No one could blame you if you never saw her again.'

'Ah, blame.' Whether it was the word, ominous in such a painful situation, or whether neither had anything more to say or, even, that they were simply too tired to talk, there fell a long silence.

They were in the dark countryside, the trees a greater depth of blackness than the sky, and no stars or moon to rival the hard-edged beam of their headlights. Janice's head was back against the headrest, her eyes closed. Perhaps she slept. They had a three-hour drive ahead of them, from west to east of southern England. Even the villages they passed through were mostly dark, and it was only when they came closer to London that a red glow was thrown upwards from thousands of homes round hundreds of streets.

Janice got out when Rob stopped at a service station. They were not too far from home now and, feeling this, she seemed determined to shake off her previous mood. Standing outside the car, she brushed her hair, smoothed her skirt, tugged at her jacket, looked at herself in the wing mirror and smiled.

'That's better,' said Rob.

She turned her smile to him. 'It's always the same, just worse this time. But now it's over.'

They drove on.

'That wisteria is like a garland of welcome,' said Janice, as they drove up their driveway and stopped at the front door. She got out of the car and stood under the heavily hanging bunches of flowers, their pale mauve luminous in the dark. Mary did not want her to tell Sissie so she must not feel guilty.

They had left the house so early in the morning that the letters and newspaper had not yet arrived. Rob carried them into the kitchen, glancing at the front page as he did so. Sissie. There she was, another photograph to add to Janice's collection. Without bothering to look at it properly, he called out, 'Sissie's on the front page again.'

Normally Janice would have hurried along to have a gloating look but tonight, instead of answering Rob, she went upstairs.

The newspaper lay on the kitchen table with its dramatic second headline, 'Sissie's Fall Kills Designer'. Under it was a long thin picture of Sissie as she had paraded with broken tooth, tattered costume and bleeding knees and arms. Rob found glasses and a bottle of whisky, bread and butter, cheese and plates and disposed them on the table so that, quite naturally, they formed a protective wall round poor Sissie's desperate image. When he had had a reviving gulp or two, started a sandwich and still there was no sign of Janice, he shouted up the stairs. 'All right, are you?'

'I've found the best place for me.' The voice came back, faint but content. 'Bed.'

So Rob lost interest in kitchen life and took his glass and plate up to the bedroom. Tomorrow would be a brighter day. Dues paid to dark secret.

Chapter Four

In which Sissie seeks Home Comforts.

L IKE A TATTERED bird of plumage Sissie lay on the doorstep under the arching wisteria. The early-morning sun glinted sharply off the silver on her blouse, the sheen on her Lycra-thick leggings, the taut pull of young skin unpadded by flesh, fitting tightly over long and elegant bones.

The milkman found her there. 'I thought she was dead,' he told his wife later. 'Eyes closed, whiter than the skimmed milk in my bottles. Thin so you could see her bones – and the length of her! She took up the whole doorstep and overshot the edges.'

His wife, at this point, told him not to exaggerate and that, in her view, it wasn't good for him getting up at 4 a.m. every morning and he should look for another job.

'It's true she wasn't dead,' he agreed, 'because she opened her eyes and when she saw what I was carrying, asked for a pint of milk. "Don't pay," I told her, so she gave me a French note – look, I've got it somewhere – for the times we cross from Dover to Calais to buy our six-packs.'

'You got talking, then?' His wife was becoming a little more curious.

'She said she'd come from France on an early crossing and she didn't want to wake her parents yet. Just then a cat came out of the shrubberies and she saw where I was looking. "That's right," she said, "I can be what the cat's brought in." She laughed then, not a happy laugh, and I said I had to get on with my deliveries.'

'You did.' The wife put a pot of tea in front of him.

The milkman looked at its comfortable roundness and thought it was exactly the opposite to that poor skinny girl, with black eye and missing tooth. 'Funny though,' he said to conclude the conversation, 'I felt I knew her face from somewhere.'

The bright morning sun did not last. Sissie began to feel cold. The cat seemed to feel it too for it climbed on top of her, turning round and round in search of a warm and soft place. Eventually it decided on what passed for a tummy and, curling up, began to purr contentedly. Apparently, it was in no hurry to get inside the house. Sissie had not been home for over a year so she had no idea whether her parents had a cat or not and whether this black and white creature sitting so confidently on top of her, as if waiting for the door to open, was actually an impostor.

The combination of milk inside and cat outside was soothing and Sissie felt the aches in her body less and her tiredness more. As her body relaxed, the rolling waves of the Channel crossing rose again and rocked her in a slow cradle-like swinging. This time she fell into a deep sleep.

Janice and Rob had overslept. Oversleeping was not part of the plan. They favoured punctuality, precision and purposefulness. Snapping at each other with polite hostility, they bruised about the house, knocking sharp edges, wishing they could be at work with this disorganized transition behind them. By the evening they would be restored to good humour. Neither had time to look at yesterday's paper and, as Janice swept through the kitchen on her way to collect fresh milk from the doorstep, she dropped it into the bin.

The front door was not so easy to deal with. Resistant. Stubborn.

'Yoweee!' The cat screeched out and, using Sissie's tummy as springboard, bolted across the garden and dived into the shrubberies from which it had emerged.

'Owwhhh!' screamed Sissie, the shock of waking, the indignity, the pain, as the cat's tiny talons tore railway tracks in her flesh, calling up fury she had not felt before.

Janice put her head round the amount of door she had been able to force open and saw her daughter's black eyes glaring up.

'Sissie!' It was so unexpected, so unlike her usual conquering-hero-returns-home, so frightful really, the sight of her bedraggled, and worse, at a time when Janice just wanted to push the day into a proper routine, that she too felt a surge of rage. Like a child she wanted to cry, 'It's not fair!' Not on top of yesterday when Mary had been difficult, and then waking up late. Usually so strong and competent, she felt herself at a low ebb and knew that one slip and the pack of cards would tumble down. She should never have suggested that Sissie had a right to know the truth.

'Sissie, what are you doing here? What have you done to yourself? Where have you come from?'

'Milk delivery.' Sissie gritted her teeth and handed over a bottle. 'I had a disaster so I came home.'

'A disaster?' Janice felt like crying. So feeble and so unlike herself. If only she were dressed or had drunk her coffee or Sissie wasn't so very, very tall. But, then, she had the addition of those platform shoes. How could you hug a girl who towered over you? Her own daughter, Ruth, was just the right height. Even Adam, her son, would hardly reach Sissie's shoulders. Oh dear. She mustn't think such thoughts. Sissie had come home, it seemed, for comfort.

'Rob!' Janice called. 'Sissie's here!'

Ducking from her great height, Sissie stepped over the threshold. A little patchwork bag, embroidered and beaded, swung from her less injured shoulder. It seemed to be her only luggage. 'I'm dying for a cup of coffee,' she said and then, remembering it would not be French but home and the colour and texture of old paint water, she grimaced.

Rob met the grimace as he came down the stairs, tie in hand. He guessed it was not for him but, combined with the deathly black-eyed pallor and the shocking hole in the gum, it impeded his friendly welcome. For years he had thought of himself as her father but for the last few he had remembered he was not.

'Can I use my bedroom?'

Sissie's bedroom. What was that? Rob's junk room.

'Well, there's still a bed in it.' Janice led the way. Poor Sissie. What disaster had befallen her? But what was the time? And how late was she going to be for work?

'Where are the others?' asked Sissie, drooping down onto the

27

little bed which had been hers as a child. Even now she had not removed her shoes, which seemed too heavy for her narrow legs and ankles.

'The others?' Janice presumed Sissie meant Ruth and Adam, but even she must know that it was university term and they would be away. 'I'd better dress,' she said instead of answering.

'Oh, I'm so tired.' Sissie yawned. 'I didn't sleep on the boat. Until an hour or so ago, I hadn't slept for forty-eight hours, not since it happened.'

It happened. The words were ominous to Janice. She had studied *The Rime of the Ancient Mariner* at school and always retained a vivid image of the ravaged old man who stopped the busy wedding guests and insisted on telling them his ghastly history, quite spoiling their day. Something had 'happened' to Mary. Once was enough in any family.

'Oh, darling, if only I had more time!' As a child, Sissie had not been given to confidences. Self-contained and quiet, she had stunned them all with the news of her successful audition with a model agency, chosen from thousands, even though they'd been more interested in her hands. Janice could see her now, shiny bright eyes, swinging dark hair, long, lovely body. She had learnt to admire her at that moment and not to interfere. 'We can talk this evening,' she suggested. 'That is, if you're staying.'

'I need a doctor,' said Sissie, head back against the sprigged counterpane. 'And a dentist.'

'Oh, yes, you do.' Janice sighed, blinked away warmer feelings. She could hear Rob coming up the stairs behind her. They drove to work together each morning unless one of them had a meeting somewhere else in the country. 'I'll leave the telephone numbers on the kitchen table. Sleep will be the best medicine, whatever – whatever's happened.' A little kiss, a peck, and she was gone. Rob too.

Sissie shut her eyes. Abandoned again. First Sebastien, now her parents. She could tell already that she would not miss Sebastien in the future. His body, for example, had always been too like her own, pale and bony and beautiful. Sometimes when they made love and lay naked and entwined she could hardly tell which were his limbs and which hers. Perhaps she would miss his mind, although she

28

thought she knew it well enough now to take away with her. His love of Manley Hopkins, his knowledge of art. He was a cultured person, thought Sissie imprecisely. He knew the difference between Michelangelo and Raphael, between Tintoretto and Titian, between Duccio and Masaccio. How happy she had been the evening Sebastien had called her his Primavera. Then later that night Rudolf had said the same, his accent making the words at first incomprehensible. Swathed in the lightest of chiffons, bound in silk ribbons, strewn with flowerettes, she had felt the very incarnation of spring.

Ah, the two men in her life! Rudolf and Sebastien. And now she had lost them both. 'You will not like England,' Sebastien had finally pronounced. 'You didn't like it before and you will like it even less now. You've got used to admiration and making lots of money and being Somebody. You won't like being Nobody one bit. If you were honest, you would admit that you're scared of people seeing you looking ugly and that it is not England you're going to or any great change in your life but a doctor and a dentist and a burrow to hide in while they fix you up. You'll be back soon enough, and I'll be waiting here in your rented horse-strewn apartment.'

This harsh judgement on her character was what Sissie would have expected from Sebastien. Warmth was the soft scarlet of a Masaccia cloak, not a feeling in his heart. Let him live in her apartment, recite poetry, take in another pretty, confident girl who had not yet fallen off her catwalk.

Tossing and turning on her too small bed, Sissie did not want Sebastien at her side, but she could not quite control a replay of the past. It was weakness, she thought, and eventually staggered out of bed.

Circling the house, nosing out old corners, she soothed herself with the innocence of childhood. Here was the paler spot on the carpet where Ruth and she had once peed when they couldn't be bothered to go to the lavatory. Here, on the third step from the bottom of the staircase, was where she and Ed Staines had exchanged a first kiss, hearts thumping, more in terror of discovery than in erotic arousal. That night the silence and darkness of the house had only masked the presence of the family, four strong, sleeping sensibly in preparation for another day of positive action. She had been the outsider then, as she was now.

The house was emptier but not silent. A blackbird chirped insistently, a descendant, presumably, of the one that used to wake Sissie on spring and summer mornings when the curtains were too thin to keep out the rising sun. How long did blackbirds live? The one from her childhood had always been invisible. Creeping burglar-like, the feeling of trespass growing steadily – had she felt that, too, as a child? – Sissie left the house for the garden, down onto the crazy-paving path. It was the only crazy thing about the house, chosen and laid with the utmost sanity by her father. It was not difficult to locate the tree, delicately fronded and pale green, from which the blackbird belted out his message of defiance. How much had it grown since her childhood? Standing outside her bedroom window, she felt as if she stood outside her own life. The blackbird remained invisible, although the leaves that veiled him were so light.

'Montres-toi!' Sissie shouted, and clapped her hands. The singing stopped abruptly and was replaced by a busy rustling as the bird, no fool, escaped from the back of the tree. There was no diversion now from the doctor and the dentist. Sissie made her way to the kitchen and the telephone numbers that could be her passport back to the world of starry fame. Perhaps Seb was right. That was her world, where she belonged, where she became strong and powerful.

As soon as Sissie had shut the front door behind her, the blackbird darted back from his banishment and began to issue his warning signals from his accustomed place. At the foot of the tree, Sissie's platform-soled shoes, like Lilliputian scaffolding, lay abandoned. Ten seconds later, the cat that had sat so cosily on Sissie's lap streaked across the lawn, low and flat from pointed nose to tip of tail, and, mounting the shoes, turned vertically up the tree trunk. Once again the song stopped abruptly.

Chapter Five

In which Sissie goes in search of a new Tooth and falls prey to a Truly Sensual Human Being.

THE TOOTH-CROWNING dentist in the town remembered Sissie from her childhood. He had a lascivious mouth and liked to induce sensuous relaxation in his patients with a liberal dose of gas and air.

'I just squeezed you in,' he announced meaningfully.

Sissie had come to him at the end of the day. 'As you can see, it's an emergency.' Her tone was formal.

'You will have to visit me several times,' responded the dentist, staking his claim.

His name was Mr Plumb and Sissie thought how well it suited him as his smooth reddish face with black shiny eyes bent over her open mouth. He smelled slightly of peppermint, disguise for a less hygienic odour which was still just discernible, sweet, sour, rusty, cauliflower.

'Take good deep breaths,' commanded Mr Plumb, pressing the rubber nozzle over Sissie's nose. 'An injection may not be enough.'

Perhaps I should be in hospital, thought Sissie as she felt herself slipping away into Mr Plumb's clutches. But she had already been to hospital, sent for an X-ray by the doctor, and this had seemed so much easier. What was it Rudolf had said to her once? 'The worst is before you accept.' Eyes closed, mouth tortured by a variety of hard cold instruments, Sissie let herself float into gaseous regions and it was Rudolf's face that hung over her. He had inspected nearly every part of her before taking her on as his model, the model he most desired to show his beautiful creations. Tears welled behind Sissie's eyes. He had not looked into her mouth in quite such detail as Mr Plumb, perhaps, but, then, she was not a horse. At any rate, he had pronounced her perfect. 'Parfait!' Or, at least, as near perfect as a human being ever can be. He had seen so much ugliness in his life before he came to Paris. That was why he had to create beauty and she, Sissie, was part of it. 'Perfect! Parfait! Perfetto! Perfettissimo!'

The tears trickled out of Sissie's eyes and ran down the side of her face into the white napkin Mr Plumb had placed round her neck. Eventually he noticed the increasing damp and looked with admiration on someone who suffered so deeply, silently, bravely. 'Not much longer now,' he comforted, pressing her cold fingers.

Sissie did not hear him. Her perfection had died with Rudolf. He had been the first person to point it out to her – although she had always had a strong suspicion that she was less ordinary than other people. He had given her perfection and she had lost it in his service and then pointed him the way to death. The quiet tears changed to hiccuping sobs, which caused Mr Plumb to retreat from the mouth in some confusion.

'Is it that bad?' he worried, appealing for contradiction.

'Oh, yes. Oh, yes,' gulped Sissie, in heartfelt tones, as swabs and steel clamps were removed hastily from her mouth. 'Much, much worse. You see. You see, now I'm not perfect any more, no one will ever love me again!' And she gave herself over to a luxury of tears.

Mr Plumb had known this before, the release of sadness under the influence of gas and air, but in twenty years of practising, he had never known quite such an intensity of feeling, such a superabundance of watery grief. Perfection, she talked of, but did she not know what a truly perfect false tooth he would give her? The best that simulated ivory and orthodontic artistry could provide. He would tell her this when she was a little calmer.

Mr Plumb left Sissie's side to look for a thicker, drier towel. Up till six months ago his wife had been his assistant, not particularly efficient but always on tap. Unfortunately she had come to hear of a little flirtation – well, a little more than a little flirtation – with the daughter of the antique dealer three doors down the high street, and she had left him, teenage son in tow. He had protested innocence but Shirley Plumb had remained absolute in her determination. 'It isn't the first time and it won't be the last. It's the way you're made. You think you need sex of more than one variety. Sex is your hobby.'

Mr Plumb had pointed out that cutting diamonds was his hobby but she had remained inexorable and left the next day. It was a sad blow for Mr Plumb, not least because his other hobby was bridge and he had trained up his wife to be a very respectable partner. He missed his son, too, who was a bright boy, although inclined to take his mother's side.

Feeling disconsolate himself, Mr Plumb brought over the towel to Sissie and mopped her up in a general way. 'You have been in the wars,' he said, 'but your beauty shines through.'

'It's the end of everything,' sobbed Sissie.

'Well, I wouldn't quite say that.'

'It is. It is.'

Seeing he could do nothing more with her that day – to put in so much as a temporary crown now would have been like trying to plant a tree in a well – Mr Plumb pushed away his mobile table of instruments. 'I'll give you some air. That'll brace you up.'

Sissie did not want to brace up but that is what Mr Plumb decreed and it worked, for once he removed the rubber nozzle she found herself swinging her legs down to the floor and seeing straight again. There stood the dentist meditatively surveying her.

'You still don't look good.' His white coat shone and his black hair, with a little premature grey, gleamed. 'I don't like to let you leave in this state. I hope to convince my patients that dentistry is therapeutic not simply masochistic.'

'You're not to blame,' replied Sissie, thinking of Fate with a renewal of guilt (although why guilt she did not analyse) and misery.

'I'd better give you a cup of tea.' It had struck Mr Plumb that his currently shaky reputation could do without a distraught and tear-stained young woman being seen leaving his surgery after hours. 'I live above and below the shop, as it were. If you follow me down to the kitchen, I'll put on the kettle.'

Mr Plumb had seldom made such an innocent offer and Sissie followed him obediently. Now and again her shoulders still heaved with a shuddering sob.

The kitchen was clean and tidy, the only sign of Mrs Plumb's departure a desiccated potted plant. Sissie sat numbly at the table.

The least numb thing about her was her mouth where the injection was beginning to wear off.

'I'll make the tea cool. We can't have you burning yourself,' said the dentist solicitously. 'You're staying with your parents for a while?'

'No choice now.' Sissie gingerly touched her mouth.

'Your mother is so proud of you. You're in all the papers. A very top model.' Encouraged by a flicker of interest, Mr Plumb leant close – after all, he had already known the intimacy of her mouth. 'Sometimes it's hard to believe that a butterfly like you should emerge from our dull little town.'

Under normal circumstances, such a man's admiration would have been beneath contempt but circumstances were desperate. Pushing aside the tea, Sissie sighed. 'I'd give anything for a glass of wine.'

'You must be feeling better.' Mr Plumb poured glasses of something dreadful produced from a cupboard.

'Oh, I'll be off in a moment,' replied Sissie, misunderstanding his remark. 'I suppose you have a wife who will come back and cook you a nice supper.'

'I did.' Mr Plumb swilled back his wine. 'No longer. If it isn't prying, may I ask if it was a man who gave you your injuries?'

'It was not.' Sissie held out her glass to be refilled. She supposed she should return to her parents – where else was there, after all? But she found herself unwilling to leave the comforting of this attentive dentist, this foolish ladies' man. 'My teeth were always perfect as a child.'

'I remember. Don't forget you had first-class dental care. Of course, teeth are not all I know about. Perhaps you would like to see my diamond-cutting equipment?'

'Not now,' replied Sissie languidly, elbows on table, head in hands. The combination of pain, unhappiness, wine and gas and air was making her irresistibly sleepy. 'You don't have a spare bed, do you?'

'A spare bed!' exclaimed the dentist, shocked, which made a change as he was the one who usually did the shocking.

'If I could lie down for a little while, I'm sure I'd feel better.'

'Well, I don't know . . .' But Sissie was on her feet and heading in unstoppable somnambulist fashion for the stairs.

'I suppose you could use Tom's room.'

The room was small and smelled of stale teenager. Nevertheless, Sissie flopped thankfully on the bed. 'So kind of you,' she murmured with a pitiful sigh, before falling into a sleep as deep as if she'd been drugged.

Flummoxed, Mr Plumb hovered at the door and then returned slowly to the kitchen. Should he ring her parents and tell them to remove her? But surely she was too old and grand for that. Or should he convey her back himself? Unable to decide, he poured himself more wine and made himself his staple diet, a large cheese and chutney sandwich, chutney being the odour that Sissie had sensed under the peppermint.

Uncaring of the eating habits of this wolf in dentist's clothing, Sissie slept upstairs while the evening light dimmed and faded away. Soon she began to smile in a lopsided way for she was enjoying the mirage pleasure of sexual dreams. If she had been awake she would have been properly annoyed to find this dream dentist tenderly caressing her, stroking her inner arms, her inner thighs, but in her sleep, free of shame, if not all anxiety, she looked into his plummy eyes and allowed herself to be broached. Someone admired her, someone thought her perfect still.

Mr Plumb finished his cheese and chutney and took a call from a doctor acquaintance, inviting him to make up a bridge four. Despite the short notice, he saw it as a step forward in the rehabilitation of his reputation in the respectable communities and was keen to go. But how could he leave or explain the presence of a Goldilocks in his son's ex-bedroom? Or even his ex-son's bedroom. 'Give me five minutes and I'll let you know,' was the best he could do.

So now he stood in the bedroom once more and, bending close, whispered urgently into his guest's ear, 'Do wake up, dear. Do, please.'

Slowly, luxuriantly, without opening her eyes, Sissie raised her arms above her head. Then brought them down where they came into contact with Mr Plumb's smooth, handsome face. 'Hold me, touch me,' murmured Sissie, and pulled him gently towards her.

Where are you, respectability? The sweet youth of Sissie's arms wound itself round the dentist's neck. Such an invitation had not come his way for some time. At least he could kiss her, neck, shoulders, arms, light flutters of homage on her bruised skin, and still keep his bridge options open.

Enveloped in the sweet-sour smell of chutney – for there had been no time or incentive for disguise – Sissie half opened her eyes. There was no point in pretending this was Seb who kissed her so sensuously, so sensitively. Perhaps this was the older man who would think about her rather than himself, who would wish to make her happy. But, of course, it was Mr Frightful, Awful Plumb, the dentist who had tickled her disgustingly as a child. How could she bear to let him touch her, even if with such delicacy and understanding?

Sissie woke up further and, as Mr Plumb's encroaching fingers stroked her hips in soothing admiration, a counter-wave of despair made tears start up once more in Sissie's eyes. What depths was she plumbing that here she lay, naked and responsive, under the fingers of such a man? This emotion, of degradation and enjoyment and despair, instead of making her punch her would-be lover and run, caused her to wind her arms more tightly round his neck and pull him, chutney and all, towards her.

Where is my self-control? Mr Plumb asked himself, hopelessly. Lost in the joy of making love, an art form he revered above nearly everything, he answered his own question by easing down his trousers and sliding into bed.

'Mind my ribs, my cuts, my bruises,' muttered Sissie, eyes shut, drowning in tears, at once happy and in acutest misery.

'Oh, yes! Oh, yes!' breathed the lucky dentist. 'My angel! My princess! My nymph! My Sugar Plum Fairy!' He did not even hear the telephone, which rang downstairs for a considerable length of time since the doctor was a deliberate man and not inclined to give up his good intentions easily.

Meanwhile, back at Sissie's childhood home where the remains of the blackbird lay strewn across the lawn, Janice and Rob waited and wondered. Eventually, they ate their supper, guiltily.

'Perhaps she's been kept in at the hospital,' suggested Janice, the crisp lettuce sticking in her throat.

'I thought she was seeing Dr Clint-Smith?'

'But he might have sent her to the hospital.'

So, after they had finished their meal, staying calm, they rang the hospital and, having no luck, rang the doctor, but somehow they didn't think of ringing the dentist.

'She's more trouble than the other two put together,' said Rob.

'You can hardly say that when we've only seen her twice in three years. She's a credit to us. Such an outstanding success.'

'Pride comes before a fall.' They had both caught up with the front page of yesterday's paper while disposing of the bird's beak, laid on the sitting-room rug by that stray cat who wouldn't leave them alone.

'That's only a temporary set-back,' insisted Janice, defending her dream. Reality would have been much too tough.

'Well, where is she now?' asked Rob, jerking open the dishwasher. 'She comes here, unsettling us both, and then disappears – for all we know, back to Paris for another three years.'

'Oh dear.' Janice plonked down at the kitchen table. What had happened to her resilience, her joie de vivre? Perhaps she was entering menopause. 'I just wish I knew she was all right.'

Fortunately, neither Janice nor Rob could possibly imagine that their super-model daughter (or as good as daughter) was thrilling to the touch of a small-town Romeo. They knew Mr Plumb's reputation but it was beyond their wildest dreams that Sissie, so young, so beautiful, so successful, even if currently battered, could give in to the tacky allure of a dentist whom even Janice found unappealing. It might have been different if Plumb had been a Parisian dentist, who smoked Gauloises and drank Pernod and raw red wine. If he had smelled of garlic instead of chutney, there would have been something unknowably foreign about him that might have seemed exciting. Outside those who entered Mr Plumb's bed, only the most perspicacious could guess that his ridiculous lascivious manner hid a loving reverence for the body of a woman and that, in conjunction with one, he showed a long list of the most splendid virtues: sensitivity, kindness, gentleness, generosity, imagination, unselfishness, energy, understanding, sweetness, humility and many others besides.

*

'I could get you struck off the dental register.' Sissie noted the ugliness of Plumb's son's furniture with a further twist of unhappiness. And yet, if she cared to admit it, her body was relaxed, charmed and altogether improved.

Mr Plumb stroked her pale, perfect buttock; he was still confident with the sense of a job well performed, and knew she didn't really mean it. 'I hope your ribs have not suffered?' he enquired solicitously.

'Do you do this often?' asked Sissie, fighting to discover energy, even anger. Was there any hope she had been raped? At very least, seduced. She feared not. Gathering the sheets under her chin, she looked at Plumb with her dark, bruised eyes. Was he as bad as she feared? Yes, he was.

Seeing her look, Plumb slid out of bed and fell onto his knees beside her. 'I understand what you're feeling,' he said, imploringly. 'I'm not what you're used to.'

'That's an understatement,' muttered Sissie. But what did it matter, really? Any of it? What she was used to was not so good either and, besides, she didn't have it any more. Again her tears flowed.

'Oh, please,' cried Plumb. 'Why are you so unhappy? Just a few minutes ago, you were so—'

'Just don't remind me of it,' sniffed Sissie. 'Or I may accuse you of rape. I suppose the best thing we can do is pretend it never happened.'

'But it did. It did!' cried Plumb, still carried away and not thinking quite straight.

'I know.' Once more losing her purpose, Sissie wiped her nose on the sheet. 'But it will be better if we pretend it didn't.'

'I see,' said Plumb, coming a little to himself. 'But I did make you happy?'

Sissie took pity on his pleading dog eyes, and gave him the benefit of a slight nod. It was not his fault, after all, if she was having a breakdown.

'I'll do anything you say, anything!'

He would. She saw that and, in her disconsolate depths, an idea came to her, a kind of bedrock survival plan into which only someone

38

who had fallen from the heights could be prepared to sink. 'You know, I'm retiring.'

'Retiring?' Plumb attempted to look business-like.

'I *am* retired now, of course, while I wait for my tooth.' Sissie sat up cross-legged on the bed. 'And I need somewhere to live.'

'Retired?' echoed her lover again.

'Don't worry, I shall not be your PG for long.'

'PG?' Plumb looked up at her and his voice had become fainter.

'Paying guest. While you fix my tooth. I get on with my parents perfectly well, but they can't give me what you can.' At this point they caught each other's eye and Sissie, red-faced, looked away and then back. 'Not that,' she said, 'because that, you must remember, did not happen. But I upset my parents. I shall pay you well, of course, because I am so rich I can't even count the hundreds of thousands I have earned.' For some reason, the thought of all this money made Sissie weep again but she managed to staunch the flow long enough to get across her plan. 'We'll make it all sound very official because, from what you've told me, you need to hang on to what shred of reputation remains to you. Officially, I shall be visiting the hospital too, and resting in order to regain my health.' Here a few more lingering tears fell.

Mr Plumb saw he had lost control of his life. Sissie sat naked in front of him, her slim thighs spread and nearly flat to the bed, the dark curls of her pubic hair gleaming a little damply, the rose-coloured tips of her high-set breasts pointing towards him. In the dimness, he could hardly see the gap in her mouth which, anyway, he had grown to love, or the lacerations of her fall. He feared and yet also hoped that, if he rubbed his eyes, he would awake and she would have vanished.

To test this, he stretched forward and clasped the ungrazed knee. The contact of flesh was enough to put his ever-ready body into Start. But Sissie took hold of his hand and, studying it coldly as she might a piece of anonymous flotsam, put it to one side.

'I shall be honoured to have such a PG,' said Plumb.

39

But Sissie had curled back into the bedclothes and gone far from him.

So Sissie had found a place where she could still be a star, worshipped, adored and serviced as far as she required. Once, but only once, in the days that followed, she allowed Plumb's tongue to enter her mouth where he soon found the gap in her teeth and gently massaged the gum. She felt flooded with well-being but would let him go no further. Better, far, to wet his son's bed with the tears of failure and ignominy. At lowest points, it crossed her mind that she was broken down beyond repair.

However, on Saturday evening, she felt strong enough to descend to the kitchen. Over white wine, cheese and chutney, she even felt prepared to make a little conversation.

'Why did you become a dentist?' she enquired of Plumb, who was staring at her with greedy eyes.

'Ninety per cent of all dentists are men,' he replied, as if this was a satisfactory answer in itself.

'How very peculiar.' Sissie licked the delicate tips of her fingers. 'Perhaps women have more sense than to spend their lives looking into other people's disintegrating mouths.'

'Not at all.' Plumb was hurt. 'My point is that dentistry is a very masculine profession.'

'Really?' mouthed Sissie doubtfully, through chunks of chutney – there was not much else to eat and, now she was no longer a super-model, she could afford to put on a pound or two. Nevertheless, she was in no position to doubt Mr Plumb's masculinity and he was the first dentist she had ever known intimately.

'I'm so glad you're feeling better.'

'Please don't think any such thing. But tomorrow I may go out.'

'Come in, Sissie dear,' invited Janice. Sissie noticed the formality at once. Her mother and father were both changed and spruce and now the door was held open for her as if she were a dinner guest. Had they heard something about her relationship with Plumb? Was it a sign of disapproval?

'Hello, Mum.' From her great height she stooped and kissed her mother and then, spotting Rob hovering behind, kissed him too.

'They've fixed your tooth, I see.' Janice was obviously flustered.

'Just temporarily,' said Sissie airily, 'while the permanent one is made. I thought I'd spend some of the waiting time visiting Ruth and Adam.'

By this time they'd reached the living room, which showed its usual immaculate face. Sissie slid herself into an armchair.

She had spent the middle of the day shopping, having procured large sums of money through the bank. The shops, catering for a middle-aged, overweight and conservative clientele, had proved a challenge to her powers of creative dressing. The boys' schoolwear shop had produced drainpipe cricket trousers and a V-necked sweater, while Woolworths girls' counter had provided a pink and lime green Lurex turtle-neck sweater, which she wore underneath. A lilac coat worn inside out completed what she considered a thoroughly dashing outfit worthy of a disciple of Rudolf. Shopping had done wonders for her morale.

'You certainly look a lot better,' said Janice, as Rob poured them drinks.

'Actually I've broken two ribs.' Sissie put her hand to her chest. 'But they don't believe in strapping people these days.'

'You look better,' repeated Janice.

'Yes, you do.' Rob handed her a glass of Riesling.

'I feel better.'

What had happened? Silence entered the room with a weight impossible to lift. Janice was thinking of Mary, of what might have been and how she had done her best all these years and what had she to show for it but this pink and purple alien sprawled like a huge, decorated spider in her best armchair? She knew she must make a further effort, that her job as mother would never be over and she really did love the little girl Sissie, who must be somewhere inside all that Lurex and fluff, but she just could not find the energy.

Rob also wished to speak, not only because he felt a sense of duty but because he could see that Janice was suffering and he loved Janice. But he was ever a man of few words and could think of nothing to say.

Sissie minded the silence least of anybody but all the talk of looking and feeling better had made her feel rather ill so she drank her wine in silence.

41

In the silence, a faint mewing was heard.

'There's that damn cat again,' said Rob.

'It won't go away so you might as well let it in.' With relief, Janice found she could move and talk once more. On her way to the kitchen she gripped Sissie's shoulder. 'It's lovely to have you here. I hope we're going to see more of you, now that you've decided to work less hard.' The warmth in her voice pleased her and Sissie, who smiled upwards.

'Is that what I'm going to do? Work less hard?'

Once Janice had left the room, Rob's face became more severe. 'Whyever do you want to dress like that? Calling attention to yourself.'

'I suppose I'm used to people staring.' Sissie was unruffled, although rather surprised. Rob's criticism had never disturbed her but he had made no such comments since she'd left home. 'I look different, anyway. I always have.'

After all these years, such words still had the power to make Rob shift uneasily and then, to cover his confusion, rise from his chair and pour them both more drinks.

'So when I was discovered . . .' continued Sissie with unusual earnestness.

'Discovered,' murmured Rob.

'Discovered as a model,' Sissie explained, 'I began to feel part of something. By becoming more odd to most people, I became less odd to myself.'

Rob was flattered by her confidence, so unlike Sissie, so unlikely to be given to him. She had always been closest to Janice – blood tie, of course. 'There's your wine, dear.'

Janice noticed the happier atmosphere in the room when she returned crying, 'Sup-per! Sup-per!' in the way Sissie remembered from childhood.

'Bangers and mash,' announced Rob with relish. And Sissie found that a diet of cheese and chutney can make a red-blooded meat-eater of even the most dedicated carniphobe.

'Ruth will be pleased to see you,' said Janice, wondering if this would be the case.

*

When Ruth opened the door to her little room, where she had gathered two of her best girlfriends in unconscious self-defence, she was amazed to see Sissie followed closely by Mr Plumb.

'Darling Ruthie,' Sissie waved a bottle of champagne in either hand, 'here I am, me and Plumb come all the way to Bristol to visit you.'

'I know Mr Plumb. He descaled my teeth only a fortnight ago.'

'Of course. Comme je suis bête! May we come in?' for Ruth stood blocking the door.

'Oh, yes, please.'

'Mind your ribs,' murmured the dentist, attentively, removing the bottles from Sissie and, after looking in vain for a table, handing them to Ruth who set them on the floor. The room seemed very small with all of them crowded in and, since there were only three chairs, Ruth's friends joined the champagne on the floor.

'This is Gilly and Sue,' introduced Ruth, 'and this is Sissie, my famous sister, and Mr Plumb, our dentist.'

'Oh, Ruth. Ruthie, do open the champagne.' The gap between the sisters seemed very wide, yet how happy they'd been as little girls, eight and five, skipping round the bay tree in their garden, going off to school hand in hand, lying awake at night planning how many children they should have and what sex and what colour hair and eyes. They had learnt to ride together, learnt to swim together, gone to tap-dancing together, glanced sidelong at boys with the same subtle estimation. They had been friends and chums and mates and almost best friends until Sissie began to grow. Was that it? As simple as that.

At thirteen Sissie was under five feet, at fifteen she was barely under six feet, her body drawn upwards in elegant elevation. She could no longer look sideways at boys but only downwards from a great height. At school sports, she was forbidden to compete in the high jump or the hurdling and, after a while, even running was banned to her. She was a freak show and no one admitted her beauty.

'Trust you to bring champagne, Sissie.' Ruth was recovering. She could see that the bemused expressions on her friends' faces were changing to awe and excitement, understanding that Sissie was something special. Her outfit, of fisherman's wading boots over white long-johns, topped by a black lace bustier and a fuchsia angora stole, had been assumed as a defence against their academic elevation and it worked. She was a bird of paradise, beyond judgement, and if she wanted a dentist as escort then good luck to her.

'Mr Plumb, would you like to open the champagne?'

'Please call me Eddie.'

'I call him Plumb.' Sissie threw off the stole and turned eagerly to Ruth. 'Tell me all about it. All. All. All of you. What are you studying, for example?'

'We are all reading social anthropology with economic theory as a subsidiary subject,' replied Ruth, a little primly.

This seemed to take some of the wind out of Sissie's sails, but she rallied after a second or two, particularly after Mr Plumb had cried, 'Pop,' and then, 'Pop, pop,' as the champagne corks flew.

'We've seen so many photographs of you,' volunteered Sue.

'It must be awfully hard work being a model,' suggested Gilly.

'Sissie's decided to give it all up.' Mr Plumb entered the conversation with aplomb. Without his dentist's white coat, his dark handsomeness was not quite so impressive but, on the other hand, he looked less ridiculous.

'Have I really?' Sissie seemed vague, looked at her sister as if she'd know the answer.

'You've lost a tooth, broken your ribs, been bruised and battered all over. Enough is enough.'

'But at least I didn't die,' murmured Sissie sorrowfully.

'Oh, yes, we read about that.' Led by Ruth, all three girls gave Sissie sympathetic grimaces. 'It sounded terrible. We felt so sorry for you. And then Mum said you were back in England. Are you really going to give up being a model?'

'Become an ex-model. Surely I'm too young to be an ex anything.'

'I suppose it gives you plenty of time to start something new. But haven't you got a lovely flat in Paris?'

'It's only rented and filled with horses. Anyway, Sebastien's keeping that warm.'

'Sebastien!' Sissie's negligence as she pronounced her ex-loving lover's name did not take in Mr Plumb. Sebastien! A man keeping her flat warm! His face went bright red and then settled into lines of

44

woe. He had known all along it was fantasy. But now he could put a name to it. Sebastien. A poncy, stupid, Frenchified twaddle of a name. Despairing, he rose to his feet and said he would check the car and get a bit of air.

No one missed him, except Sissie, who felt a slight coolness along her I-am-being-cared-for side. What if her tooth fell out and no one was there to shove it back in? Instead, they settled down into the sort of conversation that Sissie imagined should take place in university rooms. She heard about the clubs they had joined, the clubs they disapproved of, their views on the Third World, the USA and, coming a rather poor third, their own world. She learnt about the exams they feared the following term, the parties they had given and been to, the sporting exercise they had or had not taken.

'You're so busy,' sighed Sissie.

Pleased with this response, Ruth led them off to a Chinese restaurant, where the owner paid due deference to Sissie and gave them a table in a back room festooned with turquoise and yellow satin lanterns whose brilliant scarlet tassels tickled the tops of their heads and fell like earrings round Sissie's shoulders.

She did not eat, the smell of monosodium glutamate hanging as heavily in the air as the lanterns hung lightly. But she was happy to be in the well-disposed company of her sister and her sister's friends, and it was only at the end of the meal that anyone wondered about Mr Plumb.

'Oh, he'll be fine,' said Sissie airily. 'He prefers eating cheese and chutney sandwiches.'

This obviously intimate detail of the dentist's private life spurred Ruth into a brave questioning. They were walking along Clifton's charming high street and had fallen behind the other two. 'I suppose you've seen a lot of Mr Plumb because of your broken tooth?'

'That's how it started.'

What started? thought Ruth anxiously.

'But now I'm his PG,' continued Sissie.

'His PG? Do you mean paying guest?'

Ruth's shocked disbelief spurred Sissie on to lift the corner on her dark night of the soul. 'He's very sexy, don't you think?'

It was hard to deny Mr Plumb's sexiness. It was the most obvious thing about him. It was what made him ridiculous, what put him outside the bounds of any sexual attraction. He was a caricature of a sexy man, his eyes too longingly black, his mouth too lusciously red, his skin too smooth, his hands too caressing. Such a man should not approach her extraordinary, brilliant, successful-beyond-the-bounds-of-imagination sister. It was too ghastly to contemplate.

'Oh, Sissie. He's dreadful. When I lie in the dentist's chair, I live in dread of his hands slipping along my neck.'

'I know what you mean.' Sissie looked at her sister, at her expression of sense and sensibility, and felt herself teetering on the edge of a deeper, darker hole in which, perhaps, Plumb was not as bad as all that. 'He is rather awful,' she agreed before opening her eyes and curving her lips to make the face that had launched a thousand ads. 'But he does have his talents.'

'Mum always said he was wonderfully quick with the drill,' said Ruth hopefully.

'I was not referring to his *dental* talents.'

Fortunately for Ruth's sensibilities, at this point they arrived back at the university digs where the man in question could be seen standing, sentinel-like. He was holding a plastic shopping bag in one hand and dangling the car keys in the other.

'I've done some grocery shopping,' Mr Plumb greeted them. 'And I think we should be off before dark.'

He did not ask where they had eaten and the girls did not tell him. Sissie kissed Ruth warmly enough to last for another three years.

Only Mr Plumb lowered the tone by reaching into his breast pocket and extracting two cards printed with E. A. Plumb, Dental Surgeon, which he pressed on Gilly and Sue, squeezing their hands as he did so. 'Special rates for you two. Ask Ruth for a reference. But I can tell you you won't find a better descaler, remodeller, bridge-builder this side of London.'

Mr Plumb did not accompany Sissie on the day she went to see her brother. She had not warned Adam of her arrival and, after much searching high and low, on a campus that looked more like a concentration camp than a seat of learning, she discovered him undergoing 'Rowing Trials' on a large river whose name she did not know. She shouted from the bank her name, rank and number, as it were, but he seemed curiously reluctant to hear.

If she had been dressed as for her Bristol trip in thigh-high waders, she might have been able to get closer and have greater success. But, since the weather had moved on into a warm phase, she had chosen a frou-frou organza skirt worn with exquisitely tie-dyed tights, which she had rescued from the local craft market and did not dare entrust to the water.

'Adam!' she cried repeatedly. 'It is your sister, Sissie, come to see you! Sister, Sissie, come to see . . .' But he stayed persistently on the far side of the river and, since Sissie could see no bridge for her to reach the other bank, she could do nothing but shout.

After a while all those *sss* began to sound silly even to her, like the hissing of geese. Moreover, the sunshine was dispelled by clouds, which soon dispensed a spattering of rain with the promise of more. This was just how Sebastien would have behaved, locked in his own occupation, immune to her presence. It reminded her that Adam and she had never had anything in common as children. He had been a dull, unimaginative little boy, perfect casting, in her view, to be her admiring acolyte. However, instead of enjoying her wild adventures, which Ruth always had the grace to do, he had taken most pleasure in shopping her to their parents.

Gloomily, she returned to the station and from thence to the waiting arms of Mr Plumb. Except that when she entered the little house on the high street, there was an expression in his dark eyes that was other than passionately, desirously soothing.

'I hope you're not making a secret fetish of me,' complained Sissie to Mr Plumb, several minutes after they had been alone together. To spite his anxious looks, she rolled down her roll-on roll-off sweater so that her exquisite shoulders (no longer bruised) and the tops of her delicate breasts appeared.

Mr Plumb groaned. He had had a hard day at the drill but that was not it. That morning his cleaning lady, Mrs Irene Patterson, had paid him her weekly visit. If he had not been so busy and Sissie out of the house, he might have made precautionary preparations. As it was, he had hardly been aware of her organizational bustle upstairs until, at his lunch-break, she had descended and sought him out in the kitchen.

Normally she paid him the deference due to a skilled practitioner, an attitude not discouraged by the free dental services she received at his hands. She addressed him as 'sir' and clearly took his side over his wife, who had departed before her arrival. As far as Mr Plumb had considered his cleaner at all, it was as a good old soul, the surprisingly bright condition of whose teeth belied what he imagined to be her advanced years.

But there in the kitchen, apron off, bunched up and held in front of her as if she might throw it at him, had stood a veritable virago of indignation looking a couple of decades younger than the six he had assigned to her. He did not like to remember all her words but part of a sentence stuck obstinately in his memory: '. . . when one finds evidence of two in a bed and up to things sacred to marriage . . .'

'Mrs Patterson,' he had defended himself, noting unconsciously that her figure, without the apron, was firm and shapely, 'I don't know what you are thinking. But Miss Slipper is my paying guest for a short period and what she does with her private life is not for me, or you, to judge.'

This had seemed to him rather a brilliant rebuttal and it had seen Mrs Patterson off the premises. But now, with Sissie's glory facing him, his heart was split in two so he groaned.

'Do stop groaning,' said Sissie irritably. 'And, if it comes to that, when will my new tooth be ready?'

She went upstairs and, finding her bedclothes thrown in a tousled heap on the floor, became thoughtful, which in her case meant immersing herself in a deep, very hot bath. Mr Plumb followed her up and, finding the bathroom door locked, knocked humbly.

'It was my housekeeper,' he said.

Sissie did not answer, for she was contemplating her future. How long would her temporary tooth hold? If she abandoned Mr Plumb, would another dentist fix a new one just as easily? Should she sort out things with Sebastien now that she was less battered? Where should she go next?

'I had a call about your tooth today,' said Mr Plumb, trying a

48

different tack through the door. 'It will be here tomorrow or the next day, depending on the smooth running of the post office.'

That answered one question. She should wait for her tooth.

'Shall we go out to dine?' suggested Mr Plumb, aghast, even as he spoke, at his daring. In this little town, to be seen eating chicken tikka together would be tantamount to being caught in adultery. 'There's quite an attractive place on the outskirts of town. It is run by Rex and Leo who have a very original menu. For example, you can order a "red platter", which consists of rare roast beef, pink beans, red cabbage.'

That night, as Sissie lay awake in the dark, Mr Plumb near at hand (although never more allowed in hand) she sincerely wished she had known of Rex and Leo's establishment earlier. They not only ran an elegant restaurant – coloured platters seemingly an invention of Mr Plumb – but also had several tastefully decorated rooms, which they let out to chosen guests. She could have rested there so well, in loving non-commitment. She pictured Rudolf, her patron, her mentor, her friend whose untimely death had set her off on the path to a local dentist. Yet again huge tears began to roll down Sissie's face and, anxious to avoid Mr Plumb's condoling caresses, she slipped from his bed – his son's bed, to be exact – and slid downstairs to the telephone. Her mind was made up.

'Seb?'

'Tenez.'

Was that Seb's voice? If so, why was he telling her to hold? For certain, it was a young man.

'Yup.' Sissie had forgotten Sebastien's annoying habit of answering the telephone as if it were interrupting a thought of genius.

'It's Sissie.'

'Hi.'

Sissie ground her teeth. 'Who answered the phone?'

'François.'

'François who?'

'I don't know yet.' He hardly paused. 'You're not returning, are you? Your beauty restored, perhaps. "Her flower, her piece of being, doomed dragon food".' Clearly pleased with his quotation, he stopped as if waiting for commendation.

'I'm waiting for my tooth,' said Sissie, annoyed at the idea. 'But you – and François – if he's still there, can expect me in a day or two.'

'François will be charmed, I'm sure. Are you stopping or just passing through?'

'Ça dépend.'

Mr Plumb, arriving downstairs, white towel tucked round his waist, stood marvelling at Sissie calmly chatting on the phone at four in the morning and, moreover, in a foreign language. And yet he sighed, too.

Sissie heard the sigh. 'Ah, here's Plumb,' she said into the phone. In answer to a question, she added, 'No, that's his second. Actually, I don't know his first.'

Could this be true? Mr Plumb sighed more deeply. He thought of the huge sum he'd spent on their dinner, of his lack of sleep, of his handsome housekeeper's disapproving yet gleaming eyes, of the inevitable disloyalty of the young. 'I'm going to bed,' he said.

The next morning, the tooth not having arrived by the first post and the sound of drill and water-hose making it clear that her host was occupied, Sissie decided to take a swing down the high street. She soon spotted a little shop called At Home Hats. It seemed an odd idea to wear a hat in the home but the sun was remarkably bright for England in May and her much improved health gave her renewed interest in protecting her exquisite white skin.

The shop seemed to hold few hats and all of them either canary yellow or royal blue boaters. Surmising this to be the local trend, not what she fancied, Sissie was about to leave when she spotted a woman in a dark corner peering at herself in a long mirror. She was wearing the yellow variety and there was something vaguely familiar about her.

'Sissie!' cried Janice.

'Mum!' cried Sissie, surprised by how pleased she was to see her.

'I'm using my lunch-hour to buy a hat for a wedding,' explained Janice, taking off the boater and inspecting it meditatively.

'I wouldn't get that one. You might as well plonk a lump of butter on your head.'

'At Home Hats is the most stylish shop in town.' Janice attempted a defence. 'But I'm not certain the yellow flatters my skin tone. And the blue seems so hard. Mrs Dworkin says they're *the* colours this season.'

At this point there was the sound of a telephone being put down and Mrs Dworkin appeared in person from an inner room. 'So, have you decided?' she demanded.

How well Rudolf would have dealt with this inflated symbol of the sales-person's ignorant conceit! thought Sissie. In homage to his memory, and in defence of her mother's skin tone, she faced Mrs Dworkin imperiously. 'My mother dislikes the yellow and mistrusts the blue. I agree with her.'

'Now, if you had something with a bit of pink or cream,' muttered Janice placatingly, as they reached the door.

'Last year, we stocked pink and cream,' roared Mrs Dworkin, recovering from the unusual shock of criticism, 'as you, Mrs Slipper, know very well, since I sold you a pink hat with a cream bow! This year we are royal blue and canary yellow!'

'She is a bit of a bully.' Once they were on the pavement Janice recovered her composure quickly and turned to concentrate on her daughter.

Mother and daughter, arm in arm, found themselves passing The Garden Room, a charming café, and entered companionably. Janice's pride in Sissie's triumphant success was based on the knowledge that she had always been different, special, if you like. To admit that was no criticism of Ruth and Adam, as Rob seemed to think.

For two years she had been Mary's daughter. Mary and Thomas's. Sissie may have forgotten that – had, of course, forgotten that – as if the ghastly tragedy had never taken place, but she, Janice, would never forget and whenever she looked at Sissie, she saw her, despite her incredible beauty, stamped, through no fault of her own, with an original stain. Success, let's face it, was the best antidote.

'Oh, it is nice to see a bit of pink!' exclaimed Janice. This was an understatement. Floribunda roses ornamented walls, ceiling and the oilcloths covering the tables. The cruets were shaped like rosebuds, and when the waitress appeared, she wore an apron of the same material as the tablecloth.

'They do a lovely quiche,' advised Janice.

'Served with a side-salad of rose petals and washed down with rosehip cordial,' suggested Sissie.

'I'm having a glass of wine.' Janice didn't mind Sissie mocking. It was exciting to have her to herself now that she was restored to power and strength. Janice did not quite like to admit how she had hated seeing Sissie's plumage in tatters, how she had fled from the sight because one victim in the family was all she could cope with.

'You look magnificent, dear,' she said proudly. Which Sissie certainly did, apart from a bit of bruising. But then, as Janice thought to herself, Sissie had always had such a delicate skin. As white as her father's. A frightening image appeared in her mind and, although quickly suppressed, it left behind the ever-lurking temptation to reveal what Mary insisted must be hidden for ever.

Drinking a gulp of wine, most unusual at lunch-time, she asked herself whether she had not earned the right to do what she felt was best rather than obey Mary. Poor, unhinged, well, strange Mary. Sissie might not appear again for years and she was old enough to be told the truth. Surely, she was old enough? Or would it be merely a selfish way of lessening her own secret burden?

Janice drank more wine in gulps and didn't really listen while Sissie complained about Sebastien. What did she know of such people? But by the time that Sissie had become silent Janice had decided that she had assumed voluntarily the role of guardian of Sissie's history and that only Mary could give her permission to lay it down. Replacing her glass, she asked Sissie, although hardly expecting or even wanting a proper answer, about her plans.

'I'm in thrall to this new tooth,' grumbled Sissie. 'Really, I don't think Plumb's very efficient.'

'Oh, Mr Plumb.' Janice did not want to consider the dentist in any aspect, not least because she had a guilty conscience about the reasons Sissie had stayed with him.

'It's humiliating to be in thrall,' Sissie seemed to enjoy the word, 'to a tooth.'

'I know what you mean.' Janice decided to be sympathetic after all. 'There's nothing more annoying than hanging about because someone hasn't pulled his finger out.'

Sissie, finding this figure of speech not quite to her taste for reasons she did not pinpoint, smiled a little grimly. 'I don't think I can hang about any more, tooth or no tooth.'

'The world is your oyster,' advised Janice, who had succumbed to a second glass of wine. She thought, with pleasurable nostalgia, of the glorious photographs of Sissie in Paris, New York, Milan and even more exotic places. No doubt, once this little upset was over, she'd be back to all that sort of thing.

'I suppose you like your job,' suggested Sissie, spurred on by the unusual experience of seeing Janice outside the home.

'I like the independence. You know, earning a bit of money for myself.'

'I can give you money. Would you like some of my money? I've made a lot, you know.' Sissie wondered why she had never thought of this before. Her parents had always seemed to have everything they wanted. That must be it.

'No, thank you, dear. We're fine.' Janice's earlier temptation to reveal all was slipping away and being replaced by a niggling depression. Yet she still could not admit fully to herself that something was wrong with Sissie that even the most beautiful photographs would not put right. Instead she began to suffer from a generally gloomy sense that nothing would change. Nothing ever changed. If dramatic revelation was really what was needed, she, Janice, had not the right character for it. Perhaps, by keeping her promise to Mary, she was proving herself a coward.

Sensing Janice's mood, which she assumed to be due to imminent farewells, Sissie had an idea. 'I'll tell you what. I'll send you a beautiful hat from Paris. When's your wedding?'

'Ten days, dear.'

'That's another reason for leaving. An excellent reason.' Sissie leant back in her chair as if she had made up her mind. Today, despite the bright sunshine, she was dressed all in black, black tights, black T-shirt, a black shoe-lace round her long slender neck and two blackbird's feathers dangling from her ears. The effect was devastatingly, heartrendingly beautiful – but also outlandish and peculiar.

The waitress became so obsessed that she forgot to pay attention to her other customers, which brought the owner out of his office to give her a sharp reproof.

'I'll pay.' Such a wad of notes Sissie produced from her little swinging bag. 'Yes, I think I'll go off now,' she said after the transaction, in which she grossly overtipped the besotted waitress. 'But I won't forget the hat, so don't you go buying anything canary yellow or royal blue.'

It was a moment, however small, of reversal, when daughter becomes mother, and Janice accepted it for her own. How could she say at that moment, 'I am not your mother. You must start your life all over again, with a different mother, very, very different'? How could she say, 'You must change the story of your life. You see, your true mother is called Mary, my elder sister Mary, and the thing is that your father isn't Rob either because, as it happens, not her fault, your mother killed your father'?

No, it was not possible, Janice told herself. Mary was right. It was impossible. Sissie's early years meant nothing any more.

Janice looked at Sissie towering so grandly above her and decided that her feeling of disappointment and anticlimax was not because she had failed, her courage weakening at the prospect of truth, but because she had been thwarted of the excitement of revelation, a base motivation, best repressed. Yes, that was it. It had been a narrow escape. But truth, thank God, had not come out but been ousted.

'Sissie dear, I must return to work.'

'You must,' agreed Sissie, her restlessness increased by the shadow of Janice's closely regulated life.

Mother and daughter hugged as best they could and, as they pulled away from each other, Janice felt her eyes warm with tears. Just for an instant she allowed herself to know that the secret was a barrier between them and the reason that Sissie had gone so far away. And was going away again now.

'Goodbye, Mum. Send my love to Dad.'

Janice blinked and smiled and, since she was the sort of woman who lived her life on principles of practical good sense, she soon decided that Sissie's life was far more wonderful than she could ever imagine.

Chapter Six

In which Sissie flies into the Blue with a Mysterious Author.

S ISSIE ORDERED a bottle of champagne and launched into the rare roast beef for which Air France's first class is justly famous. 'I shall fly forward as a meat-eater,' she told herself. 'Paris will be a mere stepping-stone to a new stage in my life.'

Sad, it was, that this bright optimism should be quenched so soon! For on Sissie's second bite of her sandwich she felt a hardness more than meat or even chewy crust and, having discreetly removed the mouthful, discovered her temporary tooth embedded in the beef.

'Oh, no! No!'

The first class was scarcely inhabited but an elegantly dressed man sat across the aisle from Sissie. He had been eyeing her admiringly for some time – she was once more in her frou-frou skirt and tie-dyed tights – and when this sorrowful objection at destiny broke involuntarily from her lips, he leant across sympathetically.

'Please. May I help?' His accent was foreign, his tone mellifluous, his eyes the amber of the beads of a necklace, his hair more tortoiseshell, streaked from dark to golden, his suit, worn with open-necked white shirt, in perfect taste.

Italian, thought Sissie, putting her hand across her mouth, in the arts, fashion, films, pictures – or just very rich. Yet when had she cared to impress? 'It's my tooth.' She indicated where she held it. 'Well, not actually my own tooth. A false tooth. A temporary false tooth. It's come out.' Despite not wishing to impress, she spoke through closed mouth.

'What secrets we all have!' The Italian smiled, showing a set of perfect gnashers right back to the wisdom teeth. 'Whenever I meet any beautiful woman I always take the first opportunity to raise my top set.'

Sissie did not quite take his point until he slipped his forefinger under his front teeth and lifted them enough to expose the smooth pink gum beneath.

'Weird,' murmured Sissie, feeling upstaged, which, she supposed, in the cause of gallantry, was what he had intended.

'As for your sweet little singles tooth, spread a bit of this on it and shove it straight back in.' Sissie found herself taking from her new friend a little tube that looked like glue. That was glue. While she obeyed his command, he continued to talk – to hold forth might be more accurate – telling her about his friend with one leg who always unhooked the false one and presented it to any woman in whom he was interested so that she knew the worst. 'She was not allowed to keep it, of course, but to feel its weight in her hands and imagine what it must be like attached to his torso. Apparently, odd though it may seem to you and me, this very often had an extremely arousing effect on women.'

By the time the Italian – although he spoke English perfectly – had moved on to his own failed experiments with a Mexican's luxuriant hair stitched to his scalp, Sissie had fixed the tooth to her satisfaction and surprise. After testing it a few times with the tip of her tongue, she dared to speak naturally.

'I'm afraid it was a punishment for eating roast beef. You see, I'm a natural vegetarian.'

'No human is a natural vegetarian. You may impose such a regime on yourself, but God created man omnivorous. To change the subject, may I sit next to you?'

'No, I don't think so.' Sissie frowned. It struck her as depressing that her tooth might have introduced another man into her life. One Plumb was enough.

'I like that. A woman who can say no. But perhaps I can offer you my smoked salmon?'

'Oh, all right,' said Sissie ungraciously.

'And even,' he added as the stewardess reappeared, 'another inadequately sized bottle of champagne.'

Sissie looked at the watch on the stewardess's wrist. There was half an hour to go. Perhaps she should let him sit by her.

He was over in a flash, but not too close and with none of Plumb's early-days' lasciviousness, which was a relief. In fact, now that he was closer at hand, she saw that he had a distinguished, intelligent face. Maybe he was an academic or a writer or a journalist – a high-class journalist, who wrote long, internationally acclaimed articles about the Mafia.

'I can see you are wondering who and what I am.'

He seemed to expect an answer to this so Sissie made encouraging noises through her smoked salmon (which she was eating with the greatest care).

'It is not an easy question to answer. Even my name has a certain ambivalence. For example, I could introduce myself as Carter Blackstone. On the other hand Enrico di Stefano might be more appropriate. On the third hand – and I did meet a man who had the good luck to possess three hands, who made an excellent living in a wide circle of Southern India without more effort than raising a finger – there is a case for Girish Manekshaw to make one of his rare but important appearances.'

'Do you mean you're a con-man?' asked Sissie, putting the choice of names together with the teeth-raising episode.

The distinguished Italian, although this description now seemed less likely to be true, laughed heartily. 'Nothing so formidable. I'm afraid I'm merely an author. Inventor of fictitious lives but, as myself, a nobody, hardly real at all. Blackstone, di Stefano and Manekshaw are some of the names I am published under in different parts of the world.'

'I thought you might be a journalist.'

'I see your face fall. This is unusual. Most people, even young and beautiful women, are fascinated to meet someone who can conjure people out of thin air, give them faces, bodies, thoughts, feelings, make them meet, fight, love, die. People say to me: "How do you do it? I can't imagine how you do it." They wish to make me admit that it is all facts, if I were only honest, facts taken from the real world, altered a little and popped into the pages of my novels. As Jesus Christ discovered, human beings are, at heart, doubters. It was to persuade them otherwise that I began my secondary career – some might say my more successful career.'

'What's that?' asked Sissie, showing only polite interest. An announcement, rising above the author's voice, had just informed her that they were starting their descent for Paris.

'It began in a small way. I was persuaded by a friend when we shared a room during an international fiction conference held in Houston, Texas, that I had a particular gift for conveying to the uninitiated the art of fiction. "But I am a writer, not a lecturer," I protested. "I was not thinking of you as a lecturer," he insisted, his face shining with enthusiasm, "I was thinking of you as an Inspiration." So that is how it started. I began travelling the world and talking about fiction, fiction in its very widest sense, uncovering the secrets, bringing, to those who are interested, inspiration.'

'How very nice!' said Sissie, listening to the change in the engines, waiting for the clunk of the descending wheels. Upwards, downwards, forwards, backwards.

'I can see you're not interested,' said the author without rancour. 'I fear the combination of your extraordinarily exciting appearance and being air-borne made me talk too much. I shall resume my seat.'

He had become so formal that Sissie half expected him to kiss her hand but he was gone speedily across the aisle before she had said a word. Perversely, she began to miss him at once and wonder why she had been so discouraging. He was engrossed now in an important-looking book despite their imminent landing. It showed a level of intellectual concentration that impressed Sissie. Striving to see the title of the book without drawing attention to herself, she had made out the one word *Magic*, when the plane hit the runway with a bump and a bounce.

At once the stewardess was shepherding her off and it was only as Sissie reached the door that she turned and saw the writer still sitting reading. 'Oh, goodbye!' she cried, loud enough to rouse him from his book so that he gave her a smile and a small wave. Definitely she had lost him. A serious man who had admired her.

Diverted by such thoughts, Sissie progressed somewhat absent-mindedly through baggage reclaim and passport control and was caught ridiculously off-guard when, on entering the airport proper, she was trapped by a dazzle of photographers' flash.

'Eh, voilà, Sissie! Faîtes comme un giraffe!' shouted a raucous voice.

Posing automatically – How was her makeup? Had she, indeed, applied any at all? Would her tooth jump out? – Sissie spied, amid the group, her agent, the formidable Madame Bertrand.

'Sissie dit: "Je ne regrette rien!"' shouted another voice, with no regard for the truth. But long experience had taught Sissie never to speak while being photographed. 'Le retour de Super-model Sang-lante!' shouted another liar.

Photographs first, explanations after. Madame Bertrand had made a fool of both of them. She had arranged this circus without instructions, without warning. Was it supposed to be cajoling, flattering? Was it threatening, a 'You must pick up the reins of your career'? Or was it a punishment – 'Why did you allow your heel to fly off and stop the great Rudolf's heart'? Madame Bertrand was fiendishly crafty but this time she had miscalculated.

As the photographers thinned and faded out to file their film, Sissie walked forward to Madame B. (as she was generally known) with her beautiful swinging lope – unused recently but not forgotten. The agent, sinewy in a navy suit with white beaded lapels that Sissie recognized as one of Rudolf's, revealed her teeth in what she liked to think of as a smile.

'Chère Sissie. Et voilà. On n'oublie pas.'

'Madame.' As the last photographer slid away, Sissie allowed her immobile camera face to be replaced by angry animation. 'Je ne veux pas. I do not wish it! I did not wish it. Je n'ai pas donné la permission.'

'La permission!' Madame's pencilled eyebrows shot up towards her streaked hair. 'Vous parlez de la permission?' And, as if to make sure she was understood, she changed into English, which she spoke just as well as French. 'It is not permission I am looking for, it is gratitude. Do you think it was so easy gathering such a welcome for you? You run away. You do not even attend Rudolf's funeral. All of Paris is there but you, his beloved, his star, his murderer, stayed away. What do you think people made of that? "Lâche Anglaise" was the most charitable judgement I can recall. Cowardly, disloyal, cold-hearted. It took money, believe me, to persuade those photographers along. It took money and influence, of which I have a certain amount, as you know, and which I chose to use on your behalf and now you dare to talk about la permission. Eh bien, ma chère Sissie, tu es vraiment bête!'

Her passion, justified in her terms certainly, would have made more impression on Sissie if she hadn't just spotted Sebastien lurking on a chromium-plated stool. He seemed to be studying his own face reflected in the shiny surface of the bar. The sight allowed Sissie to ignore the potentially disturbing thought that, in her wells of despair, she had not even considered the idea of a funeral for Rudolf.

'So it was Sebastien who informed you!'

'I see there has been a misunderstanding.' Madame B. put on the white kid gloves that were her trademark. 'Come to my office tomorrow morning at nine and we will talk.'

'You do not understand!' This time Sissie screeched, childish impotence against authority, 'It is over! I am over! Done! Finished! Those photographers have just wasted your money—'

'Your money,' interrupted Madame Bertrand grimly.

'—on an ex-super-model, a super-model who is model no more, a non-model, perfectly ordinary human being,' yelled Sissie, perhaps trying to convince herself as much as her agent.

At this point Sebastien slid off his stool and started his nonchalant way towards them. Sissie saw that he was carrying a book and realized that that was what he had been looking at on the bar top. Probably Manley Hopkins. She raised her guard again. 'What I am saying is that I no longer wish to pose, ponce, or otherwise display my face or body.'

'Well. Well. We will see. À demain, Sissie.'

'No!' protested Sissie, but as Madame had gone, her high heels clicking determinedly, she turned her anger on Sebastien. 'Rat! Scoundrel! Traitor!'

He seemed surprised by this greeting, spread his hands deprecatingly, then rubbed his chin. Typically, he made no move to touch her, not even a peck on the cheek. The book now stuck out of his jacket pocket.

'Why did you do it?'

'I suppose you mean, inform the ghastly Madame B. She happened to ring and sort of got it out of me. I always said she had a Gestapo training.'

'Seb!'

'I'm sorry.' He did not look sorry but perhaps he was. Perhaps that was why he had come to the airport.

'You knew I'd finished with the whole fashion circus.'

'I suppose you could see it as a final test. To be sure you're doing the right thing. I think you are, incidentally. I always thought your whole life a nightmare. I like your tooth.'

'It's an insecure temporary tooth, which has already been defeated by Air France's roast beef.'

The conversation was beginning to make Sissie feel extremely tired, or perhaps it was the after-effects of the champagne. 'Let's go to the bar.' Hair of the dog, hair of the man. Sebastien began to talk about a paper he was writing on Gustave Klimt and Sissie half shut her eyes.

After they had ordered a second round, Sebastien interrupted himself to announce that she would not be surprised to hear he had no money to pay for the drinks. Sissie opened her swinging beaded bag and took out two rolls of notes in rubber bands. 'I had two thousand a few days ago,' she explained.

'Pounds?' Sebastien was impressed. Although she earned miraculous sums, Sissie seldom carried much money. 'You could do anything with that. Go anywhere.' He looked up at the monitor, showing departing flights. 'Athens, Mexico City, Bombay . . .'

Hearing echoes of Janice, Sissie began plaintively, 'Why does everyone want me to be a world explorer?' And then she stopped because she had seen the title of Sebastien's book. She took hold of it and looked more closely. It was called *Magic and Fate*.

Suddenly galvanized, she leapt from her seat and, knowing he would be too lazy to follow her – particularly while he still had drink in his glass – she scooted round the corner to the nearest ticket desk. The young man at the desk was grudging. 'Officially the flight is closed but there's no problem with seats and if you're truly only carrying hand baggage?'

In response Sissie held up her bag from which she'd just removed four hundred pounds to pay for a single standby to Bombay.

'I see.' It was not for him to comment on a girl going to India so lightly burdened. Or to enquire where were the malaria pills, the guidebooks, the trainers, the light-weight sensible clothing. 'So here's your ticket, boarding pass, passport. I'll ring through to the gate and tell them you're on your way but don't delay for a second.'

Sissie did not delay for a second and was totally out of sight by the time the airline official noticed that his extraordinary customer (what length of legs!) had left behind a book. He was just wondering what to do with it when a young man, with broad, bony shoulders and a superior expression, swept it up in passing. 'C'est à moi, je crois.'

Meanwhile Sissie sped, fast forward, underground and over-ground, down escalators, up escalators, through corridors and tunnels, until, just in time, head bent low, heart pounding, she projected herself back into the aeroplane that she had abandoned less than an hour before.

'I am so glad you decided to return,' said the author warmly, 'because now I can finish telling you the story of my friend with the wooden leg.'

Happy, and only a little surprised to be accepted so comfortably, Sissie settled down to listen. She was still gasping for breath after her run so she was glad to accept the passive role of listener.

'The wooden leg was a tragedy, of course, but my friend, who was, incidentally, a distinguished Argentinian diplomat, set out to make good use of it. He had inherited large estates, but their value was diminished by their position in the mountainous region of Y. Anyone less determined than Signor X would have been satisfied with sheep and goats but Signor X considered such animals only fit for peasants and began to build up a herd of dairy cattle. Unfortunately, they soon ate all the thin coating of grass and it was then that he had his stroke of genius: he would breed small cows with large udders. For this he needed a good supply of the strong small bulls from Spain. The only problem was that these bulls were more expensive than gold, too delicate to travel, and protected by a purposefully tangled web of export barriers. In short, it was imposs-ible to supply his need.'

The author sat back in his seat as the plane nosed forward and then headed powerfully upwards into the sky. He looked at Sissie seriously. 'You will now ask me, very sensibly, "What about the semen? Why do you need bulls when semen will do the trick?" And

I will answer, "You are quite right and that is where the wooden leg comes in".'

He paused for a moment, checking, it seemed to Sissie, the plane's altitude, and then, seeming satisfied, continued, 'Semen is also heavily protected, particularly the valuable strain that my friend needed. However, he soon found a black-market source so only one difficulty remained: the means to get it from Spain to Argentina.'

'He put it in his wooden leg!' cried Sissie, inspired.

'Exactly.' The author patted Sissie's hand in grave congratulation. 'Backwards and forwards he went over the border and not even the most suspicious customs official ever suspected that the distinguished diplomat with the limp was transporting a priceless load of bull's semen on his person.'

'In his person,' said Sissie, giggling.

Still grave, he nodded agreement and a silence fell.

'Don't you want to know what I'm doing here?' she asked, after the silence had begun to seem oppressive.

'Coming to India, I presume.' Eyes close on her, the author added, 'I've never found questioning very helpful. Even the most imaginative of us can only ask those questions to which we can predict the answers.'

'But don't you want to know who I am?'

'It is only too easy to see who you are. Even what you are.'

'Well, my name, then.'

'That too.'

Sissie frowned. She had certainly not told him her name.

'It is written on the ticket lying open on your lap.'

'But I don't know what to call you,' fretted Sissie. 'Too much choice makes things so difficult. Incidentally, I am generally known as Sissie. Come to think of it, I shall call you Enrico since I first thought you Italian.'

'That's a good start. Now, perhaps we'll have supper together and leave such anxieties behind.'

As the stewardess produced more smoked salmon and champagne, bending so solicitously that her perfume overwhelmed the smell of the fish, Sissie began to wonder if her companion were not only strange and fascinating but also a madman. Somewhere in second class sat his keeper, white coat in hand baggage, waiting to transport him to a healing guru.

'I am not mad,' said Enrico, putting down his glass. 'I pay taxes in three countries and may, shortly, in a fourth. My only eccentricity is never having been married but that is due to a mixture of luck and bad luck. Nor am I too old to say the matter is over for ever.'

'Oh, you don't seem old at all.' Sissie heard the ingratiating tone in her voice and knew she was definitely rattled. 'Actually, I'm feeling rather sleepy.'

As Sissie put on her black velvet eye-mask and wrapped herself in a blanket, she imagined night stretching as infinite as the black space through which they flew. It was a nasty shock, therefore, to be woken what seemed like five minutes later (it was actually five hours) by the unmistakable sensation of a large door being opened to the world, followed by a blast of furnace-like air and loud, harsh voices extremely close by. She could even hear them through her vermilion sponge ear-plugs, recommended to be used, according to the packet, by pit attendants in the Monte Carlo Rally. Taking off her mask provided one more horror as glowing orange light scoured her eyeballs.

Blinking protectively, Sissie saw that the noise was coming from a group of people, standing round the open door, which included several men in full Arab dress as well as the air hostess and Enrico. They seemed excited but not enough to suggest real drama, rather the animation of people who felt good in the morning. This must be a pit stop. Sissie closed her eyes wearily.

'Aren't you going to come and see the desert?'

Sissie refused to reopen her eyes, although she could sense Enrico's energetic presence over her. 'I've seen the desert.' This was quite true. About a year earlier she had starred in a ten-day fashion shoot, which had taken place in a Moroccan desert. Even her extremely large fee, engineered by Madame B., had not compensated for the humiliation and shame of the experience. For a start they had insisted on coating her beautiful white skin with fake tan so that she had turned a disgusting dirty ochre colour. Then they had dressed her in layer after layer of very expensive model clothes topped by shawls and turbans and heavy jewellery of anonymously ethnic origin.

The dresser and the photographer rejoiced together. 'It's the Spirit of the Desert!' cried one. 'Potent! Secret! Unfathomable!'

It was with some difficulty that Sissie had called their attention to the fact that it was 110 degrees in the shade, if there had been any, and, unless they wanted a dead model, they'd better give her a few air-holes.

'I suppose as we're paying Sissie a fortune we'd better let our readers get a glimpse of our star,' the director of the shoot had admitted reluctantly.

Unfortunately this had inspired the dresser, a sharp-fingered youth, to reveal one high-set breast with its pretty protruding nipple. 'Perfect! Perfect! But just a few whorls of paint, don't you think? I'm sure they paint their breasts round here.'

'You're in the wrong part of Africa, Schmittie.' The director had become quite snappy. However, the nipple had remained, causing extreme merriment among the locals who were called in later that day as supporting cast. That had been the shame part. Man, woman and child had understood at once her role in all this pantomime. She was a whore, her body sold to others to use as they pleased.

'I know you're not asleep,' said the author, in her ear, 'because I saw your eyes open like a blue mirage in the desert.'

'I hate deserts,' said Sissie grumpily.

'How very unEnglish of you. One of the best documented facts about the English, women as well as men, is their love of the desert. From Lawrence of Arabia to Wilfred Scawen Blunt, from Lady Hester Stanhope to Ethel M. Dell, the sands of North Africa have been littered for centuries with the enthusiasm of adventurous English.'

'Who is Ethel M. Dell?' asked Sissie.

'What? You have not heard of *The Sheik* or, even better, *The Sons of the Sheik*? No wonder you don't like the desert. Those two books are the greatest example of the romantic fiction genre since Emily Brontë put Cathy Earnshaw up on the Yorkshire moors with Heathcliff. Imagine this: you are a well-brought-up, perhaps even aristocratic young lady come newly from England, dressed in open-necked silk shirt and creamy jodhpurs. You are crossing the desert—'

'Why?' interrupted Sissie.

'"Why" is the wrong question,' said Enrico severely. 'To resume, when suddenly, your horse careers madly—'

'I did not know I was on a horse.'

'You would hardly wear jodhpurs without equestrian intentions.'

'I do. I most certainly do.'

'When suddenly your horse careers madly and you find yourself surrounded by dashing stallions ridden by men in flowing garments. Before you have time to give even the most modest of screams, the Arab whose eyes flash the blackest and who rides his stallion with greatest mastery, thereby showing himself to be the Sheik, snatches you from your saddle and holds you close in his strong arms, possibly uttering a sharp cry of triumph. Ahead, of course, lie the terrifying delights of his tent, silken cushions and a climactic battle of wills as he determines to have his wicked way. I will leave the outcome to your imagination.'

'It all sounds very old-fashioned to me,' said Sissie obstinately.

'It's too late for the desert, anyway.' Enrico sat down beside her. 'They're closing the doors. But I have to say that I hope you show more curiosity when we arrive in India.'

'I'm going back to sleep,' replied Sissie, suiting action to words.

There was not another stop before India but the Arabian interlude entered Sissie's dreams and took her on bounding stallions against a backcloth of blue skies and palm trees.

Sissie woke with a start to find that only half an hour had passed and Enrico was sitting across the aisle, staring at her.

'If I must invent you,' he said in a mystical voice, 'I shall call you the little lost girl.'

'I'm certainly not little. How much further is there to go?'

'Two thousand and one miles,' replied Enrico looking at his watch.

'I meant in hours.'

'Divide two thousand and one by six hundred, multiply by sixty, add forty and take away eighty-seven.'

Sissie shut her eyes.

'We could talk about our childhoods.' Enrico nudged her. 'I always find that passes the time wonderfully.'

'No!' exclaimed Sissie with a vehemence that surprised her.

'Fine. Fine. I expect it's my turn for a kip, anyway.'

Sissie felt like a kidnap victim who was refusing to talk to her gaoler.

Chapter Seven

*In which Sissie meets Shireen and Azita's Mummy and experiences
a change in her Bodily Functions.*

S ISSIE SHOWED neither elation, revulsion, depression, excitement,
nor curiosity as she drove with the author, presently called Girish,
through the slums that line the road between Bombay airport and
the city. Instead she remembered, with a sense of deep guilt, that
she had forgotten to buy her mother a hat in Paris. 'It is the one
thing in my life I have promised her,' she wailed.

'But you never went into Paris,' pointed out Girish.

'I can't tell you how hideous the hat is she will have to buy if I
don't find her something better.' Sissie wrung her hot, sticky hands
in anguish. It was the force of the sun at the airport which had
reminded her of her hat mission. She suspected that disfiguring
freckles had already sprung out across her pure white skin.

Could this be displaced guilt for the sights and sounds and smells
beyond the window? the author wondered. 'We will send your
mother a purple and silver sari,' he suggested kindly. 'My friend
Shireen knows all the best sari shops.'

'My mother wants a hat not a sari!' cried Sissie, putting her head
in her hands.

Girish now decided that the hat was a symbol. He remembered
pointing out to a student writer only recently that life was so full of
symbols that there is hardly room to fit them into fiction. If the hat
was a symbolic need, then there was little point in rational sugges-
tions. He picked up Sissie's long hand and gently stroked it.

Sissie liked the stroking. The chauffeur-driven car, although neither chauffeur nor car were in their first youth, had given her more confidence in her companion. The tangle in her head was not his fault. The feeling that she had failed in some vital daughterly test probably arose out of panic and an unusual desire to touch base. It was only too possible that her mother had fallen victim to a hideous straw boater by the end of the day. One must never confuse one's own needs with the needs of others.

'A sari would be more useful for me than for my mother.'

'I take your point. But I do not see you in purple and silver. That would be too matronly, too reminiscent of Lady Willingdon.'

Lady Willingdon was a red herring thrown by Girish to divert Sissie from the spectacle of an old beggar lady being kicked out of the way by younger competition since the car was now entering the city itself and their slower progress made them a target for the poor and insistent.

'Who is Lady Willingdon?' asked Sissie, swimming-pool blue eyes gazing over Girish's shoulder. Perhaps it was only exhaustion that blinded her to the world outside.

'Lady Willingdon,' began Girish, collecting his thoughts with a refining of his handsome face, 'was one of the last great ladies of the Raj. When we visit Delhi you will notice Lady Willingdon's Club, Lady Willingdon's Hospital, Lady Willingdon's Road, Lady Willingdon's Gymkhana Ground, etc., etc. Lady Willingdon's husband, however, Lord Willingdon, although governor of a great continent, was a man of little consequence. No one remembers him at all and, in truth, what is mostly remembered about his majestic wife is—'

'I wish I could remember,' interrupted Sissie yawning, 'why you mentioned this old bag in the first place.'

'—that she always wore purple,' concluded Girish, showing no signs of resenting Sissie's rudeness. 'We shall shortly arrive at Shireen's,' he said. 'This is her chauffeur and she is expecting us.'

This seemed to be taken as a cue for the chauffeur, previously only seen as a white-jacketed back, a shock of dusty black hair and a heavy hand on the horn, to represent himself more fully. 'Miss Sharma is waiting with happy expectation.'

'Ah, thank you,' responded the author, politely but with an undertone of anxiety for while the chauffeur faced them he had understandably less control over the car's direction: they had now left the centre of the road, and were moving, admittedly at a slow pace, into the crowds.

'Look out!' cried Sissie, shocked into noticing the outside world at last. 'You've hit an old man!'

The car had, indeed, stopped altogether and there appeared to be a bundle of rags and nakedness, which might be identified as an old man, under the front wheel.

The chauffeur looked out of his window with the generous expression of a child humouring his parent. 'He is pretending,' he announced.

'Pretending!' cried Sissie. 'But we cannot move either way without running him over.'

'That is why I say he is pretending. You will understand this man is wanting money.'

'He might have been killed!' shrieked Sissie. But, as she spoke, the rags gave a curious wriggle backwards and, in the same continuous movement, a long sinuous arm came through her window. This would have been shock enough, as unexpected – despite the chauffeur's warning – as an adder's tongue, but there was only one finger, and that barely seventy-five per cent of the original, on the hand.

'Drive on,' commanded Girish, seeing his guest's greenish tinge.

Now that Sissie had India in her view, it would not so easily go away. They drove for only ten more minutes but in that short time, totally unprepared as she was – after all, she had expected to be in Paris – she found herself closely surrounded by shouting, scuttling, wailing, praying, clawing, rejoicing, running, beseeching, squatting, living examples of an alien humanity, and that is to leave out the dogs, birds, cats, cows, monkeys, butterflies, rats and fleas. Not even to mention the cow-pat fires, tin shacks, ornate temples, plaster arches and tombs.

'Aha!' The author clapped his hands with satisfaction. 'Home from home.'

Clean white steps led up to an elegant portico around which clustered other white-jacketed men, some turbaned, clearly waiting for action. Enthusiasm turned to bitter disappointment when it was discovered that the English lady, whose height was a kind of miracle as she unrolled herself from the car, had not one item of luggage and expected none later.

Girish consoled Sissie. 'You need not worry since I have enough for two.'

Leaving the airport Sissie had been too sleepy to notice her companion's luggage, but now she watched with awe as trunk after trunk was carried up the steps and into the house. 'I learnt the value of trunks at my public school,' said Girish. 'Cricket pads, bats, balls, an entire wardrobe of clothes for every occasion, tennis racquets in triplicate, blankets, sheets, thirty-six white handkerchiefs.'

'Even a conjuror wouldn't need that many.'

'It was school regulations.' Girish looked into the distance, although he was clearly not seeing a mother picking lice from her daughter's hair.

Sissie followed the trunks into a courtyard, planted so cleverly with laburnum trees that, although it seemed to be all cool, sweet-smelling shade, well-angled beams of sun found brilliantly coloured flowers, begonias, marigolds, roses, and made them glint like jewels. Sissie felt she had reached paradise and, spotting a pile of cushions on a stone parapet, was quite prepared to unravel there for the rest of her life.

'No, no,' objected Girish, literally pushing her on. On, on, through a hallway, cool and empty, and along a corridor.

'Oh, darling! Well done! Well done, Girish and his friend. Welcome!' An enthusiastic woman's voice greeted them.

Sissie stood at the entrance to a room the other side of the corridor. She had never been less conscious of her appearance, but to those in the room she appeared quite extraordinarily poised. From laced wedge shoes, up through long white legs, cake-frill skirt, skin-tight top, to eel neck and perfect oval face, capped by slicked-back black hair, she was as perfect as the dancer in a musical box.

'Girish, *mera jaan*, why did you not tell us you were bringing a super-model?' exclaimed the voice that had spoken before. Sissie now identified her as a youngish woman in a red sari, separating herself from the throng and coming purposefully towards her, arms outstretched in welcome.

Behind the speaker, Sissie saw a group of people, some sitting, some standing but, since they wore unfamiliar clothing and the room was dark, she could hardly make out their age or sex and hesitated still before moving forward.

'Open the shutters a little, Shireen beti,' called another, older woman's, voice. But by now Shireen had hold of Sissie's hands and, still talking, was drawing her into the centre of the room. 'You see Azita and I, she is my darling sister, this all must be very muddling for you, we studied in England for years, it is our second home, you might see, and we completely adore the English mags, *Vogue, Harpers and Queen*, the *Tatler* and then sometimes we cannot resist the American too and even the French. It is a vice, I am afraid, Mummy says so, don't you, aba – that is Mummy over there on the sofa – because we really are serious people and too old for such things but, in case you are thinking I'll never stop talking, it is all just to explain how we recognize you so easily and how we enjoy so much your beauty.'

Sissie stood tall in the middle of the room, and lamps were lit around her. Now she could see clearly the vivacious Shireen, who was older than she expected, and the others were introduced to her, Azita, darker-skinned than her sister, with short curly hair and a bright-eyed humorous face. 'Mummy' was a large, complacent figure, backed by her husband, who was half the size of his wife, and one other young man and woman who seemed some kind of relation to the others.

'Now we must eat,' interposed 'Mummy', 'before our guests topple to the ground with hunger.'

Shepherded towards the dining room among this happy family with Girish, somehow dressed in a flowing white shirt and so much part of things that he hadn't yet bothered to speak, Sissie felt thoroughly bewildered, not least because she had become famous again.

Conversation, as they piled their plates with curries, salads and sauces, which looked suspiciously like chutney, was almost entirely carried on by the two sisters with interjections from 'Mummy' usually of practical advice, 'Don't forget your napkin, Azita,' 'Pull your sari over the back, Shireen' and to Sissie, 'Take more, dear guest. With your great height, you need additional sustenance.'

All was affability but it was only when they were settled on chairs and cushions that the men took part. Mr Sharma led the way. 'So, Girish, old chap, with what will you regale us tomorrow evening? You know, our English Literary Circle has built quite a reputation since you were last here. Soon the British Council will come begging for our secrets.'

'I never divulge the subject of a lecture ahead of time. Let us just say that it will be tailored to meet your particular audience.'

'What do you mean?' cried Shireen. 'I hope you are not implying we need special requirements. I must tell you that we have politicians, doctors, professors and financiers as our members.'

'That is what I mean,' replied Girish. Sissie sat on the floor with her long legs wound under her and he was perched on a straight-backed chair above. He continued, 'Your members are not only distinguished, but distinguished by the variety of ways in which they are distinguished. I must speak beyond their professions and to their hearts.'

'Entertain them, I hope,' cut in Shireen.

'The author always entertains,' Mr Sharma reproved his daughter while 'Mummy' nodded firmly. 'Last year he took three curtain calls and was only permitted to retire after he had performed an encore.'

'It was the musical bat story, wasn't it?' asked Azita.

'The bat as musician,' corrected Girish gently.

As if it made any difference. Sissie was beginning to feel left out and put out. It seemed that her fame as a model did not entitle her to any special attention. Probably, they despised her as some girl Girish had picked up, little realizing that she was the one who had done the picking up. As the conversation turned from the lecture to the changes in the city over the last year and then to various political intrigues, none of which gave Sissie the chance of intelligent contribution, her restiveness grew.

In England, she would soon have made her excuses and left, but here this oh-so-friendly family atmosphere seemed to cover a formality which intimidated her. Eventually she was saved by Mrs Sharma. 'Go, Girish, take your beautiful but oh-so-tired friend to the garden because we are going out visiting.'

The garden was even more romantic in the dusky light. It would have had a completely fairyland atmosphere were it not for the noise of the great city outside which penetrated the buildings and walls

73

that surrounded it. It was not a pretty or romantic noise, being predominantly made up of the sharp screech of street hawkers, the wail of Hindi pop music and various sorts of horn, bell and hooter, presumably fixed to various sorts of vehicles.

'What a noise!' exclaimed Sissie.

'What noise?' Girish looked round the courtyard and then up to the windows of the room they had come from.

'The city,' said Sissie, becoming irritated. 'If you want to know, I feel very odd coming all this way to see India and spending the whole day inside a house.'

'You feel like a prisoner, perhaps?' suggested Girish.

'Yes, well, a little.' His ready agreement somewhat deflated her puff of anger. The truth was that she now felt far too exhausted for any city exploration.

'Never mind, there is always tomorrow. At my lecture, you will meet the cream of the intelligentsia.'

'But I want to meet the *real* India!' exclaimed Sissie, sounding like a spoilt child even to her own ears.

'The poor, you mean. I quite understand. We all feel that at first and then we resort to the collecting box or the committee or the commission or some just turn aside. It is natural you should want to see for yourself.'

Girish walked over to a rose bush where one flower shone an almost bluish white. Snapping it off its stem, he brought it over to Sissie. 'To build on some words of Jesus Christ, the poor are always with us, but your beauty will pass, fading as will this rose.'

'Do you mean, it's time enough to help others when I look like an old bag?' Sissie's mood was not improved by a thorn in the stem of the rose which had punctured her finger painfully.

'Come.' Girish took her arm and led her inside. Through the empty and silent house, up marble stairs to a heavy door and into a high-ceilinged bedroom where a wide fan made pale curtains writhe like ghosts at the windows.

'And the bathroom is next adjoining.' Girish bowed himself out like a hotel porter.

One of the results of Sissie's quasi-anorexic history was that she no longer bled. So when she saw a drop of blood on the blue tiles of the dimly lit bathroom, she assumed it came from her pricked finger.

As if I wanted to be likened to a white rose anyway, thought Sissie, and stuck the no longer virgin bloom in a glass by the sink.

In the bedroom she found a pretty cotton gown draped across the bed. She was stuck half-way inside it, unable to pull it up or down when she heard Girish return.

'As you're there, perhaps you could give this a tug. It was definitely made for a smaller person and, frankly, I'm about to suffocate.'

'Certainly.' Certainly he was adept with his hands. Sissie emerged thankfully and took gulps of air. She was glad to see that Girish was still fully clothed. If it were sex he was after, she would take some persuading.

'Helping you out of that strait-jacket,' began Girish, walking up and down at the end of the bed, 'reminds me of the time I served as an orderly in Hoboken Hospital for Physically and Mentally Handi-capped Children. My job was to carry the children who had no legs, or none that were usefully connected to their brain. I became fond of a four-year-old girl called Lily. She was very pretty with long yellow ringlets which her mother freshened up with a hot tong whenever she came to visit. Lily used to wind her arms round my neck when I carried her and whisper nursery rhymes into my ear. One morning when I was bringing her back from physiotherapy, which was painful and therefore left her in an agitated state, I realized, to my horror, that she was not whispering "Little Bo-Peep" but instead a peculiarly nasty pornographic ditty. It was a credit to the success of my training that I did not drop her on the spot.'

'How awful!' agreed Sissie, hoping that was the end of the story.

'The next morning,' continued Girish, implacably, 'I accosted the consultant neurosurgeon, a Mr Willoughby-Smith-Stein and, in some distress, told him what had happened. Although child abuse had not been fully invented, I must have feared something of the sort. WSS was intrigued. "In brief," he said, pulling his beard, "it is not her speaking. She is merely reproducing words she heard when a very tiny child, even tinier than now, words so shocking that they have replayed in her head ever since, although quite without any conscious understanding or even knowledge. Childhood memory is one of the most fascinating areas for conjecture—'

'Stop!' cried Sissie, with an agitation that surprised her. She did not have to listen to such things. 'I was a nice child,' she found herself saying. 'My mother is very nice too. What a nice woman she is! Tomorrow I shall go shopping and buy her a present. Perhaps I will even find a hat. When I think of all the trouble she took to bring me up and then I just upped and left as soon as I had the chance. After all, it certainly wasn't her fault that I never felt part of the family.'

In her unexplained anguish, Sissie sat up sharply and at once felt an unaccustomed sensation in her nether regions. 'Oh dear!' she exclaimed into the darkness.

'I could give you a soothing massage,' suggested an insidious voice at her side. 'Massage away unwanted memories.'

'Oh dear,' repeated Sissie, quite distracted now from childish guilt. 'It seems so unlikely but I fear I've begun to bleed.'

There was a perceptible shift away in the body at her side.

'I just don't have periods, you see.' Sissie was beginning to panic as she imagined the beautiful bed sullied.

'In America, girls used to invent a flow of blood to put off would-be seducers.' The voice had become sepulchral.

'I happen to be English.' Sissie looked round wildly into the darkness. 'What I need is a few of those thirty-six white handkerchiefs you took to school in your trunk.'

'It's lucky I'm merely an honorary Indian,' Girish's tones were still doom-laden, 'and that I am neither Muslim nor Hindu or I would think you unclean and put you away till you recovered.'

'Are you going to bring me a towel or not? And please put a light on.'

Was this why she had come to India? To lie in a strange bedroom watching a strange man under a harsh light?

'When I come back, would you mind calling me "the Author", as my admirers do?'

While he was gone, Sissie lay still and thought about the ache in her stomach, which meant that now she had become part of the female race again and could have babies and was like everyone else.

'Ha, ha!' The Author popped back into the room, flourishing a box of Tampax. 'Magic!'

'Wherever did you find them?'

'Let us say it is a professional secret.'

76

Securely plugged, Sissie lay back on the pillows and, duly grateful, did not object as the Author's silhouette settled at the end of the bed. Nothing, she felt sure, could stop her sleeping, not this unusual man's presence, the fan like a lumbering animal above her head, the street noises far below her flapping curtains, not even her stomach aching and her head burning.

'Surely it should get cooler at night not hotter?' she asked, feeling trickles in every direction.

'It may be your inoculations playing up.' The Author moved closer and lightly stroked her arm.

'I haven't had any inoculations.'

'No inoculations!'

'You don't need inoculations for Paris.'

'No anti-tuberculosis, cholera, rabies, yellow fever, polio, typhoid, hepatitis A, B and C?'

Sissie let her head fall from side to side on the pillow.

'Well. Well.' The Author stood up. 'This presents an opportunity to show you some of the contents of my trunk.' In a second he was out of the room.

I would much rather have two paracetamols than all the injections in the world, thought Sissie, holding her stomach. She supposed this bleeding had started because she had begun to eat too normally. What a mistake!

'I can do them all except polio,' said the Author, arriving back with syringes and tubes and boxes and swabs and enough equipment for a medium-sized hospital.

'Oh, please!' protested Sissie, to no avail. An hour later, it was over: she was as pierced full of holes as a pincushion. 'I hope it gave you satisfaction,' she commented ungratefully.

'During my stay in Hoboken Hospital for the—'

'No!'

'I was merely going to say that the doctor has much in common with the novelist. They both identify the maladies of society, dabble in the dark, take bold leaps into the unknown and attempt to make money out of it.'

As the Author elaborated on this theme his audience slipped finally from him. Eyes tight shut, mouth fallen open, Sissie found happy oblivion. Strangely, this hardly seemed to diminish the

Author's enthusiasm for his words and he slipped under the bed-clothes beside her, 'It is a well-documented fact that the female sex remains closer to the dark creator than the male. Essentially, this is to do with her power of growing life within her body. When the ignorant ask me about the so-called woman novelist, I point to the nearest female belly and say, "A woman produces a novel from her womb, a man,"' he paused and looked down at Sissie sympathetically, '"with his head."'

'Mother,' mumbled Sissie, out of a feverish dream, and her face contorted like a child about to cry.

Chapter Eight

In which Sissie becomes an Illustration in the Author's Lecture on the Meaning of Fiction but fails to buy a Hat for her Mother.

S ISSIE COULD feel herself sweating long before she woke up. Trickles of water, little tickling worms, crawled down her body. There was also a more internal sensation. Eventually she dived through layers of swaddling and opened her eyes to find opposite another pair of eyes, almond-shaped, dark and lustrous, watchful and curious.

'Now you wake!' The voice sounded relieved, even joyous.

Sissie looked beyond the eyes and saw a tiny dark-skinned girl, dressed in a pink dress with silver threads, and red trousers, toe-nails painted a matching red.

'They left and I came up. In case you are dying here.'

'Not quite.' Sissie pulled herself up and felt her head. The room was very, very bright and very, very hot. 'What time is it?'

'Half-way through the day.' Sympathetically, the girl handed over a wet cloth and Sissie saw she was holding a bowl of water. Beside her on the floor stood a glass of pink juice and a slice of melon.

'I'm thirsty.' It was delightful to be waited on by this pretty handmaiden, the size of a four-year-old but whose composed and practical manner suggested someone ten years older. First the fruit, then the bathroom and then a look at the city below.

'What is your name?' she asked over her shoulder.

'Rita.'

'Where did they go, Rita?'

But Rita hung her head.

'I wish I had some other clothes,' sighed Sissie.

'My uncle is driver. He drives you to shops.'

It was strange to be led about by a creature whose head was barely above knee level, to be in a house empty of hosts, to be in a strange city, to sit in the back of a black car, being instructed on where to look by a sparkling little face, swivelled round from the front passenger seat.

'My uncle takes you to the shop of his uncle, who has very lovely saris.'

Sissie clasped her bag, still stuffed with hundreds of pounds, and thought how happy she was to be on such an adventure and that perhaps, after all, her mother would like a sari in lieu of a hat.

'After the shopping you see the towers where dead people lie. My uncle drives you and you can see the fat birds flying up and down.'

Rita's enthusiasm was less catching now. The car had left the quieter residential area and was pushing its way through a narrow street made narrower by stalls, bicycles, bicycle rickshaws and more people than Sissie had ever seen.

'First stop,' announced the uncle, ramming on his brakes without warning in the middle of the road so that several cyclists and a group of children chasing behind them ran into the back of the car. 'Gem stones,' continued the uncle, ignoring the confusion. 'Turquoise, emerald, sapphire, pearl, coral. Very good price.'

'But—' began Sissie.

'Very good price,' repeated the uncle, and Sissie found herself out of the car and pressed forward among a squeeze of bodies into a little dark shop. Their friendliness is quite disarming, she thought to herself, as smiling faces, packed one on top of the other, pressed around her. At the bottom, of course, was Rita's, at the top a round, noble face, which was speaking. 'I welcome you to my shop. I am told you have a fondness for coral. Here we have coral with silver. The darkest, reddest coral. Coral with silver and pearl. Coral with turquoise and pearl. Coral with gold. Coral with coral.'

Pressed and squeezed though Sissie was, no one rose above her shoulder level, which left her free to turn her head and see beyond the shop-keeper, the crowd, the wood-topped counter and into a back room where an old lady sat with a baby on her lap. With gnarled misshapen fingers, she stroked its head rhythmically.

'I wanted to buy a sari for my mother,' whined Sissie. But naturally no one took any notice of that. Half an hour later, decked with coral and silver earrings, Sissie took her leave from the shop-keeper and received the plaudits of the crowd. Now, she thought to herself, I have been kind to the uncle's friend, I shall buy a sari and some cotton trousers and a tunic for myself.

Three hours and seven shops later, excluding stops for *chai* and sweets, mango juice and chapati, Sissie knew her mistake. And yet she had bought beautiful things. Her mind became dizzy at the thought of them. She had a dark green shawl embroidered with silk flowers and butterflies, leather sandals engraved with gold that made her look like a Hindu goddess, a rich red bed-covering made of hundreds of patterned squares, bangles of every shape and colour, a carved and painted set of chess-pieces and board, spices from saffron to ginger to coriander, an exquisitely painted miniature of a lady with a blue man or god in a bower, and a woven bag of many colours in which to put them all.

'Your family has many relations,' she sighed, although not without satisfaction, to Rita who was still as chirpy as ever.

'Oh, yes. And now we go to find saris. Yes?'

Ironically, it was the saris that did Sissie in. One after another, gleaming, glittering lengths of silk were thrown open for her to inspect, making a kaleidoscope of colour that began to swirl in front of her eyes. 'I must sit down,' she whispered. But too late. Slowly, giving plenty of time for the usual admiring crowd to spread backwards, Sissie dissolved from her tower-like height and measured her length on the floor.

Out cold, she knew nothing of the hubbub and consternation, of Rita blowing cool breaths at her face, of the driving uncle telephoning the house in the grand street, of the sari-selling uncle wringing his hands over the probable loss of one of the greatest sales of the year.

The first Sissie knew was when she found herself sitting in a chair – she had been put there by many concerned hands – and facing not very sympathetic admonishment from the Author and Shireen.

'We thought you were doing a bit of sight-seeing, not stocking up for a shop.'

'The Author is anxious, you see,' said Shireen, a little more kindly, 'because he likes to be calm before his lecture.'

Trying to form adequate apologies, Sissie was distracted by the shop-keeper, who was continuing to unfold exquisite saris behind Shireen's back.

It was dark again by the time Sissie, Shireen, sister Azita, 'Mummy', Mr Sharma and several other friends and relatives arrived at the lecture hall. The family were as gracious to her as they had been the night before and when she was introduced it was as 'our Parisian model, Sissie' and there were other women who nodded and seemed to know.

The hall itself was a bewildering mixture of cheap seating with garish orange chair covers, and substantial, even modish walls with a lavish use of marble and carved wood. The stage, however, was invisible, being hidden behind a rather dirty and discoloured red curtain.

Sissie was shown to the front row with the family. But whereas she stayed put, they flittered about among their friends, chattering cleverly with unflagging animation. After a while, Sissie caught Shireen's attention. 'What time does it start?'

Shireen seemed surprised at the question. 'What time? No time. When everybody is here, when everybody is sitting and expectant.'

Sissie would get to know the curtain even more intimately than she did already and wished that the slinky suit brought to her by the Author, did not press so tightly on her arms, which had begun to swell from the needles of the night.

At last the curtains began to part, unheralded but noisily enough to rise above the hubbub around her. Instantly, with hushings and twitterings, the audience settled down on their seats. 'Oh, the excitement of this moment!' whispered Azita in Sissie's ear.

The stage was black, so completely black that it was like a hole. Into this hole stepped the Author, his cream suit flashing, his handsome face portentous.

'Fiction, ladies and gentlemen, honoured guests. Tonight, I am going to talk about fiction. Fiction as magic. Here you see it. Here you do not. If there is a person in this hall who does not believe in magic, then he should not linger but find his place in another hall where unbelievers gather. Each one of you carries the seeds of fiction in his heart. You are fiction. I, the writer, am merely the vehicle. Without you I stand in darkness. In blackness. In a vacuum. A writer is an illusionist. But the illusion takes place in the hearts of his readers, his audience, not in his own heart. The writer of fiction is the least important part of his book.'

Sissie thought this all very clever and could feel a sense of satisfaction humming round her but nevertheless wondered how the Author could keep up such a level of profundity over the promised two hours. Perhaps her reaction could partly be explained by her aching arm and her habit of falling asleep after a paragraph or two of the well-known mellifluous voice. Very soon her attention was, at best, sporadic.

It was brought back by a sharp nudge from Azita's elbow. As if in a dream, she saw that the Author, spotlit still, had come forward on the stage and was beckoning commandingly in her direction.

'Go on,' said Azita, giving her a push.

Since she had been put into an aisle seat and there were steps leading onto the stage, it was only too easy to oblige. 'But I don't want to be cut in half,' she found herself muttering. Was this why the Author had lured her to India, so that he could put her into a black box and cut her in half in front of an admiring audience, thus proving the illusory nature of fiction? Was she to be a fountain, spouting blood, not water?

'Wake up,' hissed Shireen, from beyond Azita. 'He's waiting.'

Sissie did wake up and decided to leave, to run down the aisle, take the next flight to England, and let the greedy crowd with its bossy ringmaster get on as best they could without her. But as she stood up she was almost knocked down again by a powerful sense of déjà vu. Of course, the aisle was the catwalk, the audience the baying Parisians. In a flash she relived that hideous moment when the glass heel had, like a dagger, flown from her foot and pierced the heart of Rudolf, while she, bloody, tattered murderer, had continued along the walk and out of the door. Far better to mount the stage than re-enact such a nightmare.

'Welcome!' greeted the Author as Sissie waggled her willowy model's walk towards him. Politely, the audience clapped.

'Fiction,' announced the Author, turning Sissie round by the hand so that they stood side by side facing the audience, 'in the instant that this beautiful young Englishwoman took my hand . . .'

'You took mine,' murmured Sissie under her breath.

'. . . each one of you,' continued the Author, fixing the audience with his favourite face, 'in that instant became,' he spaced each word to give greater emphasis, 'writers . . . of . . . fiction!' Into a hushed hall, he elaborated. 'Such a creature, suddenly at my side, when I had been alone for so long,' he looked at his watch, 'at least an hour, gives rise to a thousand questions. Who is she? Why is she there? Where did she come from? What is she to do with our great writer? Why is she so tall? Why is she so beautiful? Why is she dressed in a suit that is too small for her? A thousand questions in all your minds. And more than a thousand stories. She is his sister, come from America. She is his daughter by a giraffe. She is nobody or, at least, just anybody who caught his eye in a crowd. She is famous, a film star from Hollywood who wants to learn to write. She is, she is, she is . . . And these stories are just the starting point of the stories that begin about me. Her presence is the purest form of fiction. In her apparent corporeality is the essence of the unreal, the imaginative, the . . .'

Sissie listened while the Author said what she considered ridiculous things about her. She was used to being stared at, so that did not worry her, but the hall had gradually become extremely hot, the suit constricted her breathing and her feet hurt. Moreover, she was cross with this show-off ringmaster for not asking permission to use her as an exhibit. As a model she had danced to Rudolf's or another designer's tune but she had been employed to do so. Here, in Bombay, she was not a puppet for some man's fantasy or even for a whole hallful's fantasy.

'The truth,' she said, very loudly and clearly, 'is that I am a prisoner!' She was gratified that the Author's even modulations had stopped at once and been replaced by a unanimous gasp. Perhaps they had thought her dumb. Even opening her mouth had given her a nice airy feeling so that she was determined to continue. 'If you wonder why I have not escaped, I must tell you that last night, brooking no opposition, your famous Author came to my bedroom and injected me no less than eight times with various drugs. These have so affected me that I have become not only the Author's prisoner but also his slave. This is the person you see standing in front of you. Far from being the independent spirit of fiction, she is a poor, used creature, a puppet performing at the will of her master!'

Sissie was so carried away with her story that she lost touch with the mood of her audience and was extremely taken aback when the word 'master' was met with a jubilant round of applause. Now the Author's hand was on her shoulder and he was raising his voice to reach the back of the hall. 'I must congratulate you. Your under-standing puts you among the most intelligent audiences in my years of lecturing. You have learnt already that the voice of fiction bites the hands that feed it, that the novelist cannot command his own characters and that nothing is what it seems . . .'

It came to Sissie that, far from causing the Author problems, her accusation had merely given a new, exciting impetus to the lecture. It seemed that whatever she said now would be treated as fiction. She had passed into another world of the Author's creating where it would be harder to prove the reality of anything she said than it would be for a mongoose to prove he was a leopard. He had done worse than cut her in half, he had made her disappear. Moreover, since it was clear he had embarked on another lengthy bout of theorizing, she felt that her presence (or lack of it) was dispensable. Turning with her model's swing, leg swivelling out and then in, she paraded into the darkness of the back of the stage.

What a relief! It was dark but not quite so dark in a corridor that ran around the hall to the foyer. As she walked, not too fast, careful to breathe and find an even place for her foot, she could hear the rhythm of the Author's voice, although not a word was intelligible. This was a relief too. She had already had enough of him, in the middle of the night.

Outside in the dark street, noisy with sights and sounds as unintelligible to her as if she were in a nightmare, she immediately found herself surrounded by six or seven bicycle rickshaws and behind them a group of taxis honking their horns for her attention. She would have preferred one of these, but the largest of the bicycle-rickshaw men grasped her arm in such a vice-like grip that it seemed best to follow him in the hope that he would release her. By the time she had achieved her ascent into the high cart, hampered as she was by her tight skirt and the anxiety that she might have bled through the thin material, a large crowd of encouraging spectators had gathered. Once seated, things were hardly calmer as she was paraded through the streets, mountainously tall, exposed to every gaze, every comment of applause or disparagement. It was a journey of such frightfulness that when Sissie finally recognized the white house on the hill, she flung rupees at the driver, and herself onto the road, before they had come to a halt. At once another crowd collected.

'Go away!' screamed Sissie, to the curious, good-tempered faces. 'Just go away and leave me alone!'

'You are taken sick again?' Sissie scrabbled upright to see the chauffeur's sympathetic face. 'And I see, so sorry, you have lost a tooth.'

Sissie put her hand to her mouth, her tongue to the hole. When had it gone? Where had it gone to? If she had remembered its avowed temporary nature, she might have checked its presence before rising, with such spineless obedience, to stand at the Author's side on the stage. Now she became convinced that the tooth had dropped out during the first part of his lecture as she dozed through his silly Tinkle Bell philosophy. A tooth fairy would do her no good now. Besides, it was not money she wanted but the priceless temporary pearl itself.

'I must not panic,' Sissie told herself, walking towards the house with hands clasped round her bag. 'I may have been made a fool of in front of the whole of India, well, anyway, Bombay, but I am still myself, whatever that might be.' Here, stern resolutions were interrupted by an image of Shireen's face as she led the clapping against her, she now saw. Suddenly she felt certain that it was Shireen, suffering from jealousy over the Author's attentions to her, who had removed the tooth while she slept. Sissie ground her remaining teeth in rage.

Once inside the house, she dashed to her bedroom, checked her internal protection, changed into her own clothes, gathered up the spoils of her buying spree and even found time to destroy a delicate table lamp on her way out. Tricked! Abused! Destroyed! That was how she felt. But she was not finished yet. Merely exercising a right of departure.

'To the airport!' she yelled to the chauffeur, who had found time to collect round him a large group of well-wishers. She picked out a ten-pound note with a sense that he and Rita had been her only true friends in India. 'And don't forget two English pounds for your niece,' she said, the rosy mists of anger dissolving a little for her to picture Rita's eyes as she received such a gift.

The driver, picturing no such inappropriate event, palmed away the notes out of all existence.

I must calm myself, thought Sissie, once again sitting in an aeroplane, although this time courtesy of Air India. I must take off my shoes, which are killing me – an echo here of what those other shoes had done to Rudolf. I must wipe my face with one of those eau-de-Cologne sachets that are coming down the aisle, even if they do come from a sari-clad arm. I must take a grip on myself, on my throbbing arm, my hideous mouth, my aching ribs, my newly performing internal passages and make them into something better.

'Thank you,' said Sissie, through closed lips, and took not one but three sachets of saturated tissue from the hostess. The anger that had propelled her into the airport would burst a hole in the plane's fabric if it were not quelled. Sissie imagined herself sucked out into the vast darkness, holding hands with her rug-clad neighbour who would shriek incomprehensible reproaches . . .

Fiction, thought Sissie disgustedly. What do I want with fiction?

Chapter Nine

In which Mary identifies Happiness.

THE CAT SLEPT as Mary had hoped. Its strong, rounded back echoed the shape of the hill outside her caravan window. Its fur was like a coating of short grass.

'Come on,' said Mary, 'I'll give you some milk.'

Cleo woke, stretched with relaxed deliberation and then followed her mistress to the corner, where she was confident her saucer would appear.

Mary watched the pointed pink tongue slip in and out of the milk and felt a delicious warmth spread inside her as if she were the one doing the lapping. This kind of sensation had been growing ever since she had brought back the stray cat from the farm. She was black with a white face, white stocking and white belly. Her eyes were pale green and widely spaced. At first they had looked at Mary without confidence and she sat near the door like a prisoner waiting to be released. But after a day or two she had begun to explore her new home, delicately sniffing and patting areas that were unimaginably soft and cosy, so much more comfortable than the stable and the daily battle to reach the tin dish in the yard before the other cats had eaten all the food.

She tried different corners of the caravan one by one, deferring to Mary if she were there first but evidently determined on making her choice. Soon she had created a routine for herself. In the early morning she moved to a shelf by the window where she could watch the birds waking up, squeaking and fluttering. In the day she moved to the end of Mary's bed where she kneaded the woollen blanket in a way that Mary remembered was called 'making bread'. At night she curled up on the mat near Mary's little stove.

The cat's confident contentment amazed and delighted Mary. It was this, she thought, that gave her an inward glowing when she watched her. For she was the cat's benefactor. Most exciting of all was when Cleo slid through the door for a prowl to parts of the countryside Mary knew not where, and a few hours later came back. Came back of her own free will.

Mary had forgotten what it was like to live in the presence of happiness.

Chapter Ten

In which Sissie finally buys a Hat in Paris and meets two
Dangerous Conspirators. And Howard Howard in disguise.

IT WAS RAINING in Paris, unseasonably cold, heavy rain that
soaked through Sissie's sparse clothing in the few seconds it took
her to get from her taxi to the door of her apartment building. Since
her key was no longer in her bag, perhaps fallen under that bed,
already mythic, in Bombay, she had to wait for the concierge.

'J'ai perdu ma clef en Inde,' suggested Sissie, feeling the need
for human contact.

'C'est ici, Mademoiselle.' The woman – the only woman to be
unimpressed by Sissie's rise to fame and therefore unnoticing of her
fall – nodded in the direction of the post pigeon-holes.

The key was enclosed with a letter from Sebastien. Sissie took it
up to her apartment to read. She sat, steaming like a samovar, in the
unaired heat of her bedroom. It smelt of men, she noted dismally. 'I
am so grateful to you,' Sebastien had written. 'Your generosity to
me has exceeded what I deserved. François and I are in your debt.'

Farewell and thanks, thought Sissie, and not even a poem on the
mat. They had skedaddled to avoid facing her, probably impressed
themselves by the graciousness of leaving a letter. The 'François and
I' was, of course, particularly irritating.

'Fuck,' said Sissie, who did not normally swear, and tore the
letter into little pieces. Worst of all, it had made her feel old, tied by
resentment to a past. She must stop this. Rising with unavoidable
grace, she peeled off her damp clothes one by one until, naked, she
strolled along to run herself a bath. The consciousness of physical

beauty soothed and cheered her until she caught a glimpse of her face in the bathroom mirror and made the mistake of parting her lips in tender model's pout.

Zut! She had forgotten the missing tooth. Ready to despair, Sissie was diverted by the telephone. The rattle of French that poured out through the holes of the receiver made her recoil as if from something more like grapeshot than words. Certainly this was her agent, Madame B., on the warpath again. She should have known Madame would not give up one of her highest earners so easily. As the words continued to attack, Sissie looked wildly out of the window where the rain still beat doggedly. Her experiences of the last few days had put her out of touch with time. Somehow she had felt night was approaching but now she understood, from Madame's proposed meetings, that the day had barely started.

'I am not for the buying,' she said into the receiver, and put it down for a second before raising it again and dialling a long number.

'This is Mr Plumb's dental practice. Mr Plumb is engaged in the surgery at the present time, but please . . . leave your name, number and . . .' Raising Plumb, or at least Plumb's voice, so quickly made Sissie blush at her memories. The unctuousness of his tones reminded her of the sinuosities of his body, of the degeneracy of their relationship. What had it been but the waiting room for her new tooth? And then she had come away without even that. 'I want my tooth!' she felt like screaming, but instead she went into the bathroom, where she found the water gently lapping over the sides of the bath. The urgent action needed to mop up the flood, before it descended into the apartment of the bad-tempered *charcutier* who lived below, took her mind off her troubles.

When Sissie next sat by her telephone, her face was set, her hand steady. As if recognizing a presence not to be fobbed off by the unreal, it was Plumb himself who answered. 'Mr Plumb's surgery. May I be of assistance?'

'Bonjour,' retaliated Sissie, feeling this sufficient indicator of her identity.

'Sissie!' A moan of delight or despair.

'Yes, and I'm wondering whether my tooth has arrived. Frankly, I'm in urgent need.'

'You came to me in urgent need.' Plumb's tones were nostalgic, producing immediate irritation in Sissie.

'Let's be practical,' she said. 'Has the tooth arrived? Has the Royal Mail finally coughed it up?'

'Yes, indeed. The morning after you left. I attempted to call you but a French youth seemed not to understand, although I am certain "dent" means "tooth" because "dentifrice" comes from the same root. Maybe my pronunciation was deficient.'

'I was in India,' muttered Sissie, beginning to lose heart. 'Where is my tooth?' she cried.

'Naturally I wished to get it out of my surgery as soon as possible—'

'Why?' asked Sissie, drawn irresistibly into the quagmire of his mind.

'It reminded me of you. Of your delicious subtle mouth, the cavity where I could place my tongue, slipping over the gum with healing dexterity . . .'

Sissie had never heard him so lyrical and understood at once that his sexual and dental inspiration came from the same source. 'So what did you do with my tooth?'

'Sent it to your mother. I embedded it in a little box, as secure as a jewel, though not as beautiful as your mouth, so you should have no problem getting hold of it.' Suddenly his voice had changed to a businesslike formality. Someone must have come into the room. 'I suggest you make contact with Mrs Patterson as soon as possible. I did, of course, include my bill.'

His bill? Sissie put down the receiver and burst into laughter. Definitely there had been someone in the room. Had he charged not just for the tooth but for bed and breakfast – bed, in particular – as well? About to ring her mother, she remembered. The hat! Aghast, she threw on a silver-knit, wrinkle-free, micro-light, ankle-length tube dress, which made her look like a yet-to-be-laid gas-pipe, and dashed out of her apartment.

She knew just the place, an elegant boutique in the Rue St Sulpice, which she had often passed but never entered. Here she would find a delicate straw hat swirled in organza, a hat that would raise the oestrogen level in the wearer and the testosterone level in every man who beheld it.

'C'est ça!' The surprised assistant, tightly controlled in her smooth-on suit and make-up, had hardly risen to this visitation by a recognizable super-model, who spoke through clenched lips when the hat was chosen and commands were given for gift-wrapping as lavish as the hat itself.

Sitting on a nose-high designer stool waiting for this to be effected, Sissie looked into the sparkling wall of mirrors opposite and marvelled at herself. Despite Bombay derision, lengthy flights, disloyal lovers and under-furnished gums, she looked stunning, black hair like a dishevelled fountain over white face, huge blue smoky-smudged eyes, limbs so elegant in their silver coating that she could quite understand why assistant hatters had come out from back rooms to admire this shining star. After all, was she right to leave a world where she had received nothing (until a frightful accident of fate) but homage and financial reward? Should or could she sink into obscurity?

'Merci, Madame.' Sissie took the hat box, which was as light as if it contained a meringue, by the tips of her long fingers and swung out once more into the streets.

The rain had swept across the city like a steely curtain, revealing in its wake the yellow sun of summer. Rich smells of coffee, dark-grained tobacco and garlic-flavoured food spread through the clear air. A few minutes longer and wet tables were dried, covered with cloths and laid for lunch. Sissie decided she must have proper Parisian sustenance before broaching another aeroplane.

The café she chose was unknown to her, modest enough, she trusted, not to be patronized by the famous but attractive enough to produce strong coffee, nourishing red wine. With a self-satisfied, though tight-lipped smile, Sissie sat on a nearly dry chair and placed the hat box tenderly on the one next to it. Indeed, the wine and coffee were there in a second, downed in a second more, hitting her stomach with a flood of well-being. What could be more delightful than this glistening side-street, the admiring waiter, the green awning above her head, the anonymous but, she was sure, well-disposed passers-by – particularly the very old man tottering along with a rolled cigar in his mouth and a tiny hairy dog sniffing, like a connoisseur, at the gutter?

Then the combined alcohol and caffeine hit her head and there was a buzzing in her ears, followed by a roaring, a wave of heat and a banging. 'Bread!' she called, forgetting to speak French. Grabbing the hat box off the chair she clasped it to her chest so that her swirling eyes stared over the top. She realized that her physical condition had brought on an acute attack of loneliness. Now her heart was banging too, pushing at the shiny box so that it pulsed in and out as if it, too, had a life.

'Mademoiselle?' The waiter wanted to help. He stood in front of Sissie, willing to fulfil her needs. Sissie tried to focus on him. She was not used to focusing on waiters but now saw his potential as angel of mercy who might be able to lead her out from this terrifying place of desolation.

'Du pain, s'il vous plaît, et le menu.'

'Tout de suite.' He hastened away. Words had been spoken and understood between them. Sissie took a large gulp of air. When the waiter returned she was able to put aside her hat box like a soldier puts aside his shield, yet enough of her mood remained to make her stare at the waiter and notice that he was young, with regular features and hair that bounced in shiny ringlets. He also appeared to be wearing a layer of orange make-up. Curiosity is a reassuringly ordinary emotion. Sissie began to breathe more freely.

'Le menu. Le chef propose des oreilles de porc.'

Pig's ears. Sissie shuddered but not as before. The waiter was diverted by the arrival of two men, who sat at the next table. One immediately gave orders for them both.

'Entendu, Messieurs.' The waiter receded.

Sissie turned with interest as the two men began to speak execrable French together and saw that they were huddled across the table like conspirators. One was skinny with a domed forehead and red frizzled hair, the other was exceptionally broad, wearing a flashy blue jacket that strained across his bulging muscles. They looked like villains, Mr Brains and Mr Brawn, emerged briefly from some secret place for essential sustenance.

'Qu'est-ce que vous regardez?' Mr Brains's face was leaning into hers, ginger eyes bulging accusingly.

Did she deserve such aggression? No, she did not. Best to put her nose in the air. 'I'm afraid I don't understand a word of French.'

The two men leaned away and, behind her chair, she felt the

ringleted waiter take up position like a guardian angel. Mr Brains and Mr Brawn conferred. 'I guess maybe you come from England?'

'What's that to you?'

The waiter bent low and whispered in her ear, 'I know who you are.'

'Tant mieux.'

'I thought you didn't speak a word of French.' Quick as a flash, Brains responded and Brawn leapt to his hammy feet.

'She's a super-super-model!' cried the waiter.

'Tell me another.' Brains spoke and Brawn pointed a finger the size of a sausage roll at Sissie's mouth.

'I don't know what business it is of yours,' grumbled Sissie, fingering the hole.

'Play them along,' whispered the waiter in her ear and, during this moment, Brawn unrolled the canopy, previously showing only a foot or two, down and down, until every chair on the pavement was in perfect shade.

'Merde!' exclaimed Sissie, as the soothing sun moved out of reach of even her lengthy legs. 'Usually the sun is my enemy, but today it is my friend. I have need of that sun.'

The waiter hesitated, looked almost desperately at Sissie, and then made up his mind. 'Gentlemen! The lady at the next table has need of that sun.' His accent was American, full of those long Southern sounds invented by a joker.

His politeness did not placate Brawn, who rattled the bars of the canopy as if he might tear one down and use it as a lance.

'Peace,' suggested Sissie. Next thing would be a gun and then there'd be blood on the pavement. She stood up slowly, not forgetting to pick up her hat-box shield, and stood above them. 'Bring these gentlemen a bottle of Dom Perignon, two glasses and an extra one for me.' Unravelling her little bag with some difficulty from behind her hat box, she extracted several large notes and thrust them at the waiter. He looked at them wonderingly. They were rupees. Brawn half took a step forward as if he suspected a joke. They all watched as Sissie produced, from her still bulging rolls, dollars, pounds and, eventually, just about enough francs.

'You get about,' commented Brains with a discernible Irish brogue. Brawn stopped his Tarzan act abruptly.

95

'I certainly don't feel very English any more.' This seemed so to please the Irishman that he signalled for the raising of the canopy.

'I meant it about the champagne,' Sissie told the waiter.

'What is it that you are carrying?'

'It is a hat for my mother. I'm taking it to London today.'

'London today,' repeated Brains mildly, and he attempted a smile. 'Perhaps you will sit with us?'

This was living, Sissie thought, as their food came and her champagne and the sun shone once more on the sidewalk café in Paris. Furthermore, her tooth problem no longer seemed important and she found herself opening and shutting her mouth quite unselfconsciously as they agreed on Ireland's supreme place in a united Europe. 'Ireland is the cradle of the world!' she cried, raising her glass. Soon afterwards she felt moved to show them her mother's hat and was thoroughly gratified by the warmth of their appreciation.

'Grrhhh!!' appreciated Brawn, who was essentially a non-verbal being.

'You must model it for us!' encouraged Brains.

So Sissie rose joyfully to her splendid height and plonked the pink and white meringue on her head (which accorded ill with her post-modern silver tube, but never mind). Up and down she paraded, in super-model, swivel-hipped style, up and down the pavement. Such a performance she gave as she had thought she never would again. The American waiter was first out to watch and another waiter and some passers-by, including a lady with a ladder and three young girls who, after a bit, shouted, 'Sissie! Sissie! Bravo!' Then the kitchen staff came out in their long aprons, and several faces appeared at windows along the stretch of street which had become such a delightful catwalk.

At length Sissie returned to the table and collapsed there, laughing. Removing the hat, she laid it carefully among the tissue, for it was thoroughly christened now and ready for more mature use.

'You are a professional model?'

Sissie turned to the accountant and noticed that his smile was not as congratulatory as she expected. 'I've finished with it. My tooth, you see.' She smiled again to remind them.

'Ha! Ha!' Brawn revealed an unexpected gaiety as he leant across to pat Sissie's hand with a wide warm paw.

'This fellow here once knocked out six teeth with a single punch,' said his companion.

This did not seem as funny as all that to Sissie.

'Eh bien, Mademoiselle Sissie, we must return to work. Nevertheless we would like to return your champagne hospitality with a little reward of our own . . .'

Thus it was that Sissie found herself engaged to meet two villains outside the gates of Père Lachaise cemetery for a picnic tea over the grave of Oscar Wilde.

It was only when they had gone, sloping off down the pavement, rather under the shadow of the wall, their disparate natures even more peculiar at a distance, that Sissie's spirits began to sink. Tottering a little, she started back to her apartment.

'I guess you've forgotten about transporting your hat to your ma?' asked a drawling voice at her side. Sissie, opening her outer door, turned, surprised.

'Waiters should be seen and not heard,' she began crossly and then she saw her hat box. Words failed her at the thought that she had left the restaurant without this symbol of filial gratitude.

'I need to talk to you, ma'am. Can I come to your apartment?'

So direct. And yet she felt no desirous waves coming from him. Perhaps her lack of tooth was a safeguard against the sort of marauding men who used to cause her aggravation. 'Why not?'

'I appreciate it.'

He appreciated it. Sissie laughed.

Once inside the apartment, he began to study the fur picture of a stallion. 'There are plenty of horses in Texas and plenty of pictures, too, but I never saw one like this.'

'You can't think I chose that revolting object!' exclaimed Sissie, in tones of horror.

'I know very little about you.' He withdrew from the stallion's fixed glare and knocked into an equestrian door-stop at his feet. 'But anyone entering this apartment, which has, at only a first casual count, seventeen equine images, might be forgiven for making the assumption that you have a special feeling for horses, just as someone watching over you earlier—'

'I rent this place!' interrupted Sissie, reacting unfavourably to his rolling, Southern-style voice.

'—would draw the conclusion that you are a model who has a taste for red wine, champagne and pink hats and just loves your ma.'

'At least you could tell me your name,' said Sissie, slumping beside the hat box on to the sofa.

'Howard.'

'Howard what?'

'Howard Howard, as a point of fact.'

'Howard Howard, why is your face so orange?' Sissie began to giggle.

Howard sat down, with his knees apart like a cowboy. 'Would you care to tell me about your tooth?'

'That's the other reason I'm going to see my mother, to collect my tooth.'

'It gives you a – shall I say? – an unconventional appearance,' continued Howard, his deliberation hinting at an important sub-plot known only to him. 'I believe that is why your new friends felt they could trust you. They do not have trusting natures.'

'You mean you know them?'

'They are known to me.'

'You sound just like a secret agent!' Sissie jumped up and stood, nostrils flaring rather like the bronze colt perched on the desk behind her. 'Of course, that explains the orange make-up.'

'I wish you wouldn't carry on about that.' Howard sounded defensive. 'I recognize now it was a bad idea but it seemed to go with this. I have a naturally pale skin like most blonds.' As he spoke he inserted his forefinger under his front hairline and carefully eased back the hair growing there, pulling it backwards over his head until he held in his hand a wig of ringlets.

'Terrific!' exclaimed Sissie who, in her profession, had seen more wigs than most. 'I wouldn't mind an introduction to your wig-maker.'

'I guess I'll clean off the make-up now.'

While Howard was in the bathroom uncovering the Real Him (presumably), Sissie went to her room and packed a few clothes for London. She was bored, she decided, of travelling quite so light.

Howard, already back in his chair, gave the suitcase a disapproving look. 'They won't like that, ma'am.'

'Those villains will have to lump it. And don't call me ma'am. I'm not the Queen Mother.'

Howard sat forward intently. 'I'm here to warn you that you're involved in a serious matter. Those two men, whose identities I shall not reveal to you for your own protection . . .'

This did seem to be serious, even ominous. Sissie sat down again. 'So what are they up to?'

'I can't tell you that either. But let us say that it is life-threatening.'

'Not my life, I hope.'

'I can tell you that they want you to take some material into London for them.'

'Oh, that old chestnut! People always expect me to take drugs or whatever. I never do that!'

'I see.' Howard's voice did not express the approbation she expected.

'If I'm not going to the cemetery, I might as well pick up my hat and—'

'Hold on. Hold on. Who said you weren't going to that cemetery?' Howard came and sat close to her so that only the hat box was between them. 'What we want you to do is keep your assignation at Père Lachaise cemetery and accept whatever they give you. Let us just say you have the opportunity to be instrumental in saving the life of a man who not too long ago won the Nobel Peace Prize.'

Sissie felt cornered. Already she could see herself quaking on the tombstone, sullying her mother's hat with some vital piece of bomb or whatever it might be. 'You win.' She unrolled upwards, the glory of her body, which he had temporarily forgotten, making Howard gasp.

'At least they could never disappear a girl with your attributes.'

'Flawed,' said Sissie, opening her mouth. 'But thanks anyway.'

'One word of advice: wear the hat through Customs. You'll find a plane ticket inside the box. Bonne chance!'

Sissie walked slowly through an avenue of mausoleums. They towered massively, stonily, hardly the most cheering companions for a girl embarking on a dangerous assignment.

Not long ago she had done a modelling shoot among the

headstones and busts of this most fashionable of graveyards so she knew her way around. Here were Eloïse and Abelard, between whom she had wound her long limbs – modelling hand-knit winter woollens; here were La Fontaine, Molière, Daudet, Balzac ... Counting off the greats of her acquaintanceship, Sissie distracted herself from the difficult present and was quite taken aback to see her tea-time hosts on the horizon.

She supposed they had chosen Oscar Wilde as a compliment to her Englishness but Epstein's elegant statue served to show up their disreputable seediness. The Irishman, who was coming forward to greet her, looked as if he needed hanging on a line and beating like a dusty carpet.

'We are so pleased to see you!' he exclaimed. 'Look, we have a Thermos and cups.'

'Oh, such a beautiful day!' said Sissie, smiling foolishly and swinging her hat box. Could they not spot her duplicity?

'You are frowning,' said the Irishman anxiously.

'I had meant to bring a suitcase but I forgot.'

They gathered round the statue, and the afternoon sunlight dappled down through the trees as if they really were spring-time merrymakers. Sissie was wondering when would they get down to business when they heard the sound of marching feet. Behind the tombs, behind the trees and statues, trod a whole procession, some with banners, some singing, all heading somewhere purposefully.

'Le Mur des Fédérés,' growled Brawn suddenly, revealing that he could speak, after all. 'They put the Communards against the wall and shot them dead.'

'I see,' said Sissie briskly. 'Well, thank you for my tea and now I must be off or I'll miss my plane.' She started walking and as she walked Brains drew her aside. 'I wonder if you would take a little present over the water . . .' Quick as a flash he had the lid of the hat box open and under Sissie's curious gaze, pushed a white chiffon rose into the centre of those already there. 'It will be collected from you at Heathrow.'

Sissie had been through Charles de Gaulle Airport under all kinds of circumstances, drunk, stoned, in love, chased by photographers, ill, exhausted and dressed as a medieval virgin with two long plaits and a complicated golden chastity-belt between her legs and round her waist – this was for a rival airline to Virgin whose plan to mock backfired when Sissie made the chastity-belt seem a desirable fashion accessory. In fact, Sissie had seen sides of the airport that even the baggage-handlers couldn't imagine. But what she had never done was pass through Customs wearing a hat on which a piece of essential bomb-making equipment snuggled into the heart of a rose. It took a perfect model's discipline not to scream when the detecting arch screeched protestingly at her passing through.

'My belt buckle, as usual,' she simpered, half closing her eyes to acknowledge the security official's appreciation, which had dropped from her hat to her glorious legs. One sort of scrutiny was all he had time for, she presumed, and no inclination to suspect a new kind of saying-it-with-flowers.

'That's quite a hat,' he said, meaning something else.

'It's for my mother.' Rewarding the official with a heartfelt smile of relief, Sissie picked up the box and glided away to the aeroplane. The official stood watching her go. Had she really been short of a tooth or was it merely a trick of the light?

Chapter Eleven

*In which first Sissie's Mother's Hat is disappeared
and then Sissie.*

T HE HAT WAS back in its box when Sissie came through British
Customs, Green Route, nothing to declare. She swung it
challengingly from her fingertips. 'Come and get me,' her pose
suggested or, as it turned out, 'Ha, ha, you can't catch me!' For,
snaking through the turbulence of placarded chauffeurs and welcom-
ers with widespread arms, a young man, Harrods plastic bag to the
fore, tried an inefficient snatch and grab. Inefficient because, within
a yard of his prey, he found himself bodily apprehended by three or
four burly gentlemen, who removed him so speedily and so thoroughly from Sissie's vicinity that, without the evidence of the green
bag lying at her feet, she would hardly have believed her eyes.
Nevertheless, feeling her job well done, she headed for the nearest
exit to a taxi, only to find herself in the arms of further burly
gentlemen as if the whole world was suddenly filled with broad-
shouldered, clean-shaven men with flat backs to their heads.

'I have several fairly painful injections in my arms,' she reproved
the man to her left, but he was too busy hustling her along corridors
and across Tarmac under wettish skies to concern himself with
words.

'This is all too ridiculous!' Sissie shouted crossly, as she found
herself bundled into a car and side by side with Howard Howard.
'It's dark and I'm cold and wet.'

'It's steaming hot in here,' pointed out Howard, reasonably.
'You will appreciate I need to pluck your rose.' He was still wigless,

wore a suit with impeccable lapels and, even in the dimness, Sissie could see that he was more handsome than she remembered. In his hand he held a little telephone.

'By the time I get to my mother,' said Sissie, 'it will be darker and colder and wetter.'

Howard did not care about any of this, it was easy to see, while a man in the front opened Sissie's hat box and began to pull apart the flowers. Howard listened to some incomprehensible message on his telephone. 'The person who was to meet you is no longer operational. This car will take you on, ma'am.' Howard slipped out into the night.

That seemed to be that. No hope of a CBE for what she'd done or the US equivalent. At least the hat box sat snugly on the seat beside her.

'Make yourself comfortable,' advised the driver, in the tone in which hotel receptionists pronounce, 'Have a nice day,' when they want to get on with the next problem and, on the whole, Sissie could see no alternative. She might even sleep.

The English trees and hedges, the small town with its floodlit church tower, the small village with a tractor parked awkwardly flew by in Sissie's dreams. Meanwhile the driver took instructions over his telephone and ended up, after not too long, in Janice and Rob's neat driveway.

'I think I heard a car!' called Janice from the bathroom. She held a large turquoise powder-puff in her hand with which she was directing Essence des Jolies Fleurs at her naked body.

'You've got ears like a weasel,' grumbled Rob, who was already in bed and half asleep.

Finding dressing gown and slippers took him so long that Janice had time to shout for a second time, 'The car's gone, I think.'

'I'll have a look anyway,' replied Rob, in his responsible voice.

Sissie stood swaying on the doorstep. The night was dark. No cat came to comfort her.

'Oh, it's you again,' said Rob, before remembering that he always behaved well towards the cuckoo in his nest. 'Come in out of the cold.'

Sissie blinked in the bright light of the hallway. 'At least it's not raining.'

'It doesn't rain inside houses,' said Rob.

'I only came for my tooth.'

'Who is it?' called Janice from the top of the stairs.

'It's me, come back for my tooth. I lost the temporary in India and I have a present for you.'

There was the silence of hesitation as Janice decided not to take on the idea of India and then a sweet fragrance. 'Darling, you do turn up at odd times!' Janice's spirits sank as she saw that Sissie, if no longer bruised and battered, had a less than powerful air about her. 'Your tooth's in the parcel on the hall table.'

'Oh, no, it's not.'

The two women turned to the masculine voice of authority.

'I forwarded it on to you in Paris. Well, it seemed sensible since you hadn't said you were coming back.'

Sissie sat gloomily on the last step of the stairs.

'Oh dear.' Janice put a hand on her shoulder. 'And you've come all this way for it.'

Rob, looking down on them, felt a sharp stab of jealous and protective irritation (would Janice always have to give more?) and thought he had been right to get that tooth out of the house, reminder of the disgusting Mr Plumb.

'Your dental friend wouldn't fix it for you, anyway.'

'Now, Rob.' Janice rose warningly to her feet. They were such a loving couple when they were on their own. But it would not have been fair to suggest that Ruth and Adam caused the same disruption as Sissie. An image of her mother, Mary, overweight, desolate, not quite sane, came to Janice. Like mother, like daughter? Was it possible that the Golden Girl could, after all, have something in common with the Tragic Mother? Like father, like daughter would be even worse. She had last seen her brother-in-law, Thomas, a week before the tragic event – she had used to call it the 'tragic accident' until Rob had objected that this did not accord with the court's findings – when he had been, as usual, drunk. His thick black hair, so like Sissie's, was held back by two little girls' hair-grips decorated with pink rosettes. He said he had stolen them from Woolworth's to see if the assistant objected when he wore them past her check-out counter, but more probably he had taken the grips from his daughter's room, his elder daughter's room, that is, Sissie's elder sister. Janice seldom thought about poor Lou now and, if she did, stopped as soon as possible.

'Now, look here,' said Rob, 'I suggest bed for everyone. As Sissie knows, she's more welcome here than she is anywhere, but she does have responsibilities and she should know she caused her mother a lot of worry.'

'I can always find another dentist,' intervened Janice, her enticing smell at odds with her woeful expression.

'There was offensive talk,' continued Rob, by nature so mild and kind and often generous.

Sissie looked up at them from below. Was it possible that Plumb could be important enough to cause all this unpleasant emotion? No, he was not. She would give her mother the hat and leave in a dignified manner. Love, she saw, was not enough.

'I've brought Mum what I promised,' she began, looking for the round box, and then looking again. But there was no sign of a box. Absolutely no hat box. 'Wait! Wait!'

Out Sissie dashed to the driveway while Rob sighed and Janice shivered in her silky dressing gown. With the door open, there was light enough to search and the cat joined her out of the night, making wild bounds in one direction and then the other, but neither of them found the hat box.

'That stupid driver must have stolen it!' cried Sissie, returning. 'He probably has a wife who has no taste and won't appreciate it at all. Or maybe he's a hat fetishist and plans to wear it himself.'

'Come in now and shut the door,' advised Janice, with one eye on her husband's back, retreating up the stairs. You must only try a good man so far.

That night everybody slept deeply, except the cat who had always enjoyed night-time adventures and was thrilled to see a car speed into the driveway, so that the gravel flung itself all over the place, and then eject a round object that whirled along like a wheel for some yards before hitting the house and falling quietly on its side. It was so well placed that later in the night, when the birds had already performed their morning chorus and the light was becoming brighter and warmer, the cat took up position on the hat box and sat there like a statue on a pedestal.

Rob, always first up, found her there and became irritated all over again. Why was the cat sitting there like an Egyptian idol or a sentinel? And how had the hat box found its way there? And why did there have to be mysteries round Sissie? How he hated mysteries and secrets in his life! His sister-in-law was one and, if Sissie wasn't careful, she'd turn into another.

Picking up the hat box in one hand and a bottle of milk in the other, Rob strode (as far as his slippers would allow him) into the kitchen. There he removed the hat, this present, this gift, this symbolic gesture – even he half knew that – and submitted it to the clear light of day.

At once he saw that all was not well. It was obviously a hat with a secret. The base was sound, a smooth cream straw, curvaceous in every direction, but the adornments, the swathing and flowering, had clearly been tampered with. He could hear the announcement he would soon make to Janice and Sissie. 'This hat has been tampered with.' Although an uncritical eye might have been taken in by the show of the whole object, the pinkness and whiteness and shimmering softness – in a hat, mind you, a hat for the head – he could see that the tamperer had not even bothered to cover his tracks. One rose was hardly affixed to its mooring and the chiffon, which was designed to act as a kind of veil, had been twisted and screwed and put under a flower which was definitely wilting, not like the others at all. Even the colour was wrong, a sort of pallid cerise with a touch of lime green.

Of course, Sissie was the expert on such things but it was not a present he would have been proud to give his mother – who really was his mother, not his aunt who'd looked after her niece out of the kindness of her heart. Such thoughts went through Rob's mind, ignoble, perhaps, but understandable, as he made two cups of tea and the hat sat awaiting its fate in the middle of the table. It was a short step to conclude that only he knew of the hat's return and that he had it in his power to dispose of it as he would. Its demise would be unremarked.

'Darling,' called Janice from the bedroom, 'are you bringing the tea?'

'Just a moment!' Prompted into frantic action, Rob tore at the hat box, discovering at once that it was a stiffer proposition than the hat, until he had reduced it to manageable pieces which he stuffed into a plastic bag. Then, one last look at the hat, long-suffering but not long to last, and it was stuffed, squashed, delicate membranes crushed into the same bag and Rob was out to the dustbins. It was Thursday. Even now he could hear the gigantic motion as the dustcart approached down the road. In a matter of minutes, Sissie's disreputable gift would be chewed up in the jaws of the lorry, thrust into its stomach with tin cans, fish-skins, chicken carcasses and sodden cat litter.

'Coming!' called Rob, rubbing his hands together because they rather hurt from tearing up all that cardboard. 'I'm bringing your tea.'

Sissie was sad when she awoke and this made her calm. Only her mother was hanging on to say goodbye. 'I'm sorry about the hat,' said Sissie sadly and calmly. 'That's what comes of saving the life of a Nobel Peace Prize winner.'

'Don't worry, darling,' said Janice, who, if she were not going to be late for work, had no time to think how she would have liked a hat from Paris. 'What you must do now is sit down quietly and think what you are going to do with your life.'

Inevitably Sissie rang Mr Plumb's surgery bell with a sense of foreboding. The door was opened by a substantial-looking woman of middle age, who took one fierce look at Sissie and then shut it again.

'Don't do that!' called Sissie, and above her head she heard the rattle of a latch being opened.

Standing back on the pavement, not so easy as it was crowded with passing morning shoppers made bulky by bags of cauliflower and potatoes, she looked up and there was Plumb's glowing face, framed by the open window.

'Plumb, darling Plumb!' Sissie lied. 'I must have another temporary tooth!' She bared her mouth for visual explanation.

The face did not speak but mouthed passionately, making words, Sissie presumed but, try as she might, she could not lip-read a single one. Meanwhile, she was shoved off the pavement into the road by a censorious old man with a stick and a hard wicker basket filled with tins of dog food. For a moment her position was perilous as a dustcart lorry, filling the whole narrow high street, was approaching implacably. By the time she had hopped back on the pavement, Plumb's face had receded behind closed glass. Lurking at his shoulder was a substantial white-coated figure.

Eyes blurred with tears of self-pity, Sissie looked away into the chomping jaws of the receding lorry. It was too much to see a shred of pink chiffon caught between a side tooth, too reminiscent of that exquisite concoction with which she had wanted to crown her mother, although she naturally did not suspect it could be the sad remnants of the hat itself. Tears dripping now, Sissie barged her way down the pavement until she found a telephone box.

'Mr Plumb's surgery.' A grim female voice answered the phone.

'I would like,' gulp, 'to speak to Mr Plumb, please.'

'Mr Plumb is with a patient.'

'This is an emergency.'

'Mr Plumb's patient is an emergency.'

The phone was put down. Sissie stopped dripping and gulping. She understood the battle was on. She dialled again.

'Mr Plumb speaking.'

'I do not lust after your—'

'Please.'

'I just need you to shove in—'

'Shove in,' repeated Plumb, his voice quavering. There was a commotion in the background.

'Another temporary tooth,' continued Sissie rapidly.

'It'll cost you two hundred pounds, plus the price of a tooth,' interrupted the grim voice, which Sissie now recognized as belonging to Plumb's housekeeper, Mrs Patterson.

'Cheap at the price,' she responded cheerily.

In a matter of minutes, Sissie was stretched out on the dentist's chair, which displayed the length of her beautiful legs to number one advantage. She could see that Plumb certainly thought so. His black eyes, liquid with desire, hung above her. If her mouth hadn't been held open with two steel clamps and filled with wads of cotton wool and an instrument for sucking out her spittle, she would have laughed at his anguished expression.

'Your hands are shaking,' accused Mrs Patterson from behind him.

It was true. Sissie could feel the tremor as the tooth approached. Plumb was sweating too. As he bent closer a droplet fell from his forehead into her open mouth and was gurgled down by the liquid sucker. It left behind a faint taste of salt.

Sissie shut her eyes. Thank heavens the plastic nozzle dispensing gas into her lungs seemed to be more effective. Away Sissie disappeared into a dream of sunlit lawns edged by neat borders filled with cream and pink roses.

It was the lightness of Sissie's little embroidered bag that made her certain she must embark on a more consistent course of action. There was, she noted, as she sat drinking soup in the same high-street café where she had entertained her mother, only a very small roll of money left. She had frittered away a great deal over the last week, despite the contribution made to her airfares by the US Central Intelligence Agency. It was not that the pile of her earnings would be seriously diminished by a few thousand here or there but that there was purposelessness in it, which hurt her pride. Neither was her pride boosted by a review of the men in her life.

Rudolf, her mentor, had passed out of it altogether, helped by her own shoe's dagger strike. (But the shoe was made to his own design so he had to take some of the blame.) Seb, with whom she had thought herself conducting a love affair – however much at the whim of the poetry of a Jesuit priest – had preferred a French person of the opposite sex to herself. Plumb had also preferred someone else, a florid elderly person with the temperament of a Turkish soldier, which was hardly a compliment to her own world-famous attributes. Sadly, she decided that there was always a Plumb waiting for girls who slip off catwalks. Nor was the Author much better for he had turned out to be a bottomless well of deception while Howard Howard – if he counted in this list at all – well, who was Howard?

Watching green-pea soup drop off the end of her spoon, Sissie fell to thinking about Howard Howard. She had to admit that the enigma of his various personae had left her curious. Presumably he lived in Paris where she supposed she must return, yet again chasing the Holy Grail of her pure white tooth. Howard also owed her one very expensive hat. But how do you set about finding a secret agent?

Sighing, Sissie put back her roll of money and, under the gaze of the same admiring waitress who had attended her before, took to the street in search of a taxi for Heathrow.

What time was it? Or day? What place? What country? Sissie felt at home in an international airport where nobody could be certain about these things. She settled herself at a table in an area which was pretending to be a tapas bar in Seville, with plastic vines interwoven with castanets around the serving bar and waitresses wearing frilly black knickers on their heads. The waitresses were, it seemed, purely for decoration because none came near her, and she was just about to rise to her feet when a large presence descended into the empty chair at her side.

'C'est libre?' The voice was brown-sugar gravel of the type that pretentious hostesses serve with coffee. The face was harder to describe because it was covered by a frizzy chestnut beard.

'Non. C'est occupé.' Sissie gave him the hard look perfected when advertising deodorants in the earliest phase of her career.

The beard wagged a bit, reflecting, perhaps, the chin's indecisiveness. 'Mademoiselle.'

'I am English.' Pick-ups come in all sorts and Sissie knew most of them although, because of her height and glamour, she tended to attract only the upper end of the market. This bearded man, however, did not quite make sense. His beard was too full for the smooth hair on his head and for his youthful body.

'I would like a word, ma'am, a private word.'

Sissie sighed and smiled and leant back in her chair. 'Howard!' she cried. 'Howard Howard. And don't call me ma'am.' She looked at a screen on the wall. 'But my flight is already boarding and I have paid for the ticket out of my own money and all my clothes, save what I sit in, are in Paris and so is my new exquisite pearly tooth!'

'But you are wearing a tooth,' Howard pointed out, narrow blue eyes peering above his beard like a tall man looking over a hedge.

'Only temporary,' cried Sissie gaily, and then remembered something far more important. 'I will forgo all the aforementioned good reasons for me to go to Paris if you will give me back my hat! My mother's lovely flower-strewn – slightly over-strewn in its latter hours – hat!'

The blue eyes became perplexed. 'You have your hat.'

'No. I do not. It was carried away by that chauffeur, better named hat thief or a possible fetishist.'

'Calme-toi,' advised Howard, which is a maddening thing to say in any language, and particularly maddening when produced in a Texan accent.

'No, I will not.' Sissie leapt to her feet. 'Yes, I will.' She sat down again. 'I trust you, Howard.'

'Let us say that I hold your safety of paramount importance, that anything I do is for your own good.' Howard stood up. 'Follow me, if you please.'

Sissie followed Howard willingly, even complacently, with not even a backward glance for a waitress who had been encouraged by a huge drunken Finn to unhook a pair of castanets and try her hand at a touch of Spanish dancing. Neither she nor Howard noticed that the Finn (at least, he wore a yellow sweatshirt on which was printed Finnish Fitness Team) was watching them far more closely than he was the castanets.

'Ssh,' cried Sissie, as they spun along the shiny airport floor. 'I can hear my name.' She stopped to listen so Howard had to as well.

'Would passenger Sissie Slipper travelling on AF673 to Paris proceed to gate number five immediately as the flight is ready to depart.'

'That's what comes of being famous,' boasted Sissie.

'Now everyone knows you're here.' Howard sounded petulant and began to move even faster. 'I have a car waiting,' he called over his shoulder.

More to entertain herself than anything else, Sissie swung into her model's walk behind him. It was, after all, the quickest way to cover the ground.

Howard stopped a few metres ahead, his beard in a frenzy.

'They were calling for you,' said a voice in Sissie's ear. She turned to see the representative of the Finnish Fitness Team at her elbow. He was so tall that for once Sissie felt herself dominated. She also had an uneasy feeling that she knew him from somewhere else.

'Thank you,' she said placatingly, and abandoning her show-off walk, caught up with Howard at an ordinary run.

'It's becoming clear you have no instinct for secrecy,' he hissed, much less politely than usual.

They had now reached a side-door out of the terminal, opposite which a car gave the impression of rocking backwards and forwards on its wheels, as a runner in a race rocks on his heels.

Sissie was hardly pressed inside under Howard's guiding hand before it shot forward. A hundred yards behind, a figure stood stolidly, his blank pink face above his yellow barrel chest making him look like an egg in an egg-cup – or, at least, that's what Sissie thought as she leant out of the window and waved goodbye. And then she thought that this giant of a man who had whispered in her ear looked remarkably like Sven, poor Rudolf's lover.

Chapter Twelve

In which Mary is made Daring.

THAT FIRST TIME, Mary thought it was chance that the cat came with her when she set out for a walk. It was a warm, sunny evening, the sea turquoise and the sky braiding yellow at the edges. It was Saturday and there were still pleasure boats on the water, little white speedboats leaving a wake like a kite's tail and pedal-boats, flat as plates, bobbing on the surface. The summer season was opening and, if she wanted to avoid other walkers, she would have to set off later and later. Already the caravan site, during the winter months so peaceful, was filling up with more people, more caravans, more noisy children.

But still she had the headland to herself, the path spongy from recent rain, the air fresh and mild, a few late primroses still curling up from under the grass. When she felt something brush against her, she thought it was only her skirt, which was long and full, but then Cleo began to wind in and out of her legs, using them like the bending poles she and Janice had ridden their ponies round in the old days.

'Silly cat.' Mary stroked Cleo's soft fur and felt the body under it taut with confidence.

From that evening on Mary was accompanied on her walks, not always so closely for Cleo liked to bound away, pawing at flies or chasing invisible mice, but she was somewhere in the area, using Mary as a pivot on her outing.

After one such walk, in the late evening, Mary opened the drawer in her table and took out the photographs of Sissie which Janice had insisted on leaving over the years. She had often determined to throw them away, but at the last moment had lost her nerve, brushing them away out of sight but never out of mind. Once, long ago now, she had tried to lose the few she had then in a hospital incinerator. That had been a dramatic scene. She had screamed and yelled and wept, in the way she used to do, and eventually she had been forced to submit to a knock-out injection.

The photographs began when Sissie was six, which was the first time Mary had allowed Janice to visit. Sissie, long-legged, staring with those eyes, mouth clipped shut, a lanky girl with a solitary air. Was that imagined? Was that something Mary invented to increase her self-torture? Mary spread out more of the professional photographs across the table, shuffled the model's exquisite face like cards, put them face down and face up, patterned them into a series of receding fans so that Sissie's face peeped round corners, one-eyed Jacky, giving her mother a wink and a nod. But however she played with them, made the face sing for her supper, dance across the table in strict formation, pop out where least expected, from behind advertisements for insurance plans or bottles of whisky with pheasants on them, she received the same message from the blankly beautiful eyes: loneliness and betrayal. In a violent gesture, Mary swept the photographs from table to floor.

Chapter Thirteen

In which Howard Howard directs Sissie to the Kom-Ombo Suite
up the River Nile

HOWARD HOWARD held Sissie's hand in his warm golden grasp. He had removed his beard so that she could look at him with pleasure.

'So why have you brought me to this . . .' she paused and rolled her magnificent eyes round the forgettable little room which was positioned neither high nor low in a forgettable apartment block '. . . to this *safe house*, if I may hazard the expression?'

'Quite,' responded Howard.

'The man is apprehended,' prompted Sissie.

'Three men are apprehended.' Howard took back his hand and gazed, with an expression of self-satisfaction, at the ceiling. 'Those Paris picnickers can put away their Thermos.'

'Then why have you brought me here? It is not, I may assume, for recruitment purposes.'

Howard appeared to shudder a little at the idea of Sissie as a secret agent and brought his eyes down from the ceiling. 'We are worried. I am worried for your safety. Are you aware of making any enemies?'

'Enemies?' Sissie thought of likely enemies and the image came of Plumb's harridan housekeeper. 'No,' she said, firmly.

'Your own personal enemy?'

'No,' repeated Sissie, wondering whether all this was a ruse for Howard to jump on her with wild and voracious cries of Texan lust.

Perhaps disappointingly, she had to admit that his blue eyes were far too serious for that.

'My department recognizes our responsibility for your safety after you executed our assignment, so we are working out a further assignment, not associated with the service, where you can utilize your talents with complete confidence in your safety.'

'My modelling talents, you mean?'

'Certainly.'

'But I require an audience to be a model. Not just you, dear Howard, much as I enjoy your company.' Sissie, whose long black eyelashes were a natural endowment, raised and lowered them like Indian fans.

Howard became flustered. He could see she was flirting with him but any temptation to respond was hampered by the listening device planted in the lamp between them.

'We have in mind a foreign photographic assignment on board ship.'

'On board ship!' Sissie stood up with excitement and Howard, eyes level with lustrous, thinly coated thighs, felt the situation could become out of control. He must stay calm and remember that the listening device could not see. He could not be expected to know that a model's body must be interpreted differently from that of a woman in another profession – secretary, doctor or cheese-cutter. Sissie had been flirting earlier but the exposure of her inner thighs to Howard's fast flushing gaze (surely that was a dark tendril of pubic hair?) was predominantly a sign of her thrilled reaction to the words 'on board ship'.

'A ship where?' she asked, shifting her ground a little so her legs parted.

'On the River Nile,' gulped Howard, who wasn't supposed to tell her a thing.

'On the Nile!' Now Sissie moved away, causing a small explosion from Howard as he let go his breath.

'You will be safe on a ship far away.'

'It sounds so romantic, on a ship far away.'

'You will be modelling for a mass-circulation American catalogue specializing in swimwear, underwear and nightwear, although they do—'

'That's not romantic, that's humiliating!' Sissie interrupted him with her own explosion. 'I don't think you can appreciate who you're dealing with. Trying and failing to deal with.'

Howard sighed. He suspected she was right. She was beyond him, out of his ken, off over the horizon. After all, he had grown up in Dime Box, Texas. 'You'll be paid well,' he suggested.

'I have far more money than I can spend already.'

'Then what do you want?' Howard cried despairingly. His brief was to look after her, reward her for good service rendered.

Sissie hesitated just a second and then advanced on him, arm outstretched in avenging angel posture. 'What I want . . .' Her voice was so loud and she was so close to the lamp in which the listening device sat secretly that Howard feared for the listener's ears. Not that he cared, for once again those beautiful gleaming thighs were near enough for temptation.

'What I want is a hat for my mother! Indeed, not a hat but the hat that you just tortured and then stole from me. You may not have a mother or, if you do, you may not care for her, but I do. For her, I buy nothing but the best and this was the best hat in Paris and now it has gone!'

Reaching her climax, Sissie burst into tears, spouted tears in a way she'd managed to resist since leaving Plumb's confines.

Howard's most lustful dreams took the cold dousing full frontal and shrivelled for then, if not for ever. He stood up and put his arm round Sissie's shoulders. Since she had taken off her shoes and he wore boots, whose slightly pointed toes and slightly lifted heels suggested a proximity to ranch-life, they were of a level.

'There, there, honey, it's all been too much for you.'

'Don't you honey me!' With relief, Sissie turned her sorrow into rage and she stamped on his foot, which hurt her more than him. 'You don't know how tough I am. I have been at the top of an extraordinarily tough profession. If I have survived, which I had brilliantly until poor darling Rudolf misdesigned a shoe, it is because I do not drink to excess, I never do drugs and I am meticulous in my personal habits. I am clean, punctual, pleasant. I may not be the greatest intellectual. The psyche of international killers may evade—'

'Please, Sissie, you don't have to tell me this.'

'Yes, I do.'

'All right, you do. I believe you. I was just doing my level best to offer a little sympathy—'

'Wrong way.'

'About that hat. It was transported back to your parents' house.'

'It was?' Sissie sat down suddenly on the floor. 'And then it vanished.' Her voice was meditative rather than accusatory.

Howard tried to get back to business. 'If you would care to consider this Nile trip, your exit from here would be facilitated.'

'Oh, what does it matter.' Sissie lay back on the floor and looked at the ceiling. 'What sort of boat is it?'

Howard slid down on the floor beside her. 'A regular cruise ship, air-conditioned, sun-deck, swimming-pool.'

As Howard lay on the floor, hip to thigh with the most splendid creature he had ever seen, he remembered that the mike had real trouble picking up sounds from below and they were well below.

Sissie gave close consideration to the man at her side. 'How old are you? Do you believe in God? How many brothers and sisters do you have?' These were the sort of questions she had failed to ask Plumb.

Pressing his face as close to the carpet as possible just to be on the safe side, Howard drawled into the pile, 'Twenty-eight last Tuesday. Positive on God. One step-brother and one step-sister, both in Texas, both ten years younger.'

'They can't both be ten years younger,' objected Sissie.

'They're twins.'

What, after all, did 'positive on God' mean? Did it mean his parents had brought him up as a Christian and he signed it on his hospital forms? Or that he went to church on Sunday? Or that God loomed large in every moment of his life? Quite honestly, 'positive on God' opened such a wide range of further questions that Sissie felt exhausted. Whatever had made her initiate such an excursion into another's point of view? Surely she would be better judging by the superficial as was her normal practice. Plumb and the charlatan Author must be merely written off as aberrations following the dreadful shock of Rudolf's death and her disgrace and humiliation – or rather humiliation and disgrace. However unsatisfactory Sebastien had been as a lover, she had known a good deal about him. Hadn't she? Sissie gave a little despairing flutter of the eyelids, which smote Howard to the heart.

'It will be a tremendous trip! A tremendous experience!' He smiled encouragingly.

'And why did you join the Secret Service?' asked Sissie.

'No problem,' replied Howard, sitting up a little. 'Let me put it this way. There was once an immature nineteen-year-old who was touring Asia to gain life experience.'

'I bet he was American.'

'This young person spent a week in Sri Lanka. On the fourth day he was enjoying tea with a local driver on the verandah of an old colonial guest-house.'

'What sort of tea were they drinking?'

'Ceylon, of course. Why do you ask that?'

'I just don't want you to overlook any details.'

'I understand. At the next table were four Buddhist monks, costumed in the traditional saffron robes with bare feet in sandals and shaved heads. The driver whispered to the young man, "You see those four monks. I'm here to tell you they're not monks." The young man was not so wet-behind-the-ears ignorant that he hadn't already taken on board the men who were twice the height and width of his friend were foreign, most probably American but there were monks of all nationalities in Sri Lanka. "How do you know?" he asked. "Because they smoke and swear and talk roughly to their driver." "So everyone knows they're not monks." "Yes, sir." "So, what are they?" "American secret agents," answered the man lowering his voice. "And everyone knows that too?" "Sure. It is obvious. If you look you will see for yourself." The young man looked and the driver was absolutely right. They were as clearly CIA agents as he was a young person travelling for life experience. He could even see a gun bulge on one and, sure enough, another was smoking. Their spirituality quotient was zero. "They want to go and make trouble among the Tamil Tigers further north but the drivers won't take them." "So how will they get there?" "They will pay the drivers a lot of money and then they will take them."'

'Is that the end of the story?' asked Sissie, as Howard became silent.

'Yes, ma'am. That's how I entered into my ongoing profession.

They approached me to help them with the drivers and one of them gave me the card of someone he said I should look up back home.'

Sissie half shut her eyes. She hoped Howard wasn't beginning to remind her of the Author, telling stories stronger on undertones than overtones. It was a show-off technique and not, she thought, Howard's usual style.

'You may like to know that my information suggests that the Muslim fundamentalists in Egypt are unlikely to shoot more tourists.'

'Oh, thanks.' The irony was dimmed by Sissie's sudden inclination to reach out and stroke his masculine face and test the muscles in his arms and the hardness of his chest and even, perhaps, his buttocks and thighs and . . .

'Why are you looking at me like that?' asked Howard, mouth tickled by the pile of the carpet. 'I suppose you think I want you knocked off by Muslim fundamentalists.' He was talking a little wildly because Sissie's thoughts had led to a delicious expression in her eyes and a seductive rippling in her limbs.

'Are you married?' asked Sissie, still attempting, despite her languor, to think responsibly. 'Men in America get married all the time. Perhaps you're a proud father?'

'I've never been in one place long enough to be serious about a girl.'

Howard rolled slightly back from Sissie. Above her handkerchief skirt, she wore a ribbed sleeveless T-shirt, which clung to her slender waist but left exposed a smooth band of midriff and hip. Her concave and hairless underarms reminded him of the pink inside of a conch shell. He would have liked to place some part of himself there, best of all become reduced in size so that the whole of him could creep in and crouch in Paradise.

'Now you're looking at me oddly!' cried Sissie. This was disingenuous since she was quite experienced enough to recognize lust.

'I apologize.' Gathering himself up, Howard assumed an upright position on the sofa, hands trapped between his knees.

Sissie also sat up, although still on the floor. 'What are your ambitions in life? Do you wish to be president of your great country or make the world a better place? Possibly do one first and then the other.'

'I guess I'm a straightforward person,' said Howard directly into the microphone. 'One foot in front of the other.'

A wave of disappointment forced Sissie to her feet and out of the room. Entering the kitchen, she briefly laid her hands on the wall and her head on her hands.

Howard watched from the door. Since there was no listening device in the kitchen, odd but that was the way it was – perhaps due to economies in the service – he took a meaningful step towards her. Sissie saw it and entered his arms at once. Just a brief kiss, she thought, to cheer herself up. If there'd been champagne in the fridge, she might have preferred that, she told herself.

But Howard kissed her so sweetly, the line of his body so reassuring against hers that she felt more than she intended.

So, perhaps, did he. However, his training held. 'I have a plan,' he said, putting a hand across his face as if to smooth it into unkissable contours. 'A plan of the ship.'

'A plan of the ship?' Of course, Sissie broke away at once. What sexual dalliance could rival the excitement of above deck with picture windows and bath or below deck with port-holes and shower? 'Can I be forward and aft and port and starboard? Will we slip through the black waters like a golden meteor? Will I be Cleopatra to your Enobarbus? Will this ship live up to my expectations?

> '"The poop was beaten gold;
> Purple the sails, and so perfumed that
> The winds were love-sick with them,"'

recited Sissie, who had learnt the speech with Seb. Howard retreated back into the living room.

'Your suite is marked in red.' Oh, he had not meant to produce this from his breast pocket, under which his heart beat too fast!

Sissie snatched the plan and feasted on the amenities. Swimming-pool on A deck with whirling Jacuzzi, within reach of sunken bar, atrium and sunbeds. On B deck, a little dull, exterior walkway, covered sun-deck and lounge. On C deck, the Abu Simbel Royal

Suite, that must be mine or, perhaps, the Kom-Ombo, Karnak, Menderak or Abydos. She read with satisfaction but finally looked up at Howard, who was staring at her in a hungry way himself – her lips were so silky sweet, her body so sinuously tender. 'Ah,' she murmured, lips pursed,

> '"For her own person,
> It beggared all description: she did lie
> In her pavilion – cloth of gold of tissue –
> O'erpicturing that Venus where we see
> The fancy outwork nature."'

'I have a job to do,' responded Howard, taking a step backwards and nearer the bug, this time for protection.

'How long shall I be borne down this great river?' asked Sissie, apparently losing interest in Howard's body or perhaps she was picturing her arrival at Kom-Ombo, the temple of the crocodile god, Sebekh. At least she had now unfolded a plan of the Nile with illustrations of suitable tourist stops. 'And when may I leave?' Suddenly excited, she jumped up and down and shouted these words at the top of her lungs.

'She may leave at midnight.' The voice was disembodied, sepulchral, as if out of Tutankhamun's tomb itself. 'Air Egypt flight number 315,' continued the voice on a more contemporary level.

'I suppose that's base calling,' suggested Sissie, and then stopped as she caught the implication.

'From my pocket,' agreed Howard, removing a small black instrument. 'The miracle of modern science.'

Sissie did not feel like levelling accusations but saw no choice. 'Someone has been listening all the time! While you pretended to care about me, you were putting me on display, breaking all the rules of decency. What if we had made love? What if—'

'I surely do care,' Howard interrupted and, solemnly taking her arm, led her back into the kitchen. There, he held her close and kissed her in a warm, loving way. 'Sugar, you are the woman of my dreams.' He looked deep into her silvery blue eyes and spoke the same words with even greater deliberation. 'You are the woman of my dreams.'

'But not of reality,' she replied, surprising herself with a tone of genuine sadness.

'What does a secret agent know of reality?' Businesslike again, he lifted the cloth covering the table to reveal a medium-sized case. 'This should meet your immediate needs. The clothes you will model await you on the *Royal Rhapsody*. The ship, that is.'

I like the royal and rhapsodic ship, thought Sissie, and yet what a come-down there is in all this. How shocked poor Rudolf would be that I, his pride and model of joy, should be reduced to parading in front of uncultured tourists from the States. I, who have dripped with silver, pearls and gold in front of princesses, marchesas and, most of all, divorced wives of multi-billionaires. Worse was to come, as she opened the case and found it full of nylon easy-care cruisewear, bought by someone who had a taste for orange, lime green and a sort of brownish-mauve in which all hope would certainly be lost. However, there were two white cotton nightdresses, which she could probably adapt for day wear.

Meanwhile, Howard had returned to the living room where he had adeptly removed the listening device, warm in his hand from all its hard work. He twitched aside the curtain to the street and spotted a dark car parked and waiting. He could justify escorting Sissie to the airport but no further.

'The car is already here, Sissie.' She stood for him like a vestal virgin, robed all in white, her black hair plaited neatly down her back, her expression resigned. 'Have you not found a more substantial garment?'

'Nothing wearable,' replied Sissie briefly. This setting out into the unknown, if not a habit, was certainly becoming less out of the ordinary. She too twitched back the curtain and saw the car. 'Perhaps my mother's hat is sitting on the back seat.'

'It was delivered to you!' cried Howard, anxiety making him irritable.

So they went crossly down the ill-lit stairs and sat side by side and silent on the back seat of the car where there was, of course, no hat. The gentle hum of the air-conditioner, the softness of the evening light or rather dark, for night was furling the city's edges, did nothing to soothe them. They were already out in the deeper darkness of the countryside when the chauffeur's offer of a piece of black toffee reminded Sissie of a further grudge.

'I'm only wearing a temporary tooth, you know. Although searching for you, it is true – not *you* – ' she interrupted herself at the sight of the chauffeur's red and twitching ears, 'I was predominantly on my way to Paris because this disloyal Plumb, soi-disant dentist, sent my exquisite pearly replacement to my home whence my father—' Yet again she interrupted herself but this time only with silence because she was bored with such an ineffectual moan and plea and whinge. What did Howard care if, draped with revolting garments, underwear and swimwear posed above the Jacuzzi beneath the atrium, colonnaded perhaps with swinging baskets, all eyes admiringly on her, the delectable cynosure, her tooth took things into its own hands and fell out? What would Howard care about that? Even if his dull imagination could picture such an occasion, which it could not.

Glumly, Sissie and Howard entered the airport. Howard obstinately carried the suitcase with its despised contents. Such was their glum, that they failed to notice the same large Scandinavian fitness expert, who had whispered into Sissie's ear on her last visit, settling at a nearby table. Neither did they spot the obviously vengeful looks he cast in Sissie's direction.

'I suppose you don't have an address I can write to?' Sissie was drinking a chocolate milk-shake and the words came out with a chocolate bubble or two but it was a major climb-down nevertheless.

'I shall be in touch,' responded Howard, rightly shame-faced at the insulting behaviour forced on him by his profession.

Despairing a little – it was late and she was tired – Sissie wondered what it was about this actor manqué which had commanded her attention to the extent that she could already predict missing him. She, Sissie, who possessed the most glorious body in the business and had once been offered $20,000 to pose not entirely naked in fact not entirely clothed either, for a prestigious American glossy magazine. Moreover she had turned the offer down. What had Howard to offer on a par with that?

Under the still unrecognized (because now skulking) red-rimmed eyes of hatred, Sissie and Howard walked through Customs. Mysteriously, they found they were hand in hand, a fact unacknowledged by either and yet causing a softening in their necks so that their heads, like two birds, sloped gently towards each other.

'Goodbye, Sissie,' said Howard at the barrier to Gate 13. 'Good luck.' Their hands slipped slowly apart.

'Goodbye, Howard,' said Sissie. 'I'll think of you in Royal Suite Oko Omboto.'

'Kom-Ombo,' corrected Howard. But both recognized the feel of a lover's parting. The large Scandinavian noted it and drew conclusions that made his slow blood boil even deeper. If he'd had an Egyptian visa, he'd have followed Sissie immediately onto the plane but luckily he did not.

Chapter Fourteen

In which Sissie meets an Arab Diplomat on Horseback, becomes a
Mummy and narrowly avoids Death.

A NOTHER CITY, another time. Wearily, Sissie rose from her seat
in the plane. The air above the Tarmac smelt as warm as
Bombay but not so richly flavoured; in particular, the odour of cow-
dung fires was missing.

A tall man with rigid back and pale skin escorted her through
Customs. Above his head he held high a sign on which was written
in scarlet, as if letters of warning, DANTE, TOUR LEADER. Since he
was at least double the height of anyone else in the undeniably
crowded airport, Sissie felt he would have been easily visible without
the addition of a notice but she assumed, in her tiredness, that it
was a compulsory formality of his profession. Often compared to a
giraffe, Sissie felt it particularly true as she followed Dante: two
giraffes wading through a herd of . . . perhaps buffalo, since the
forces beneath them, if not tall, were certainly powerful. This was
Egypt.

'We will go directly to the *Royal Rhapsody*.' Outside the airport Dante took down the sign from above his head and addressed
Sissie with a compassionate attempt at a smile. A canopy of stars,
each as brilliant as a theatrical spotlight, hit them where they
stood. 'Then I must return for the main body of the party and the
lecturer.'

Obediently Sissie followed him into a coach where, all alone,
they traced the dark streets of the sleeping city.

'I suppose it is three or four in the morning.'

'You have come during the only hour when Cairo is quiet.'

'You are not Egyptian?'

'Italian from Milan, now resident in Shepherds Bush. You will be pleased to hear there are three TV video lines into your cabin. To your left you may see the great river of the Nile.'

What Sissie saw were the smooth white walls of a great ship, layer upon layer, as it seemed to her, a wedding cake, each layer filled with black glassy windows or the dark caverns of walkways and decks.

'Kom-Ombo,' she murmured.

Pale Pied Piper, Dante led his motley guests onto the ship. The sun was up but still wan, drawing colour from the rosiest cheeks, fading the holiday garishness of tourist hats and shirts and bags. The Egyptian crew, making an avenue of spotless uniform from shore to gangway to ship, looked sympathetically on these battered samples of a richer culture.

Sissie blinked and stretched. So day had come. She lay where she had slept, disregarding the prison of Kom-Ombo, on the top deck, shaded by a yellow and white awning. In her eyeline there appeared a small white-clad figure beating a gong. 'An ancient rite in worship of the rising sun?' she suggested hopefully.

The boy paused for a moment. 'Breakfast call.'

Sissie turned away her head and shut her eyes.

On the deck below, the corridors filled with somnambulant guests, obedient to the clamour of the gong. They had showered, undressed, rested, redressed but were still subdued by shock. In the large, circular dining room, they piled their plates high with rolls and oranges and bananas and ham and cheese and eggs and butter and jam and olives and yoghurt and cornflakes, and some were so exhaustedly incapable of sensible selection that they added a sprinkling of plastic grapes that were there for decoration. A large-bellied man with bewildered eyes managed to chew one down with a show of pleasure.

In such a state, it was easy enough for Dante to lead them to their coaches and send them off to see the Pyramids. Around their heels snapped two brisk Egyptian guides, their terrier qualities mitigated by large smiles and accessible expressions.

Sissie leant over the deck's balustrade and watched the scene. The sun was hot, the city loud, but her white nightdress floated coolly round her legs and she wanted to see the Pyramids too.

Sensitive to her every mood, a young waiter (who should have been slicing oranges downstairs) caught her wistfulness. 'It is easy to follow them by taxi. There are also shopping opportunities.'

'No shopping opportunities.' Sissie shuddered. 'But I will take a taxi.'

In and out of her suite, where the cool blinds soothed the glare and the unbearable cruisewear had not improved, a wash and brush, a spray of this and that from the well-appointed bathroom cabinet and Sissie was dancing down the rope-slung gangway, watched approvingly by ninety per cent of the crew (sailors, waiters and housemaids) plus all those who happened to be on the quay. It was her destiny, after all, to be centre stage on a narrow slippery path. She did not slip, however, and there was a taxi, warmly attended by a smiling driver in a long blue robe.

'Thank you, thank you,' he said.

'Thank *you*,' retaliated Sissie and 'Thank you' again as she saw a very nice straw hat waiting for her on the seat. Weakly repressing nostalgic thoughts of Howard, she placed it carefully on her head. Peering at the city from under its brim, she had admiring eyes for very little, although the towering minarets encouraged a sense of fellow feeling. It was a pleasure to find herself released from buildings into the sky and sand of the desert. A fairly tame desert, she was happy to see.

'We stop here a moment,' said the driver, unnecessarily, because this road was blocked by a group of horses prancing about in a typically show-off Arab-stallion way. Behind them, Sissie caught her first sight of the Pyramids and, oohing at their splendour, got out of the car to take a better look.

'I distinctly remember your expressing an aversion to the desert. And that's my hat you're wearing.'

A voice spoke above Sissie's head at the same time as her hat was lifted and removed. It was a rider, astride a large bay horse.

'Oh, you're so clever!' Screeching like a petulant child, Sissie pushed past the stamping hoofs, the shiny, sweating coat around which circled a veil of flies, and strode in the general direction of the Pyramids. Ancient Egypt was what she had come to see, not the smirking arrogance of a con-man, so-called Author, who had treated her worse than a performing monkey, all in the name of *Magic and Fate*.

'I'm sure I told you I lectured on Nile cruise-ships.' The voice was above her head again; the flies attracted to her dark hair made a coronet of black stars above the Virgin.

'I am sent hither and thither!' moaned Sissie.

'Take these!' A pair of baggy cotton trousers descended to her feet.

Side by side with the Author, astride a dappled grey mare that dipped prettily along, Sissie rode towards the Pyramids. In generous mood, the Author passed back his hat to her. 'We must not grill your face, not if you are to model for us this evening, gracing the lumpen tourists with the elegance of true class.'

This reference might have deepened Sissie's ill-humour but they had just rounded the corner and could see not only Pyramids (for, after all, she'd seen a diamond as big as a pyramid in Paris) but the battered boxer's face of the great Sphinx.

The crowds increased and she soon picked out the *Royal Rhapsody* team, trudging stoically from one Pyramid to another. It was fun to clap her heels into the mare's sides and dash past. The horse had quite a turn of speed and soon she was past the largest crumbling Pyramid and heading for another and then that was behind her. Exhilarated, she paused on top of a dune to give her horse breath and was affronted to find the Author at her side.

'I suppose you're called Ptolemy in Egypt.'

'Ha, ha. The ruler I have most in common with is Akhenaten who built a new city in 1350 BC. He was a sophisticated ruler and had no time for the rigid tradition of the old pharaohs. On the tomb paintings the servants bend double to worship their god-pharaoh. He wore especially elaborate clothing and his limbs and stomach were sinuously curvaceous instead of straight. Some see this as a sign of decadence and a disturbingly androgynous nature but I find it a sympathetic sign of an ordinary human with frailties that all of us . . .'

Sissie stopped listening and propelled her mare out into the undulating sand. Even the Author galloping atop a parallel dune, could not spoil her pleasure. Settling down into a regular canter, she headed for the tip of a further pyramid. No one had told her these sturdy stone edifices stretched so far into the desert that she could leave behind tourists, touts and all humanity. For half an hour or so, Sissie rocked through the soft golden sand, below the hard blue sky, passing untended Pyramids like abandoned ships in a sea of sand.

Eventually it was time to turn, her gallant horse flagging, her own legs aching. It was then that she spotted two horses coming at her very fast out of the sun. They were like fighter aeroplanes, turned into black and menacing silhouettes by the brilliance of the light behind them. Her horse whinnied and shifted ground uneasily. Sissie held her still and faced the enemy.

They were boys, she saw as they neared, dressed in shifts with bare feet dangling, riding with neither saddles nor bits but only scruffy halters tied together out of string. When they were within a few feet of her they changed direction and rode in opposite circles round her. The effect was dizzying, impossible to look at both at once, essential not to lose sight of either. Round and round they went while the poor mare stamped her feet and shook her head and a crowd of flies began to gather.

Sissie had just decided to break out of the magic circle, playing Red Indians with a whooping provocative cry, when a third horse appeared on the skyline, approaching at an unheadlong canter. As he slowed to a walk she saw he wore European riding clothes but no hat and rode a black stallion.

The boys performed one last wheelie and then sped off to a small distance where they waited, watching as their master approached.

'I hope my boys did not frighten you,' said the horseman suavely. 'It is not sensible for a foreign woman to ride out here alone.'

The Sheik, thought Sissie, remembering the horrible Author's story on the plane to India. Was this the Romance that she lacked in her life? 'I did have a companion,' replied Sissie, trying to make her voice bell-like but the tremor from her sweating mount seemed to have entered her vocal cords. 'He fell behind.'

'I am returning to Giza now so I can accompany you.'

'Thank you. That's very kind. Although it may give my horse a heart attack.'

His expression remained grave. 'Tutankhamun tends to have that effect on mares.'

Side by side they trod the shifting sands and Sissie's heart pulsed peripatetically. Was it to be squeezed yet again by a man who came out of the blue?

'Do you live in Cairo?'

'I am third attaché at the Egyptian Embassy in Paris but I am home on leave.'

So he was acceptable as well as romantic – no smash-and-grab merchant.

'And you?' he asked. 'You are visiting?'

How crude was the truth! I am modelling hideous cruisewear on the good ship *Royal Rhapsody*. Was it necessary to so dispel myth and magic? No, it was not. 'I am cruising up the Nile on the *Royal Rhapsody*.'

'A Thomas Cook ship, I believe.'

Sissie took a long breath. 'We are mostly academics on board, with a particular interest in Akhenaten's relationship with the Ptolemies. I am accompanying my father who is assistant keeper of the Egyptian department of the British Museum in London. I, like you, work mainly in Paris in the study of ancient oriental fashion. Voulez-vous parler français?'

As she told these lies, Sissie had never looked more beautiful, her slender pink limbs glowing through the fine white cotton, her face shaded and mysterious under the broad-brimmed hat, the long black plait lying heavy on her back but ending in curling tendrils that sparkled in the sun.

Talking now English, now French, they walked their horses sedately down the plateau, across the dunes, towards the three great Pyramids of Giza.

'And who might have attacked me?' asked Sissie.

'Nobody, now I am with you.' His eyes were dark and hot and just a little like Plumb's – perish the comparison.

131

He did not want to talk about his country's problems, she could see that.

'Perhaps you would like to be taken off your boat? There are one or two things in the Cairo museum to which I can get special access.'

What a voice he had! Deep, caressing, masterful, yet she could not risk discovery. 'Malheureusement, this is my last day in Cairo.' Sissie had already described her half-dozen or so expeditions to the museum.

'At least you must let me lunch you at the Mena House Hotel.'

'Je veux bien.' In truth, hunger had come to spoil the idyll in the dunes. Sissie could not even remember when she had last eaten. Skirting the Pyramids, they took a back alley that smelled of decaying food, bad drains, or worse, and of ill-kept animals, goats, camels, cows, pigs, chickens – quite apart from the dogs and horses. Turning left, they rode down a driveway towards a pink-washed hotel, draped in purple bougainvillaea.

Hair bound up with flowers, eyes painted in the Egyptian manner, Sissie sat behind a plate piled high with couscous and peeled tomato and chicken and shredded this and that. She was as dignified as Queen Nefertiti until she began to eat, when her host could only gape at the speed and efficiency with which she demolished her plateful.

'You are a woman of contradictions,' he commented, looking on the bright side.

'My life is hardly my own,' mumbled Sissie, through her latest mouthful. 'I once wanted to give my mother a hat but even that seems beyond me.'

'Ah, the mother,' said the Sheik darkly, and he leant back in his chair and half closed his eyes. 'If you could find a hat to please your mother that would be a miracle indeed.'

'That's not my problem at all,' said Sissie earnestly. 'My mother is perfectly easy to please. But I don't seem to be able to get a hat to her. I bought the most beautiful number in Paris, pink and white organza, like ice cream decorated with roses . . .'

She stopped as she saw that her companion was not listening but concentrating on putting his heavily booted foot over her sandalled toes. She sighed, picturing Howard's pointed Texan numbers. Somehow she had lost the enthusiasm for being thrown across the saddlebags. What she felt like was the silence and cool of the Kom-Ombo suite.

Propping eyelids up with fingers – now the Sheik was whispering endearments in guttural French – she saw a long train of people emerging from an inner room in the restaurant and proceeding to the exit. By their exhaustion shall you know them. Yes, indeed, it was the guests from the *Royal Rhapsody*, about to be galvanized for a bus tour entitled 'Cairo – Muslim City of Minarets.'

'Sissie, my dear, please introduce me to your friend.'

For once Sissie was not sorry to see the Author who leered over her shoulder. At such close quarters, she was struck how much older he seemed on Egyptian soil than Indian. As if the desert sand had dried out the juices of his skin.

'One of your fellow academics?' suggested the attaché helpfully, when Sissie performed no introductions. 'Sissie has been telling me things about Akhenaten and the Middle Kingdom that even I, a native, did not know.'

'Her thesis, as she may have told you,' the Author smiled smoothly, 'was on the god, Sekhmet, cat, lion, male, female or ithyphallic male.'

'I fear this is farewell.' As so often recently, flight seemed the best option and Sissie stood up. 'I am fetched back to my ship.' The Egyptian stood up politely.

'I gather I saved you from the fate worse than death,' commented the Author complacently, as they left the hotel.

'You are no saviour to me. You are a charlatan in shark's clothing.'

'What you cannot appreciate about me,' continued the Author, as they sped along in the car, 'is that I operate beyond the normal. My region is fictional. This is, of course, why you appeal, the term "larger than life" being coined to describe such as you.'

Knowing he was quite capable of keeping up this sort of tosh until they reached the ship, Sissie closed her eyes and soon dreamt of magnificent black stallions ridden by men with hawk noses and flashing eyes – not very like her attaché, in fact, but dreams will exaggerate.

The next thing she knew, she was lying on her cabin bed and something cool was slipping over her hands. She opened her eyes to see the concentrated face of the Author; he had a brush and was painting white the back of her hands.

'Am I the only one who looks after you?' he asked rhetorically, when he felt her gaze. 'I had earlier assumed you were wearing pink silk gloves, just the sort of fashion you might patronize, but then I realized, as I had you carried up the gang-plank, that it was sunburn. Now, in case you should wonder, I am painting your hands with calamine lotion.'

Sissie was shocked and almost grateful, although she refused to show it. Her earliest days as a hand-artist had taught her the financial worth of perfect extremities and it would be most annoying to lose that option. 'Have I freckled?' she asked anxiously.

'Not yet. But who knows whether the birth of a freckle is instantaneous or delayed?'

Sissie certainly did not know so she merely continued to look anxious.

The Author rose up. 'The tour manager, the great Dante, has left a schedule for you. You will see that my lecture precedes your modelling this evening. I shall try to make my few words worthy of your wondrousness.'

The Author, or Aki (short for the dubious Pharaoh Akhenaten) as he was known to the ship, posed under a spotlight in the softly furnished salon. His audience who, as a herd and from a distance, looked vapid, brainless and generally unappetizing, now took on distinguishing features. Here was a loving middle-aged couple, hands linked and resting on the lap of her new lilac, cruisewear pyjama suit. There was a circle of four women, nearly identical under their patina of mutually agreed make-up. Here was a single male, young enough to eye a couple of girls who were stirring drinks filled with fruit chunks and miniature pink parasols. About fifty people were sitting at tables, sipping drinks and reminding themselves, as Aki flourished a dead chicken, that they were on an adventure.

'Do not suspect for a moment,' he declaimed, 'that I am here to give you a lecture on vegetarianism. Not at all. The reason that I am holding up a dead chicken, bought when still alive in the Cairo poultry market early this morning, will become apparent. I may, however, even at this stage, give you a clue. We are here to study the stupendous works of the Ancient Egyptians. And how do we study them? How? How? Through death. Death. Death is our channel. Death our ally. If the Ancient Egyptians hadn't made death their particular friend, we would have nothing to see. Death inspired them, death was ever present in their minds. Death, as it came to this chicken a few hours ago when I persuaded your excellent chef to wring its neck. Death is now present in this room. We are in the presence of death, just as the Ancient Egyptians felt themselves to be.'

At the back of the room there was a loud grunt, perhaps a protest. Aki glared, daring anyone to interrupt. As Sissie had discovered, he accepted a sleeping or quiescent audience but he hated to have his flow halted. Nevertheless an American voice interrupted, with deliberation, 'The Ancient Egyptians were interested in the death of kings not chickens.'

'Ha! That's where you're wrong. Or, shall we say, inadequately informed?' Aki's eyes gleamed and he swung the chicken, which he was holding by its legs, as if about to toss it into the audience. Those at the front cowered a little and the circle of four tittered nervously. Most were interested in the Author's answer, however, for, although presently tainted by the vulgar colours of tourism, they were educated people, doctors, teachers, accountants, who had, moreover, just listened to an informative lecture from their Egyptian guide on the marvels of the Ancient Egyptian burial grounds. They had seen slides of the Valley of the Kings and were not to be easily fobbed off by a dead chicken. They could see dead chickens in their own backyards or those of their neighbours, or their cleaners.

'At Hermopolis,' the Author lowered his voice to a dramatic whisper, 'you will walk underground, in a darkness filled with the presence of death. Under your feet you will feel dust, dust which is only partly from the desert outside. On either side you will just about make out burial niches, some larger, carved caverns where a man could stand up, others too small for anything but an urn or a mummy, a very small mummy wound in fine linen, once white but now tattered and disintegrating. You can put a piece in your pocket when your guide isn't looking – taking back to Wyoming a little bit of Egyptian death.

'As you walk on, through the miles and miles of these vaults, you will begin to think of the tiny size of these corpses and you, with your head filled with greatness and royalty, will think, "little babies" and "dead babies". How tragic, you will say "but how nice to treat them thus". And you will turn to your guide and continue, with hardly a questioning note, "These ancient Egyptians certainly knew how to send off their babies." And he will smile, a not altogether happy smile for what he is about to inform you of does not quite fit in with the splendid view he is painting for you and he will say—' Here the Author's voice rose to a sudden shriek so that several of his audience who, owing to lack of sleep, were suffering from a lack of concentration, visibly rose off their seats. 'Not babies!' he screamed. 'Ibis! Ibis! Ibis! And for those of you who don't know what an ibis is, it is a bird, a fowl, with a beak like this one.' Here he grabbed the head of the chicken and made the beak clack as if it were a dummy. 'And now you have seen the point of the presence of the chicken, which I had been meaning to save up till later but life is like that, fate is not the same as reality, magic is not the same as fate . . .'

All this he delivered without pausing for breath and, on a roll, climaxed by tossing the chicken over his shoulder. This might have been an effective dramatic device if he had been on a proper stage where the chicken would have disappeared behind the back-cloth or at very least been spirited away by a willing stage-hand. But the ship's salon boasted neither back-cloth nor stage-hand, and the chicken lay where it fell and fell with a clunk and a dribble of blood from its beak.

The audience was shaken, there was no doubt. A distinguished-looking man (the audience had come to look more distinguished as Aki became wilder) had a prolonged coughing fit; a woman said, 'Well, now . . .' as if she meant something much stronger; and her friend who wore a pair of glasses round her neck, a pair on her face and a pair with darkened lenses on her head, began methodically to clean all three with a rose-coloured tissue.

Such minor protests had no effect on the Author, who had already launched into a development of his theme, slightly less contentious, in which he was linking high office with fear of death. The mood had relaxed a little as Dante, alerted by a waiter who wanted to know if he could remove the chicken and clean the carpet, arrived on the scene. He stood, hands folded, serious and respectful. There would be no anarchy on his boat.

Sissie had been given a dresser, a young Egyptian girl whose eyes never lost their shocked expression as Sissie flitted in and out of the awful clothes. The most awful she thought she'd model first: it was an off-white catsuit big enough for an elephant, which meant that at least it reached her ankles. She tried to indicate to the girl her need for a stapling gun or even clothes pegs, and, failing the appearance of either, bound her waist with a long stole. The binding soon went from hips to breasts which gave her an idea.

'I'll need your help,' she said to the girl, who was called Nut, after a goddess.

The Author had been speaking for forty minutes. The audience had become used to the chicken. The blood had congealed on the carpet and most of them were too dazed by exhaustion and alcohol for strong reactions. Outside the ship, shimmering night had taken over from glimmering evening, and all along the quayside passengers embarked or disembarked for the pleasures of Egypt, courtesy of Thomas Cook et al. The *Royal Rhapsody* was sleeker, whiter, newer than all the others and it was also quieter – no comings and goings there – for everyone, of course, was not quite spellbound in the salon.

It was a coincidence, therefore, that two cars drew up alongside the ship close behind each other, both black in the threatening manner of deeply black cars. Out of the first stepped a large blond man, out of the second a smooth dark person with Arab elegance. The first did not notice the second because his attention was so concentrated on the *Royal Rhapsody*, although oddly, as he approached, his pace slackened until he positively loitered at the gangway. At this point, the second man slowed, too, and drew into the shadows with the intention of watching the large blond (possibly Scandinavian), whose behaviour was now distinctly suspicious. In short, he seemed to be looking for a way of boarding the ship without using the main entrance where a crewman might reasonably be supposed to be situated. Eventually he spotted a small unlit passageway leading to a door used by workmen servicing the ship to which he went as speedily and unobtrusively as his bulk would let him. The second man followed.

Sissie made her way slowly and carefully along the corridors. Behind her the little maid pushed the rail of clothes and sobbed. But, then, she had no sense of drama. Or certainly no wish for it.

The Author was taking his bows. He had subdued his audience thoroughly, so that they would soon be prepared to believe in his genius. Few had listened to the last half-hour of his talk, which made this judgement easier, and the chicken had long been removed. They clapped with hearty relief and the expectation that now they'd have a bit of fun, with this so-called Super-model (was she really?) parading holidaywear in a kind of cabaret. Man and woman, they had had enough of Ancient Egypt for the time being and they were just about allergic to death in every form.

Making an entrance had always been one of Sissie's strongest points. She had achieved it when Karl Lagerfeld had decided to blind his models with angora hats that sat on their heads like outsized tea-cosies. She had achieved it spectacularly when Givenchy gave her a hat so wide that it cut off the heads of the lilies decorating the triumphal arch. Until her downfall she was the Queen of the Grand Entrance, acknowledged as such by all the haute couturiers. So what was a head-to-toe mummy-wrapping to her? And as, departing from custom, she had her legs free from long ankle downward, she could scurry along at least as well as a high-born Chinese lady of *c.* 1900 or earlier. But the power of her entrance lay in the undulations of her body. She *undulated* into the room and, *undulating*, stood before her audience.

Why did such an apparition so arouse the fury of people by nature reasonable and, supposedly, on a relaxing holiday? The blame must be with the Author who now stood to one side, smiling contentedly. Or even with good Dante, standing on the other side, who liked to see tourists get their money's worth but tended to go one minaret too far.

'I can't bear it!' yelped a woman in the front, and began to throw peanuts. 'This is too much!' yelled another, and 'Give us a break!' issued from a man at the back, who stood up so suddenly that his table crashed over, hurling glasses, nuts and ashtray to the floor.

Meanwhile, panting along the corridor came the large blond man, panting not just from exertion but the emotion of vengeance which contorted his handsome features. Behind him, always one corner in arrears, came the Egyptian, suavely double-breasted, silent and aware that the bulge in his predecessor's less-well-cut pocket suggested evil intent.

'We're not standing for one more minute of this!' screamed the four ladies in unison. Rested now, they had more energy.

Dante, sensing serious revolt, signalled to a minion unseen for rearguard action. In less than a second a long roll of drumming issued from the walkway that circled the ship and passed outside the windows of the salon. It was a majestic, welcoming sound, which suggested that the boy who beat the gong for dinner was not only an artist but had military leanings.

At once the mood in the salon changed. Dinner was what they had been missing all along. An elderly man looked with surprise at the ashtray he was holding as if it were a missile, and put it down.

The blond ceased his aggressive advance even more abruptly. To him the beating signalled discovery, police, prison. He was not as courageous as his size suggested and it was the decision of a moment to turn and career backwards the way he had come. Unfortunately, his pursuer was not given enough warning to reverse in time and the two men collided heavily in the narrow corridor. The Scandinavian's funk was increased by the dark-suitedness of his adversary, which suggested not just police but Secret Police. Dashing upwards, like a diver looking for air, he surfaced on the top deck where, giving himself altogether to panic, he dived over the side of the ship into the murky water, making a loud *splosh*. Thus ended Sven's first attempt to deal vengeance on Sissie for the death of his beloved Rudolf.

Not that Sissie was trouble-free. Mummified, she watched as her audience streamed cheerily past her for the dining room. She might as well have been dead for all the notice they took of her.

139

'That all-softening, overpowering knell,
The tocsin of the soul – the dinner bell.'

The whisper was very soft through Sissie's head-bandaging but she recognized her Parisian sheik's accent when he continued in a meaningful voice, 'Lord Byron, poet-politician and lover of woman . . .'

Sissie thought this far too familiar but had no visible mouth to complain.

'Mmmm . . . Mmmmmm . . .' What she wanted was to be unwrapped again and given a long, cool drink before she asphyxiated.

'By thy height and thy shoes shall I know you,' continued the Sheik who was smiling raffishly.

Sissie nudged him with her shoulder. What did she care if he didn't take her seriously? What did she care if no one in this whole ship had a sense of humour? She nudged again and started shuffling towards the door. Better this handsome stranger unwind her charms than that snivelling maid who had fled anyway, or Dante who had followed his tourists with a look of suicidal calm, or the revolting Author who would certainly talk. And talk.

'You were my final triumph!' crowed a voice so loud that her wrappings vibrated round her ears. 'An appropriate climax to everything I had taught them. Our destinies are inextricably bound!'

'Mmmmmmmmm,' mouthed Sissie, meaning, 'Oh, shut up.' In her view, she was inextricably bound in only one way. Shuffling faster, she managed to get out of the room with the Sheik helpfully at her elbow. Indeed she needed him to hold her steady as she hopped down the stairs to her cabin.

Sissie had been bound from ankle to skull. The Sheik found the end of the first scarf and pulled it so that she spun like a distaff-shaped top. He found the second and the third, not speaking, taking the job with proper attention. As he unwound further and further up her body, Sissie began to wonder what she was wearing underneath. She had disposed of the elephant-sized catsuit, but what had that left? If anything.

However, the relief of developing freedom and the flow of the almost icy air-conditioning on her skin made her too happy to care as much as a sensible girl should have. Sissie stood tall and slim and naked in front of her sheik, whose handsome face looked more dazed than sexually aroused.

'Thanks,' said Sissie. 'Wow. I'd better turn down the air-conditioning before I catch pneumonia.' Frankly, it seemed too difficult to give explanations. She took her bed-cover and folded it around her body.

The Sheik sat on a chair. Once Sissie was robed, his eyes began to regain their lustre. 'I do live in Paris,' she said.

But now the Sheik's eyes were on the floor where the magazine had been thrown by Sissie's slave. 'Yes. That's me.' She sighed. 'Super-model. Not many intellectual pretensions. I'm afraid I told you one or two lies.'

At last the Sheik spoke. 'Will you come to the Cataract Hotel with me?'

'What, now?' Sissie had begun to tremble and feared, by the goose-pimples on her skin, that she had not found the right control on the air-conditioning.

'The Cataract Hotel is in Aswan.' The Sheik came to sit beside her on the bed. He put his large, well-manicured hand round her neck and on her shoulders. Then he ran both hands over her body, stopping at her breasts where the nipples stood out prominently, owing to the cold. He lifted her robe and caressed her thighs, ran his hands under the material so that he could feel her hips. His touch was warm and comforting.

'You are very thin.' His tone was dispassionate.

'Models are,' said Sissie huffily. 'Anyway, I'm not half as thin as I was.'

'And pale.'

'That is part of my beauty,' said Sissie. 'I am famed for the whiteness of my skin.'

'I have never seen anyone so long and thin and colourless.'

'What is all this about the Hotel Cataract?' Sissie asked, for his tone suggested anything but admiration.

'It was an idea.' He felt in his inside pocket and produced a Hermès diary, into which he peered soberly. 'But sadly, it must remain an idea. My engagements will not allow it.'

I am being turned down by a sheik, thought Sissie. Instead of being thrown across the bow of a saddle and snatched deep into the

141

desert where, amid scattered cushions and lit by stars glittering through the tent opening, my silken blouse will be ripped violently and my delicate female body ravished without mercy, I am being rejected. He has unwrapped my body and found it wanting. This has happened too much recently. *I must show grit – grit and dignity.*

'Perhaps we will meet in Paris,' said the Sheik, extracting a deeply engraved card from another pocket.

'Peut-être,' agreed Sissie, also standing and then moving with exquisite grace to the door. 'Merci bien d'avoir consacré votre temps.'

'Rien. Ce n'est rien.' Backing, bowing, bowing, backing, the Sheik left the cabin with diplomacy intact.

Showing neither grit nor dignity, Sissie flung herself on the bed and wept. What had she to look forward to? Dante would throw her off the ship. Howard Howard would not let her return to Paris or even England, pretending it was for her own safety, although who knew? Qui sait? And, if she couldn't return to Paris, she could not collect her new pearly tooth and if she couldn't return to England, she could not take her mother the promised hat, although the wedding date was doubtless long past and, anyway, she hadn't even a hat to give her. Fate was against her. That was it. Hostile Fate! 'Hostile Fate!' wailed Sissie out loud.

Deafened and blinded by her paroxysm of grief – if self-pity can be called grief – Sissie failed to hear the Author creeping up on her.

'Boo!' he cried, pouncing upon her with unusual kittenish joie de vivre.

Sissie peered through soggy strands of black hair. 'I expect you were listening outside the door.' She sat up grumpily.

'Rejection is always hard.' The Author settled on the bed. He was dressed in a cream linen suit but his face seemed to have grown more lined and his hair had a streak of grey. 'However, I wouldn't allow your self-esteem to be dented by the opinion of a cook.'

'A cook!' cried Sissie.

'At the Intercontinental Hotel in Paris. I recognized him at once. He cooks mainly for the hotel's Arab clients, which are many since, as you know, Algeria was a colony—'

'Rejected by a cook!' interrupted Sissie.

'Cooks' tastes generally run to the hearty and wholesome,

couscous and risotto, spaghetti and pain de campagne,' consoled the Author. 'He was probably taken in by your prowess on horseback.'

'He deceived me. He deceived me!' Sissie tried to console herself with self-righteous indignation but the Author's dark eyes were too knowing.

'You are the cause of all my humiliations, that's the point.' Sissie might have elaborated further had there not come a knock at the door.

Dante entered slowly, a column of reproach. Perhaps he expected apologies from Sissie but none was forthcoming.

'They are eating with enjoyment,' he said eventually. 'But the memory of dead chickens and model mummies may take more than food to exorcize.'

'You take too sombre a view,' said the Author, still in high spirits.

Dante was not to be soothed. 'I should have realized one never gets something good for nothing much.'

'I suppose you're referring to me.' Sissie smiled, ravishing even with the temporary tooth, but without effect.

'Mr Howard told me you were at the top of your profession and I was fortunate to get you. When I met you at the airport, I saw immediately he had not sold me short.'

'If you want to give me the sack, spare me the rod. I had hoped to travel with you as far as the Valley of the Kings.'

Dante looked meditative. 'Of course, Sissie will not be needed tomorrow as we have booked a belly dancer. And the evening afterwards could be the Egyptian Fancy Dress evening and by then they will most probably have forgotten all about your unfortunate appearance this evening.'

'I can't see there's much to remember,' pointed out Sissie, 'swathed in bandages as I was from top to toe.'

'How would it be if we both resigned,' said the Author, unexpectedly. This seemed to shock Dante and it now appeared that his lecture, in retrospect, had drawn praise from many who had dubbed it 'controversial', 'thought-provoking' and 'inspirational'. Some had even admitted to a greater understanding of Egypt's burial habit following the dead chicken's appearance and the dining room was, at that moment, filled with animated discussion.

'I play on their subconscious, of course,' remarked the Author contentedly.

'You mean you send them to sleep,' said Sissie crossly.

'So we have decided.' Dante stood and began to scribble on his clipboard. 'Sissie flies to Luxor where she meets us for the remainder of the journey being, to all intents and purposes a New Model.'

'You can meditate in front of Sekhmet,' advised the Author, and he bent to pick up a chocolate heart that lay on Sissie's pillow.

'That's mine!' she objected.

'Nonsense,' replied the Author, eating it with relish.

The small chamber, hardly bigger than a tomb, was hot and dark and claustrophobic and there was nowhere to sit but the dirty floor. Sissie had never been good at meditating. Sebastien had been rather good at it, particularly when she needed his help. But the lion's black granite head was lit by a white shaft of sunlight coming through a hole in the roof and even cynical Sissie had to admit that the effect was highly dramatic, with Sekhmet's stone eyes glittering in mesmeric fashion.

Shifting herself into a more comfortable position on the ground, for, since she had followed the Author's advice, she must hope for some benefit, Sissie determined to concentrate. Despite being at the centre of the great ruins of Thebes, it was very silent, the only sound a faraway regular click as if someone hammered a chisel into stone. That, too, was mesmeric, a beat above the buzzing in her head, born of heat and exhaustion. Keeping her eyes open with a conscious effort, she stared at the wide expressionless eyes of the lion.

At first she was acutely aware of time, the seconds and minutes moving by with almost unbearable slowness. Then she was past the temptation to rise and stamp about protestingly and into a place of such calm that she felt no wish to move. In fact, she hardly felt capable, even if she had wished to, for her body was as weighty as the statue itself. Yet, as her body became heavier, her mind seemed to lighten and float upwards so that she looked down on herself and Sekhmet.

She began to feel that this release was putting her on the edge of making an important discovery – about what she didn't yet know but she was filled with a sense of anticipation in which her calm state cancelled any fear. Meanwhile, she could still see the dark walls of the chamber and feel the gritty floor through her thin clothing.

It was this material sense which told her that her face was flowing with water. At first she thought it was sweat but then she realized it was tears, rolling from her eyes, down her cheeks and dripping off her chin. What was she crying for? She did not know. Her mind, pulled back from the edge, had come back into her body with nothing discovered. They were inexplicable tears, about something far away. Gradually, they stopped of their own accord and, in the great heat, soon dried.

Sissie stumbled outside into the glare of the afternoon sun. Finding shade under a huge chunk of displaced stone, perhaps once a portico, she opened her guide-book with hands that shook, and read slowly,

Sekhmet has both beneficent and maleficent aspects. She is associated with healing but also with disease. War was waged under her aegis. She inspired both reverence and fear. She is usually portrayed as a woman with exposed breasts and the head of a lioness; but on occasions she has an ithyphallic male body. Sekhmet statues are carved from basalt or granite, both igneous rocks, emphasizing her fiery nature. In her tame, beneficent aspect, she becomes Bast, or Bastet, the domestic cat.

Thin ripples broke the surface of the Nile. The Author stared at them from the top deck of the *Royal Rhapsody*. He was trying to decide if a proper analogy would be the menacing cracks spreading across the ground before an earthquake struck. He had been witness to just such a sight in California. The ripples were pale rather than dark but the patterning was similar, not unlike the marks on the back of a certain snake. Was analogous repetition the clue to understanding the universe? Sometimes he was close to thinking so. Today, for example, he had been moved by the similarities between the Ancient Egyptian goddess, Isis, and Mary, the Queen of Christianity. The Author stood in contemplation in the warm darkness and was forced

145

to keep his thoughts to himself since there was no one with whom to share them.

Across the smooth water passed a white sail, gleaming eerily in the darkness. It soon caught the Author's attention for feluccas seldom ventured out in the evening and, besides, the whole day had been so calm that there had hardly been a sail anywhere. But those ripples indicated just enough breeze for a wily sailor to tack backwards and forwards across the river, adding yet another pattern to the Author's collection.

Sissie sat at the front of the boat. Every time it turned, the sails flapped over her head like the wings of a giant bird. In between she heard the swish of the water or, for the few moments as they neared the Luxor bank, a mix of music, horses' hoofs and far-off cries.

Crouched like a figurehead, unmoving and wide eyes staring straight ahead, Sissie had the dignity of some noble beast. Perhaps the spirit of Sekhmet, lion or cat, had entered her. Unremittingly self-conscious, the idea soon occurred to her and made her expression move in the direction of the Cheshire Cat. She would not stay any longer in Egypt. She had learned all the lessons it had to teach her.

The Author smiled also as he recognized his heroine, and might have stayed on deck to admire her longer, except that he was due in the lounge where he was to give a lecture on 'Sex, Gender and Genesis in the Middle Kingdom.'

Chapter Fifteen

In which Nothing much happens to Mary on the Dorset Cliff-top
but it is Important all the same.

MARY STARED into Cleo's pale green eyes with the black elongated pupils. She had read somewhere that you shouldn't do it, that cats dislike confrontation and treat it as an aggressive act. But Cleo's eyes stared calmly, unblinking, while the black stripe gradually expanded into a perfect circle.

'I'm going out now,' said Mary, who had begun lately to talk to her cat. As always, Cleo followed her out of the caravan. It was a windy evening with smatterings of rain being flown in from the sea and tasting slightly of salt. When the weather was bad, fewer people were around so Mary was glad of it. She began her usual walk, up towards the headland, round the edge of it and back to her field, which, these days, was almost entirely filled with caravans. It was a long circle she had taken for three years now, never varying it, allowing the landscape to make the changes according to season or weather or time of day.

But today she felt restless, nearly adventurous. Instead of taking the left-hand part of the circle, she took the right and at the point where the path reached the top of the cliff she turned right again in the direction of another headland beyond which lay the county town. It took an hour of brisk walking before she saw it below her. The rain had merged into a white mist so that the town was reduced to a few outstanding features. Most obvious, because it was immediately below her, was a substantial red-brick building with a brick tower at each corner and a wall around its circumference. It might have been a Victorian factory or a brewery, and indeed there was one of the latter in the town, or it might have been a military barracks, and there was also one of those in the town, although it had been standing in Napoleonic days and was now a museum. But in fact it was a prison, of which Mary was well aware.

She stood for quite fifteen minutes looking down, oblivious to the rain and gathering dark. The cat had not followed her over such a distance so she was on her own, waiting and watching long enough to see the lights come on in the windows that rose above the wall. But their bright flow was insignificant in the sombre atmosphere of the building. The windows were too small, turning the light inwards instead of out.

When Mary finally turned, the path had become indistinct and, although the rain had lessened and the wind dropped altogether, the walk back would not be easy. She began slowly, trying to allow for stones that rocked under her feet or brambles that snatched at her legs. But it soon dawned on her that if she didn't speed up, she would be enveloped entirely in the black and cloudy night, which would not matter too much when the path went through a field but could be frightening, even dangerous, when it followed the cliff edge.

If she had been on her usual stretch of the coastal path, she would have known every rock, every dip, every slide into shiny wet mud or sudden ascent but this path was unknown, its idiosyncrasies uncharted by her. Neither had she been out quite so late when the sea to her right disappeared into a black void, only represented by dull thunder caused by the heavy swell left behind by the wind.

The sound was louder than she ever remembered it, the thunder rising now and again to a boom as if the waves met some obstacle greater than normal. When this happened, Mary strained her eyes down into the blackness and once or twice imagined she saw the white frill of broken waves. Her heart was beating a faster tempo and her face felt warm from the exertion. Stopping to rest, she asked herself if she were tempted now to do what she had often thought about, to cast herself over the cliff and join her heartbeat to the ocean's cavernous roar. But as she considered, an image came into her mind, of her caravan, with its fire, its light and Cleo curled up as near the fire as possible. She pictured herself coming into this scene, hanging up her wet clothes to dry, putting on the kettle, stroking the soft warmth of Cleo, and she knew that the temptation was no longer real. She had a life now, a home, a place in the world.

Now she walked along the path with new confidence, and, as she walked, she pictured again the prison and pictured those shut up inside it. She knew only too well the stale circuit of their lives, the bitter repetition of their thoughts, their obsessions, their dreams.

Chapter Sixteen

In which Sissie meets an Anthropologist, Ethnobiologist and Ornithologist but prefers a Frog Prince or a Pink Dolphin

H OWARD HELD Sissie tenderly. Above their heads the tufted wool horse flared its nostrils in disdain.

'You're just so courageous, sugar,' praised Howard, in his lovely Southern drawl.

'Sometimes I feel as if Paris is my home.' Sissie sighed gracefully and decided she liked being called Sugar and she *was* brave, if also flotsam blown hither and thither by the world. A quotation employed by Sebastien teetered on the edge of her memory: 'the swansdown feather that stands upon the swell at fall of tide . . .' Aloud she was more bracing: 'So I'm out of danger?'

'Not exactly.' Howard's face, too open and honest for an undercover agent, became shifty. 'Let us say, Paris does not pose a threat for you as of this moment.'

Sissie laughed at his caution. 'Do you mean to tell me I'm safe as I sit here on my own sofa encircled by your arm?'

It was true, Howard held her in his strong arm. He sat back, his powerful legs stretched out in front of him, ending in the stitched and pointed cowboy boots. It was the diminution of Sissie's beauty that had aroused his protective qualities. Her nose was red from the sun, her skin frowzy, her hair brittle, her hands peeling. He could not see her legs as she wore shiny patterned tights – two silver snakes grew from her mini-skirt – but he knew her feet were battered too, for one toe protruded, the cherry nail varnish chipped. Howard was guiltily aware that he had chosen her less than satisfactory last destination.

'I was planning to recall you any time,' he told her, 'since the Nile waters have fallen so low that the *Royal Rhapsody* can proceed no further.'

Putting the unsatisfactory past behind her, Sissie snuggled closer into his smooth-shaven face and, receiving a definite sense that this was giving him pleasure, she stuck out her tongue and ran it along his jawline. She admitted to herself that, ever since Howard had stopped wearing silly disguises, she had seen him as a rock of comfort. Certainly, her standards were not high in the comfort field or she might have queried Howard's integrity in sending her into such unknown quantities.

'If I weren't so busy,' began Howard, looking down at Sissie. Her shoulders, which were unblemished, rose out of the sort of frill he expected to see round a birthday cake. He imagined the white skin continuing down to her breasts, which pointed so prettily into those little pink rosebuds. Howard, who believed in keeping his sensuality under control, began to feel less protective and did not finish his sentence.

Sissie sensed the new beat coming from his body. 'Don't you think my blouse is lovely? It's another of those elasticated numbers. Look, I can pull it down to my waist.'

It was wicked and teasing of Sissie to suit action to words but she was feeling so secure and security always made her feel sexy. 'Pretend you're King Farouk,' she advised as Howard, throwing caution to the winds (at least there was no listening device), bent forward and sucked enthusiastically on her pink rosebuds. Soon they resembled hard little knobs and Sissie felt the urge to take off more clothes or at least remove the bundle of cake frill from her waist. Howard, too, felt his trousers an unwanted constriction. With those phosphorescent eyes and mouth as soft and sweet as candy, he wondered how he could ever have considered a diminution in her extraordinary beauty and they were both starting to tear off their clothes when Sissie suddenly remembered.

'Zut alors! We can't do this. I might have a baby!'

The responsible expression took over Howard's face so quickly that it was hard to believe the trembling bag of lust had been one hundred per cent in situ just a second before. 'You're right,' he said, sitting up and squaring his shoulders. 'Accept my apologies. I only came over to see you were not too shaken up by your Egyptian experiences. I assure you I had no intention . . .' His tone descended in the direction of the defensive, which grated on Sissie.

'You don't have "intentions" to make love to a woman,' she complained and, since she had not pulled up her blouse, her thrusting nipples made accusing eyes at Howard. 'You are overtaken by desire.'

'Yes,' agreed Howard, trying to get the shake out of his voice. 'You are a very desirable girl.'

'Woman,' said Sissie. And this time she pulled up her blouse.

They sat side by side on the sofa, neither quite clear on the next move. Their bodies, after all, had been aroused and needed time to settle back into calmer moulds. Were they to be serious about each other? Sissie's new womanhood had put this on the agenda and taken the erotic irresponsibility out of her love-making.

'If only I were not kept so busy in my job.' Howard clasped his big hands together.

'You would have produced a suitable contraceptive?'

'No. I meant . . .' Now he was flustered.

'I was far busier for years than you will ever be,' interrupted Sissie severely. 'Business is not the same as busyness. If you are not interested in me, please say so, because it is perfectly clear that I am *part* of your job.'

'You have always worked for yourself. What you cannot comprehend is the demands of my employer. I am on duty every waking second—'

'Employer!' Sissie jumped to her snaky legs. 'The president of the United States could not be harder to please than Emanuel Ungaro or Karl Lagerfeld or even my dear dead Rudolf. I know more than you ever will about discipline, perseverance, humiliation. You see here a shell, a husk, a travesty of what I was only a few months ago.'

'I know. You forget I have spent time with your files. You were in demand by the whole world.' All this talk was quite a come-down from the heights of passion they had started to scale but the moment had so completely passed that they looked at each other in an objective light.

Sissie sat down again and hung her hands between her legs. Why had she come to Howard like a homing pigeon? Even if he had come to her.

Howard said, his face flat and expressionless, 'I am sorry that Egypt was not a success but I, we, do have an alternative destination for you.'

'Up the Amazon, I expect.' Sissie spoke to the floor with satirical gloom.

Howard started and a flush of Pompeian red spread from his neck to his cheeks.

'You know, my agent, Madame B.,' continued Sissie, now glaring at the bronze horse door-stop, 'has telephoned three times already in order to persuade me back to the catwalk. They are booking for the autumn, that is spring/summer shows and find themselves much in need of a star. The line will be modern and fluid, they tell me, although Valentino is rumoured to be flirting with S and M, sado-masochism to you, just up my street. Now I have my new, exquisite, tailor-made tooth, the world is my oyster.'

Howard, who had seemed distracted during much of this, became interested at the word 'tooth'. 'I didn't know you had your tooth.'

'Why else should I come to Paris? Do you want to see it? I warn you, it's a work of art.'

Howard, a little confused, expected Sissie to open her mouth, but instead she rose gracefully and brought him a small leather box which she opened reverentially. 'There,' she exclaimed, as a girl might show off her engagement ring, 'isn't it beautiful?'

'Yes,' agreed Howard, looking closely.

'Notice the blue-white pearliness, the smooth-edged silkiness, the delicate golden roots of it. With this tooth I will have the confidence to conquer the world again. I will put the past behind me, forget everything but my own dazzling, scintillating . . .'

Howard put out his finger to touch the little wonder but, in a flash, Sissie had snapped the box shut. 'No touching. I guard it with my life.'

A plotting look passed over Howard's pleasant face but he changed the subject, suggesting, 'How about opening my wine?' He had brought Sissie a slender bottle, the wine gleaming pink through a gilded net. She found goblets and they drank together, except that Howard sipped and Sissie quaffed.

Quaffing, she asked, 'Where *do* you want to send me?'

Howard put down his glass. He looked out of the window where the lunch-time light was diffused by two layers of grubby gauze. The need to send Sissie far away tugged at his heart-strings, and he reminded himself severely that she had an enemy, although who or why was still not precisely clear, and that constant protection in the shape of large bodyguards, who told their client to duck in open spaces, were beyond the budget of his department, even given the favour she had performed for them. 'I have to go now.' He stood up and took his jacket and tie from where he had discarded them.

Sissie stared vaguely up at him. 'Hold my hand?' she asked.

But he would not. 'I have to work. I'll be back later.' Noticing her eyes filling with tears, he took the opportunity not to comfort but to swoop along the surface of the table where the jewellery box lay and remove it with the deftness of a conjuror. No tooth, no model, no Paris. Now she would have to go where he sent her.

'Let yourself out.' Defeated, off-guard, Sissie lay on the sofa. 'You can wake me up like Bottom when you return.'

The cruelty of Sissie's solitary awakening is too awful to contemplate. Her large mascara-smudged eyes fell at once on the table where the exquisite tooth had resided in its padded throne. The box's absence from there and anywhere else in the apartment threw her into terrible confusion. She had an appointment that very afternoon with a superior dentist in the Rue St Honoré, who had promised he'd stick it in for life. No tooth, no model, no living. Frantically, Sissie searched every dusty nook and cranny, discovering in the process some things she'd rather have left unmined – a used candy-striped condom and a love letter written to Sebastien but not by her.

'I've lost it! I've lost it!' screamed Sissie, flying at Howard Howard when he reappeared that evening. Never, never would she suspect

Howard of stealing it. He would not have the meanness or the imagination. He was the good guy in her life.

'That's truly tough. That's not fair. I feel for you, Sissie. I know what that tooth meant to you. Your whole future depended on that tooth.' Howard patted her shoulder, with a face like Judas.

'I can only imagine someone came into my apartment and stole it while I was asleep,' cried Sissie wildly. 'That ugly old concierge has always hated me. I can just imagine her, sliding in through the door and pouncing on my poor unprotected pearl, like the untrustworthy, verminous—'

'Let me take you out to supper,' suggested Howard soothingly.

Over supper in a good restaurant locale where silver fish blazed on charcoal grills brought to the table, Howard talked about the Amazon, about trees as tall as skyscrapers, about earth as soft as down, about parakeets as red as Valentino's signature and macaws as blue as the sky and yellow as the sun. He knew it well, having worked there, over the years, on an even more secret assignment than usual to uncover an important route for the drug trade. Shortly, indeed, he would be there again, but this news he did not share with Sissie.

Sissie, who pictured rainforests blazing like the fish, listened to his descriptions dully. Eventually she roused herself enough to comment, 'And why are you talking about the Amazon, anyway?'

'Because the Amazon, as you so percipiently guessed, is your very next destination.'

In the middle of the night Sissie was woken by a dream. There stood her mother, dressed in a hat made of turquoise and gold macaw feathers. She spoke severely into Sissie's ears. 'But you know I prefer sugar pink.' Sissie woke with tears on her cheeks but soon went to sleep again and in the morning had forgotten the dream.

Sissie looked out of the aeroplane's window. They were still flying high but she could clearly see the land below. At least, there was no land as such but wide drifts of shining water, separated by a herringbone pattern of dark trees that at times reached the edge of the sky. Until recently, there had been a cloudy mass below them but this had now divided itself into hundreds of identical single-turreted cloud castles, which did not obscure her view but moved slowly above the dark and light of the trees and water like chess-pieces above a chequered board.

Howard had described Manaus as a jewel set in the jungle, thought Sissie. He didn't say it was Noah's Ark.

'Excuse me, Sissie. I have come for you.'

The voice was formal and heavily accented. Sissie opened her eyes and thought she saw a bespectacled owl. The face was round, pale, half concealed by large glasses and topped by tufty brownish-grey hair. She rose at once and followed him.

'I am an anthropologist, ethnobiologist, ornithologist and one of the lecturers on the ship,' he informed her as they brought her case to his taxi. 'I believe you already know my partner.'

Outside the airport, a purple pansy night had fallen, filling the air with heady smells and unidentifiable sounds. As she reached out her hand to the taxi door, she felt a light touch and, looking down, saw a tiny green frog sitting on her hand staring up at her. Even in the dim light, she could see the brilliance of its colouring and the intelligence in its beady eyes. It seemed to have arrived from nowhere, dropped out of the sky by magic. Sissie stared in wonderment.

'Quelle chance!' The anthropologist stood behind her. 'To be visited by a tree frog means good luck.'

'I think it is a prince in disguise,' whispered Sissie but, as she spoke, the frog put on seven-league boots and leapt into the darkness.

The *World Traveller* was painted white and lights shone from each deck, striping the dark waters below. From a distance, it looked not unlike the *Royal Rhapsody*.

'I guess she's been round the world more than you and me.' The anthropologist shrugged ruefully.

'I guess she has.' This was an old ship nearer the *African Queen* than the *Royal Rhapsody*. This was a ship whose white paint peeled, revealing wooden planks, a ship where washing was slung on the lowest deck and hammocks on the top. It rose above them in a haze of yellow lightbulbs each vibrating with its own halo of insects, but this, Sissie could tell without setting a foot in it, was not shipshape, spick and span, neat as a new pin, clean as a whistle or even safe and sound.

'Is it riverworthy?'

'The water's high and the captain's German.' The anthropologist, who had been standing rubbing his glasses, started up the gangplank. Sissie hesitated.

The anthropologist turned encouragingly. 'I'll show you the cabins.'

Sebastien lay on a bunk reading. He lay in exactly the same position with the same expression that Sissie had seen a thousand times in her apartment in Paris. Yet here he was, transported to a very dirty ship on the Amazon. Could she believe her eyes?

'Oh, it's me all right.' He smiled at her bewildered face. 'Surely I told you François was an anthropologist. Look,' he said kindly, as if to ground her in reality, 'now I drink flat beer instead of flat champagne.'

Sissie sat on the other bunk and stared at her ex-lover. Clothed only in shorts, or possibly underpants, he was as beautiful as a Greek statue but he did not touch her heart. Previously she had been so impressed by his class, his beauty and his erudition that she had overlooked his succubus qualities. He lived off people. Once, he had lived off her.

'What book is that?' she asked suspiciously.

'*Magic and Fate*,' he answered nonchalantly, as she had somehow guessed he would. Oh, how she preferred Texan secret-service men!

'You were reading that ages ago.' It was an angry accusation. Anger suffused Sissie, making her already heated body burst into further rivulets of sweat.

'I shall probably read it for the rest of my life,' responded Sebastien calmly. 'It is full of clues.'

The complacency of this answer turned Sissie into a virago. Leaping forward, she snatched at his hair, pummelled his chest, kicked his toes. He hardly bothered to defend himself, like a bigger boy who knows a little squirt can't really hurt him.

François returned to this scene. It did not seem to worry him very much either. Perhaps he, too, had discovered Sebastien was a tougher nut than he looked.

'I've taken your case to your cabin,' he said. 'Shall I take you there, too?'

Sissie came to him, with just the smallest backward kick which she hoped expressed the essential je-m'en-fou-ism of her attack, or, in English, 'I can kick him or leave him.'

The corridor they walked along was dimly lit and ran along the outside of the ship.

'Oh, heavens!' exclaimed Sissie. 'We're moving. I mean, we've moved. That is, where is Manaus?'

'You were the last aboard. The captain likes to leave on time.'

Sissie stared at the dark waters rushing by.

'Ne vous appuyez pas sur les barrières!' François' warning came too late. Sissie unstuck herself from the railing to find a wide bar of varnish across her midriff.

'The captain is new to this part of the world. He doesn't realize the time things take to dry – if ever. Please follow.'

Sissie saw now that the length of the shiny railing was decorated with moths and insects caught by the gluey varnish. Many, stuck fast but still alive, beat their wings into whirling fans. Some were at least an inch wide so that she could see the desperation in eyes rolling on the end of long antennae.

François came back to her. 'I am hoping for a Hawk Tarantula Moth.'

Sissie sat at a table in the dark, fish-smelling dining room. Opposite, Captain Heine, large and dressed in a superb white uniform, talked with François about atmospheric disturbances, the five hundred members of the catfish family in the Amazon and the air-roots of epiphytous plants.

'Whatever are we doing here?' she whispered to Sebastien, whom she was already forced to view as a friend.

158

Sebastien shut the book he had been reading and laid it on the table. 'I am the boat manager.'

'You? You? You!'

'Heine is the captain, I am the boat manager, François is the lecturer and . . .' his eyes narrowed in a way she remembered from their shared past, 'and you are the housekeeper.'

'The housekeeper! Me?'

'Here's how it is.' Sebastien relented and took her hand in his. The sweaty contact was so unpleasant, however, that he dropped it quickly and wiped his palm on a paper napkin as a child wipes away a kiss. 'When your friend Howard Howard barged into the apartment—'

'The apartment? My apartment?'

'You were in Egypt still but, as he told me, unhappy. He asked my advice . . .'

'Your advice?'

'As to your next destination. As it happened, François and I had been that very evening in touch with Captain Heine who had been scouring the world for a bilingual housekeeper. I thought you would thank me, become radiant as only your beauty knows how, send up incense to heaven at the chance to become untrammelled, unconfined—'

'By sorting clothing and ordering meals?' enquired Sissie, without raising her head.

'Oh, I shouldn't take your duties too seriously. I don't. Let's skedaddle before the students come and ask me questions. I'm worn out with lying and invention. You'll manage. The captain has imported a fine team of small but strong Filipino slave girls, who save space by fitting in three to a cabin.'

Sebastien and Sissie skedaddled together to the top deck where they breathed a sweetness borne on the night air that reminded Sissie of sybaritic evenings under friendly Mediterranean skies. They found two wooden chairs and sat together like an old couple.

'I think it's orange blossom,' Sebastien sniffed like a wine connoisseur at his claret and Sissie realized she no longer wished him ill.

'Are you truly, madly fond of François?' she asked.

'François knows everything about the rainforest.' Sebastien stared up at the sky. It was the soft black of low clouds, a comfortable duvet suspended above their heads. 'He understands Nature.'

'Oh, I see,' said Sissie. And she saw Sebastien bent day after day over Gerard Manley Hopkins's poetry. 'I can't bear the thought of my cabin.'

'Sleep here, then. François says the bats eat the mosquitoes but I can't see any bats. Lie still and I'll anoint you.' He produced a gel stick and rubbed it carefully over the exposed parts of Sissie's skin. When she next opened her eyes, she was alone. She saw that they had crossed from one bank of the river to the other and fell asleep in a daze of orange blossom, lemon, pine and musk.

Not long before dawn the ship's pilot came close to the sleeping Sissie and fingered her hair. He was a Caboclos, mixed race, part Indian, part white, part African. Sissie woke to see a small man with shoulder-length hair receding out of her vision. She went forward, somewhat shakily, to the prow of the ship. They were not moving fast and the engine's beat did not break the stillness of the pre-dawn calm. Not a bird, not an animal, not a person seemed to share her place in the world. Now she could see the trees more clearly and, although their size was impressive, she was disappointed by their regular English appearance, solid brown trunk, dark green leaves. But as the sky grew lighter and the blue stripes became variegated by a hazy pink and yellow, strange things happened to the forest and suddenly she caught a glimpse of a froth of lilac, bursting out from among the green, or a cascade of yellow or an explosion of scarlet, the colour vibrating against the dark leaves. The next thing she saw were flying chips of colour, as if the scarlet and yellow had fragmented into the sky. It took her a while to realize they were birds, silenced by the acres of space around them. The ship, meanwhile, was moving all the time closer to the right bank and they were approaching the mouth of a large tributary river, which made a smooth parting in the trees.

As they drew nearer she saw movement in the water, a flurry and splashing, a leaping and diving. The glow of dawn had not reached that shaded river and yet she was sure something shone with more than a fishy silver. Now they were level with the opening and, as she leant over the rail, the sun just tipped over the rim of the trees behind her and sent a shaft of brightness into the river's mouth.

Sissie blinked and, like the heroine of a fairy story, rubbed her eyes in disbelief. She was looking at a crowd of pink dolphins, as unreal as toys in a child's bath, as pink as the hat she had bought for her mother.

'Pink dolphins,' said Sissie, speaking out loud as if to convince herself. 'I am watching a school of pink dolphins at dawn on the Amazon.'

'They jump for you,' said a voice at her side. 'They say, "join us." See, they stand out of the water and put the eyes on you.'

Sissie glanced at the pilot, come so silently again, and looked quickly back at the dolphins. No, she had not imagined them. They had come closer now, really close and she could see, as the pilot had said, the way their bright eyes stared at her as they leapt from the water and stood upright on their tails. One in particular, as big as a large man, came insistently close to where she leant over the railing.

'He wants you play. He loves you. He wants you come to him in the water.'

Sissie gasped and felt the breath going from her body. Each time the pink dolphin stood up on his tail to her, she felt more drawn to him.

'Dolphins can be the man,' said the soft voice at her side. 'Like the man, except for one thing, the hole in top of the head. We know if we see the stranger dancing at party in the hat, we know he is the dolphin man. No good girl goes with the handsome stranger who keeps on the hat.'

'Oh,' gasped Sissie, dizzily leaning, dizzily watching.

And who knows what might have happened if at that moment there had not been loud cries in many strange languages from below but advancing nearer, all conveying the excited message, 'Pink dolphins! Pink dolphins!'? The deck was crowded with huge, half-dressed students, many carrying cameras that clicked and flashed.

'Nobody photograph the pink dolphin,' said the pilot in Sissie's ear.

Sissie found she had been holding her breath and heaved air into her lungs. The dolphins had not gone at this influx of noisy admirers and continued to dance joyously at the side of the ship. But Sissie could no longer pick out her dolphin from the others. They had

161

become a pattern of pink shapes, performing leaps and arabesques for their audience as if choreographed by a master.

'Just like Matisse's "Les Danseuses".' Sissie turned round to see Sebastien.

He raised his eyebrows mockingly. 'Better than a little green frog, I think.'

Sissie wanted to see once more that shiny smooth body pirouetting so invitingly in front of her but the dolphins were no longer beneath the boat, they had dropped back and soon became smaller and smaller, as small in that great river and that great forest as the tree frog had been on her hand.

'Do not cry,' said the pilot, brown face and black hair gleaming in the ever-rising sun. 'He comes back for you.'

Chapter Seventeen

In which Sissie meets Mo's Mother, uses three pages of
Magic and Fate *to good purpose and narrowly escapes a*
Fate worse than Death.

'THAT IS NOT a sloth,' said François severely. 'It is the nest of a
termite.'

There were twenty of them stuffed into a small rubber dinghy
and parked, it seemed for eternity, down a side-river. François
provided information in three languages, English, French and
German, but reproved only in English, which seemed unfair to Sissie.

'Well, it looked like a sloth to me,' she persisted grumpily, 'a
giant sloth.' She might have added that François' glasses were so
misted up with the wet heat that he was as likely to mistake a sloth
for a termite's nest as he was for Yves St Laurent stuck up a tree.

'"The great wall of vegetation, an exuberant and entangled mass
of trunks, branches,"' read Sebastien, as at last they prepared to step
ashore, '"leaves, boughs, festoons . . ."'

'Shut up, Sebastien,' hissed Sissie. 'Can't you experience anything for yourself?'

'What a vulgar idea.'

A lecture tour into the heart of darkness, thought Sissie, and two
words came into her head: 'Noble savage.'

That evening, buoyed by a sense of virtue after raising the pay of
the overworked Filipino slave girls, she sought out the pilot, whose
name she had discovered was Mo. As she crossed the top deck to his
cabin, the sweet smells of night flowers filled her nostrils, until she
came close to him.

'Am I disturbing you?'

'We stop now. Dangerous.'

Noble Savage, she reminded herself, not Eau de Sauvage. Such powerful (yet gentle) masculinity as Mo possessed was sure to give out a powerful aroma.

'I wondered if you would take me fishing tomorrow?'

'We catch the pink dolphin?'

Sissie laughed uneasily. Now that she was standing and Mo was standing, it was disconcerting to find that his legs stopped where her thighs began. His torso, on the other hand, was the same length as hers so that if they had both been sitting they would have been the same height.

'We leave at five, the latest. I show you the piranha bites like the man.' Mo smiled, showing his own sharp white teeth.

'Oh, good,' she said, and left in a rush.

In Lapland, at certain times of the year, the sky attracts those with unquiet minds. The bulky figure stood looking upwards. He had climbed as near to the top of the ice-capped mountain as he could and now he received his reward. The black sky moved and swirled into glittering myriad colours as if fireworks had been set off from west to east, except that instead of the usual bangs and squeals and whooshes, there was absolute silence. The man's face, at first as fearsomely forbidding as the mountain, became streaked with pink and yellow, orange and green, and his expression softened as if he found soothing this explosive display of nature's power. He grunted a few words, secure in the knowledge that no one was nearer than several hundred miles and, even then, they were unlikely to under-stand his language. 'Homeland,' he said, or something similar, and seemed to meditate, turning his face to the snowy ground. Then, once more, he looked into the flashing, whirling brightness and pronounced, with veneration: 'Rudolf.'

Since he was standing in the reaches of the snowy North, to which Father Christmas is supposed to retire with his questionably red-nosed reindeer, a casual observer (no hope of this) might have been reminded of the season of goodwill. But one look at his face, growing puce and purple as the great lights faded from it, would have quickly contradicted such a cheery notion. 'I shall mourn you, here, now – but soon I will return and then my vengeance will be fatal!' The lights faded, leaving only the ice cap glowing eerily.

White vapour hung over the river and the trees, cloaking and disguising equally what remained of the darkness of the night and the emerging dawn. Sissie crept to the back of the boat.

Mo came to her side. He wore some kind of shawl and a broad-brimmed hat of which Givenchy would have been proud. Silently he escorted her into the dinghy that lay in the shadow of the ship. Someone was there already, also wrapped in a shawl – an Indian friend, Sissie assumed, not sure whether to be sorry.

Mo pushed off with a paddle. 'No engine.' His wide-spaced dark eyes gleamed at her. 'Fish have ears like bats.'

'Literally?' enquired a voice from the other shawl. They had emerged from the side of the ship and the first rays of sunlight painted colour into the dark water.

'This isn't fair, Seb. Just not fair.'

'François tells me piranhas grunt. Mo invited me along too, didn't you, Mo?'

Mo paddled impassively at the front of the boat as if the conversation had nothing to do with him.

Sissie turned her back on Sebastien and concentrated on the wall of forest passing so close. It meant more to her now. She could pick out the cocoa tree, taller than all the others, and name at least some of the splashes of colour. When her knowledge and interest ran out, she leant over the side of the boat and watched the water sliding by, green marbled paper, untranslucent, unfathomable. She bent closer and closer, trailed her finger.

'No!' shouted Mo. He dropped the oar and took hold of her finger. 'Like the white worm. You want four fingers?'

Sebastien put aside his book. 'François tells me that a certain unassuming little fish makes a habit of swimming up the penis, and once arrived, puts out sharp prickles so he can't be got down again. The only option is to cut off the penis.'

'Women are so much better designed,' said Sissie sweetly.

The boat bumped against the river bank.

'A good place for fish.' Mo jumped out of the boat, and tied it

165

to a tree. As soon as Sissie saw the string, the hook and the bamboo rod, she remembered that she hated fishing. It was the same boring activity on which her father had insisted she accompany him at the age of five or six. It was supposed to bring them together, but the cold, wet, agonizing boredom of it had had the opposite effect. With lowering spirits, she watched Mo and Sebastien throw a line out of the back of the boat. Their enthusiasm was absurd and there was little difference between the expression of the Noble Savage and that of the aesthete. Sissie raised her eyes beyond them to the opposite bank and her attention was caught by a stump protruding from the water on which a tall black bird with hunched shoulders sat silent and immobile. I know just how you're feeling. Sissie sent sympathetic thought waves over the water. Here you are in the heart of darkness and nothing ever happens.

This was not quite true. After two hours, there was quite a pile of prettily coloured piranha fish. After three hours, Sissie began to read *Magic and Fate*. That, however, lasted only until she reached the following sentence: 'A major shock to the creative psyche can part the mind so that it proceeds in opposite directions like a worm cut in half with a spade.'

After four hours, Mo, who had hardly uttered a word all morning, pulled in the line. 'Now we eat.' He took off his hat and shawl and then his shirt. His skin was as smooth and hairless as a copper kettle. Sissie's lassitude lessened. She was not prepared, however, to find herself handed a paddle.

'We get to the breakfast quicker.'

As they set off, the depressed black bird hunched its shoulders higher and higher and then extended its neck: up and up it went, carrying its hard black head and wicked beak. At last it rose right off the stump and, still with a certain lack of enthusiasm, had lift-off into the great height of the trees. 'The snake bird,' Mo, who had been watching Sissie, commented.

'It was watching us.'

'It hopes we drop a fish. Look.' Chopping the smallest piranha, he looped it towards the far side of the river. Just as it reached the water, a black mass of power materialized out of nowhere, snatched up the fish in a noisy swirl of feathers and froth and receded once more into the camouflage of the dark trees.

Sissie found that her heart was bouncing like a yo-yo.

'Now we paddle,' commanded Mo impassively.

'Quite a circus performer,' Sebastien added.

Sissie sat behind Mo, in front of Sebastien. Although the sun did not break the barrier of the trees to shine directly on them, the heat was in every particle of air. At first she could not find the proper beat of the rowing but eventually the rhythm of the muscles in Mo's back taught her how to dip in and pull out. It became satisfying, the steady beat, the water running under the boat, the dark pattern of vegetation on either side, a dramatic wallpaper unrolling at the corner of either eye. Apart from the noise they made, she soon became accustomed to the unceasing buzzing of the insects, punctuated by the oboe cry of a bird. The monotony of all this made their continuing on and on seem inevitable and stopped her from complaining about the physical discomfort. In this way, several hours passed.

Because Mo's broad back was in front of her, Sissie could not see ahead. His announcement took her by surprise. 'My village. My brothers.' A reverential pause. 'My mother.'

Sissie felt Sebastien drop his oar and stand up behind her. 'Mon Dieu! A jungle Lake Windermere.'

As they stopped rowing, the boat swung round and she could see that their river was joining a wide lake, as blue as the sky above it, as peaceful as Paradise. On one side of it two or three wooden houses perched on stilts, their doors only just clearing the water. Clustered round them were small trees, garden trees, as she put it – one with exuberant scarlet flowers, others with what looked like fruit, although she could hardly see at this distance. There was a space behind for what must be cultivated land and then the great forest flourished again.

Mo began to paddle slowly but Sissie rested, watching. There were figures, small dugout canoes. Mo put down the paddle and went to the back of the boat. A huge roar shattered the stillness. Sissie had forgotten the existence of the engine. She turned round and frowned angrily at Mo but he was having far too good a time playing the role of returning hero.

'I agree with you,' said Sebastien, evading a pall of blue smoke to come and sit beside her.

As their boat rushed forward, a group of canoes came to meet them, each one filled with four or five moving figures. 'I feel as if I'm on Lord Nelson's flag ship being escorted into the Bay of Naples,' commented Sebastien.

They arrived at the shore and Sissie found herself carried by half a dozen small but wiry bodies onto dry ground. Three or four dogs yapped continually and, in the nearest tree, a monkey danced about from branch to branch shrieking and gibbering alternately. Overhead the sun escaped the forest and blazed into the clearing. Sissie felt herself sway. In a second, the same half-dozen bodies had hold of her and carried her several yards into one of the houses where an old woman, standing at the entrance, made way for her and followed her in. Sissie lay thankfully on the swept earth floor in the cool darkness.

Mo appeared at the doorway, a black shape silhouetted against the glaring light outside. 'My mother, Madame Didi,' he said. 'My brothers, my cousins, my family. And now we make the breakfast.' He disappeared again. Sissie now understood why they had to fish quite so long for quite so many piranha.

Feeling better, she sat up and attempted to make conversation with her hostess. However, although she never took her eyes from Madame Didi's face, it soon became clear that neither English nor her few words of Portuguese made any impression. So they sat in what Sissie hoped was companionable silence while she began to pick out details of the room: the old Singer sewing machine, the hammock, the large plastic bowl and the neat pile of bowls made from coconut shells. Soon a delicious smell of charcoal-grilled fish came in from outside. Sissie felt her entrails stir.

'Beer?' Sebastien came to the door with a couple of bottles in either hand.

'I think I need a lavatory,' said Sissie.

'The jungle is vacant – well, fairly vacant.'

'But I need paper.'

'Ah, paper.' Seb retreated and returned with *Magic and Fate*. 'Try not to use pages seventeen to twenty-four inclusive, which contain one of the best expositions of the relationship between experience and belief at the court of King Freddie of Uganda.'

Sissie took the book and went outside into the cover of scrubby bushes, followed, protectively, she assumed, by Madame Didi.

When she reappeared she saw that they were to take part in a feast, a celebration. Twenty or thirty people had gathered, mostly men, although some children were scattered at the edges. They were already drinking, bottles of beer regularly cracked open by a usefully shaped stone jutting from the ground. Looking at the mound of broken glass, Sissie felt glad of her own shoes and fearful for their bare feet.

Mo tended the fire. Far more substantial than any of his relatives, who had the narrow frames of the perpetually undernourished, he stood out in Mephistophelian manner, the flames of the midday sun mixing with those of the fire. He had now stripped further so that he wore only shorts and Sissie could see sweat running down his torso and continuing through the material onto his thighs. He looked happy and energetic, prodding here, commanding there, taking a swig of beer from a bottle in his left hand.

Sissie retired under the shade of the scarlet-flowered tree. She would have liked to sit down but the parade of insects, some ant-like and carrying pieces of leaves ten times their size, others as strangely shaped as if prehistoric beasts had been reduced to miniature, kept her on her feet.

Soon Sebastien joined her. 'They're getting drunk.'

Sissie stared. His usual face of the eternal voyeur, the disengaged, had shaped into something else. 'I suppose they would. Don't you remember the Captain's joke? Drink and Diving.'

'Mo's drinking too. But I don't think he's getting drunk.'

'That's all right, then.' They stood together under the tree. Even the dogs were quiet now, laid out panting under the back of the house, which was built against higher ground. Only the monkey still shrieked and gibbered, running round in what seemed to Sissie like aimless circles, until she realized that he was imploring whoever had opened a new bottle of beer to share it with his humble friend. His attitude of grovelling desire was both ridiculous and macabre, a parody of the young Indian masters or Caboclos or whatever they were. Sissie sighed and wondered whether to follow Madame Didi, who had disappeared into the hut. It was not that she felt threatened exactly by these boys, who were half her size and whose movements were becoming so languid that they seemed most likely to keel over, but that the scene was disagreeable, Paradise tarnished, the peaceful beauty of the lake, and the luxuries of nature surrounding it, mocked by its inhabitants' idea of a good time.

Mo brought over half a dozen fish, laid out elegantly on leaves as thick as plates. 'Bad bones,' he warned, as a mother to a child, 'the piranha is angry even in death.' Bread was brought too, as hard and strong as the white flesh of the fish was delicate. Sissie washed it down with beer, which was warm and fizzy but deliciously thirst-quenching. Time passed.

'You itch?' Mo's black eyes were very close to hers.

'Terrible biting things. Terrible itching.' Sissie focused hazily beyond him. There stood Sebastien at the edge of the water, splashing his hands and face. The lake was now silver, the sky above white as a porcelain bowl.

'I will help you.' Mo held out his hand. 'Come.' Supported by his short, powerful arm, she walked towards the hut and there was Madame Didi, crouched half asleep in the corner, a neat stack of piranha bones at her side.

'Where are your sisters?' asked Sissie.

'In Manaus working. Dead. One sick. Please sit.'

Sissie sat thankfully and shut her eyes. When she opened them again, Mo squatted by her holding a coconut shell filled with some red liquid.

'The shoes off. The socks off.'

Sissie watched dazedly as he used a fronded leaf to paint the soles of her feet red and then her feet entire and up over the ankles so it was as if she were wearing red boots.

'Now the hands.'

The same process was repeated on the palms and then up over her wrists so that she wore elegant red gloves.

'Good now,' said Mo. 'No more biting.' Now Sissie saw that all the Indians were painted in the same way, although it had not been obvious because their skin was darker and the red faded.

'More?' enquired Mo, sitting back on his heels with his black eyes fixed on her. He lifted the brush and sketched the shape of a torso in the air. 'All over?' He smiled.

170

Sissie began to feel Madame Didi was insufficient chaperone and to wonder about Sebastien's whereabouts.

'The shirt off?' suggested Mo, gleaming and glistening. He rolled forward on his knees in an admirably executed yoga position, not, however, admired by Sissie. Now that he was so close, she could smell the sharp tang of his body and the fish and beer on his breath; she could see the muscles bulging independently under his smooth, shining skin. She had never had a lover with serious muscles.

'You still want the pink dolphin? Brazilian crocodile better best. Yes?' Sissie got his point. At least he had asked her the question, although his confident expression indicated his certainty that she would echo his 'yes'.

Perhaps she did want Brazilian crocodile, if it came to that. She must have set up this so-called fishing trip with a reason. Would she find peace, tranquillity and even the meaning of life if she allowed her body to be taken over by this undoubtedly masculine man? Such dithering lost Sissie the chance of replying to Mo's question with a dignified, 'Not this afternoon, thank you very much.' Instead she found herself knocked backwards by the weight of Mo's body as he launched himself towards her with all the power of his admired pectorals. It was no comfort to spy Madame Didi sneaking out of the hut as fast as her ancient, withered legs allowed her.

Deciding that crocodiles were nasty bullying animals, Sissie wondered whether to scream and kick or attempt something more subtle. Where, after all, was Sebastien? Although no knight in armour, he might at least be an unwelcome witness – unwelcome to Mo, that is.

Sissie had just opened her mouth to scream 'Seb!' – Mo did not seem much interested in her mouth and at the moment was fully engaged with her breasts – when she recalled seeing him dallying at the water's edge, probably washing off the mixture of beer, sweat and fish that she could smell so strongly on Mo. Sissie shut her mouth again. Sebastien was at the water's edge and so was the boat. It only needed her to get herself there. Swiftly.

Mo's black head had a frantic, burrowing-animal feel about it. His heavy legs pinioned hers to the ground but her arms were free. Where should she strike? A steely finger into his eye? As Sissie summoned up warrior blood, Mo raised his head and looked at her with such heart-warming adoration that Sissie might have melted – his mouth so red, his skin so lustrous, his whole body so taut and keen and happy – had she not realized that this, this moment before his final plunge, was also her best moment for escape.

'I'm off!' The cry helped her to stab with her fingers, hook with her knees, arch off the ground and lift into space.

Sissie was running, bent, stumbling, bare red feet feeling for even ground, eyes protruding for a sight of Sebastien and the boat, the boat with its engine at the back, filled with infinite promise for a speedy getaway. Sissie ran like Atalanta, dexterously avoiding broken beer bottles, jagged coconut shells, sharp twigs and even a solemn procession of ants, each the size of her little finger, who crossed her path.

Sissie ran and jumped and her black hair streamed behind her like the smoke behind a jet and altogether she was rather like a child's imitation of a fighter plane with her wing-like arms and her long, smooth body.

Behind her on the dim and dusty floor, Mo rose slowly. He was disarmed, dismayed and disbelieving that this could be happening to him in his home town, more or less in front of his mother (who thought him god-like) and this made him slow to action. A blurred look veiled his broad, handsome face, an inability to recognize the moment, so he did not put his powerful muscles in service of the chase. However, when Sissie began to shout, the veil dropped away and he was on his feet and by the door.

'Seb! Seb! Seb!' screamed Sissie. 'We're leaving!'

Sebastien, who was gingerly dabbling his feet in the fringes of the lake, looked with a frown at the figure hurtling towards him.

'Get the motor going! On the boat!' screamed Sissie, infuriated by his ungalvanized attitude.

And there stood Mo in the doorway of the little house. It was clear that, like a powerful, low-slung car, he was about to go into overdrive and would be at the side of the lake in a matter of seconds. Moreover, the gentle, booze-smitten Indians were beginning to show signs of movement, an arm raised here, a set of toes uncurled and placed firmly on the ground there. Soon they must be counted part of the scene.

'Well, get a move on, then!' Sebastien shouted, swung his shoes into the boat and then himself, pushed it out into deeper water and tipped the motor upright. He pulled the cord with the energy of a soldier pulling out his sword from a corpse. To his astonishment, the motor started at once.

The roar, music to Sissie but crudely reverberant across the smooth water and against the tall trunks all around, shocked the less drunk into further action and Sissie needed to fly even faster to keep ahead not just of Mo but of several of his cohorts who, luckily, were still only partly in command of their limbs.

She splashed through the water, giving the sludge at the bottom no time to squeeze up between her toes. Gasping, she fell across the side of the boat. It set off at once, skimming across the lake with Sissie flapping feebly like a huge fish, half in and half out.

'Heave ho!' Sebastien extended his bony arm and pulled on one of her legs. Sissie collapsed into the bottom of the boat, incidentally crushing Mo's straw hat, which he had left behind along with his blanket.

'That was a narrow escape.' Sebastien's tone remained cool.

Sissie peered over the edge of the boat as if she feared flying arrows. Three long canoes were setting out from the shore. In the first the more substantial figure of Mo stood aggressively at the prow. 'We're going much, much faster,' Sissie whispered to herself, and sank down again.

'But was it really necessary?' asked Sebastien meditatively, although gunning the engine even faster.

'Necessary! Necessary!' Sissie crouched up and bared her teeth like a puma. 'I suppose you don't consider rape a good enough reason.'

'Calm yourself. Am I not your saviour?'

'So far, so good,' conceded Sissie grumpily. Her chest hurt and her feet were sore and she felt ignominious, too.

'We'd better check the gasoline,' said Sebastien. It was becoming obvious that he was enjoying himself. Their speed set up a cooling wind and the role of saviour was novel.

Sissie sat up, mainly to avoid the noxious blue smoke coming from the engine, and gazed at the scene behind them. They had come so far so fast that they would soon be entering the river and leaving the lake behind them. It was now late afternoon and the sun was already turning the sky and the lake, in which the sky was reflected, a taffeta yellow. Unfortunately, the sweet calm of visual perfection was spoilt by the spiky canoes, angry black insects, the fast-dipping paddles like waving legs.

'They'll never catch us,' said Sebastien. 'Look, we're into the river and far away.'

They were. The boat swung round in a flashy spin of white water and splunged into the deep dark tunnel of the river. It was even warmer than on the lake, a stifling, still warmth, and although Sissie was pleased to have passed out of view of their hunters, the atmosphere was horribly oppressive.

Sebastien throttled back the engine. 'You steer.'

Sissie sat at the back of the boat and fixed her eyes on the next bend in the river. Perhaps if she willed it the *World Traveller* would appear on the horizon, comforting lights glowing from every porthole.

'We're fine for gas.' Sebastien emerged from under the bulkhead. 'So, tell me, what happened? You know, when I first saw you, I thought you were bleeding.'

'It's paint,' said Sissie, looking at her hands and feet. 'He did it.'

'Part of a ritual orgy?' suggested Sebastien.

'To keep off insects.' As Sebastien took back the steering, Sissie stuck out her extremities. Since they had slowed down, a mixed swarm of flying creatures had collected above the boat but it seemed to her that they were less interested in her than in Seb, who had already started slapping himself and scratching at red bumps.

'It looks as if he did you one favour, at least.'

'Go a bit faster.'

'Now it's getting darker I'm worried about running into floating logs.'

'Surely we'll be back soon?'

'We rowed very fast for three hours after fishing and an hour or more before.' There was a pause in which they both heard the Red Howler Monkeys ululating somewhere ahead, a thoroughly depressing sound. 'I have never been interested in forced sex.' Sebastian spoke in tones of enquiry.

'Nonsense,' said Sissie irritably. She looked up at the sky, which was still surprisingly bright, considering how dimly placed they were.

What was there to tell Seb, Seb of all people, who, although a saviour in this case, was habitually a voyeur of other people's emotions – or so she had always thought? Not that it mattered what she told Seb anyway. She had fallen for the romantic dream of a pink dolphin and Mo had translated her starry-eyed look into a desire for his body. Or perhaps she really had desired his body but had just lost her nerve. Or maybe his was the wrong body.

'I just don't like being forced into things,' she said flatly.

'Quite right,' agreed Sebastien, but his mind was no longer on the reason for their flight. 'Do you remember a fork in the river?'

Sissie did not remember a fork in the river but there it was in front of them, a fork so evenly divided that whichever side you concentrated on seemed to be the straightest path.

'I suppose coming from the other direction we just didn't notice it,' said Sebastien.

Sissie felt like crying. It was obvious that there could be other forks they just hadn't noticed. She had certainly seen nothing beyond Mo's broad back.

'Pot luck?' questioned Sebastien, expecting no answer. The boat reached the divide and passed to the right.

'I expect we'll recognize where we sat still and fished for so long.' Sissie stared ahead. She remembered the rotting tree stump jutting out of the water where the snake bird had sat. She could remember its outlines specifically and it had been opposite where they fished. Only a few moments passed before she spotted it. 'There!' she cried excitedly. But it was too late. Sebastien had shot by. 'Seb!' she began, furiously, tears now actually in her eyes. 'That was the place.'

'If it was, we're on the right track.' His voice was dour.

Turning round to face front again, for she had been straining her eyes backwards to catch the last sight of the stump as if it were an old, valued friend, she understood why he was not sharing her excitement. There ahead of them was another stump, quite as recognizable as the first. 'I see.' She sat fixed and tense. The noise of the engine, even though they were not going fast, had become louder and she realized that this was because the river was narrowing and the sound hardly left the wall of trees on one side before it met the facing wall and was thrown back again, again and again, so that she could hardly tell apart the original engine sound from its multiple echoes.

'You'd better go to the front and spot floating or submerged debris.'

Sissie went obediently. She thought how direct he was now, how terse, how unlike the clever dilettante who had squatted in Paris life. The change was amusing and, for a moment, she lost the lumpen ache of dread.

'Watch out!' called Sebastien sharply. He looked at Sissie's long slender back, at her red hands splayed out on either side, at the vertebrae he could count one by one through her thin T-shirt and he, too, wondered what had happened to them both. Why, for example, were they, two chic sophisticates, alone in this boat lost in the middle of nowhere, where all the odds would have put François at the helm, François who knew about the forest and the river and the insects, who were gnawing even now at his flesh, and, although maybe unable to guide them, would at least have given them a sense of living in a reality rather than a nightmare?

'I am watching out,' grunted Sissie.

'We missed that log by a hair's breadth.'

'There's so many.' Sissie hung her black hair over the water's edge and began to shout. 'Right. Left. Straight ahead.' It was impossible. The river was narrowing, the amount of submerged debris was increasing and the water was not running anywhere very much. A brilliant green weed, as delicate as lace, was closing over the surface of the river, embroidering round floating tree trunks, so that they looked like Swiss rolls lying on a tablecloth.

Sebastien stopped the engine. The silence was a relief, despite the circumstances. 'On the whole I would not describe this stretch of water as river.'

'More an inlet,' suggested Sissie, carefully. They were being polite to each other in a way they never had been before. The silence made it easier to see and to think and Sissie suddenly noticed her bag stuffed under the front of the boat. 'I expect I have some anti-insect spray for you.'

'Thank you. Though I'm afraid post-insect would be more use.'

'Howard provided me with all sorts.' Sissie delved eagerly in her bag but the thought of Howard made her weak and filled with dread again. 'Poor Seb,' she mourned as she doctored his ankles and calves, which were marked with rows of pointed reddish-orange bites like cones on a motorway.

'At least we know the right fork now,' commented Sebastien, as Sissie pulled down his trouser legs and wound a shawl round him for greater protection and then placed Mo's hat on his head as if that might contain some Indian magic. He turned the boat round.

Neither mentioned the increasing darkness as the faraway sky's luminous yellow deepened to bronze with a greenish purplish tone. They reached the divide and took the other fork.

'At least we've thrown off Mo.'

'I'd give us half an hour before darkness.' Sebastien looked at his watch.

Sissie began to run through the animals of the forest. She pictured her childhood bedroom curtains, which had been covered with a thick trellis of green jungle through which birds and beasts peered dramatically. There was a snake, she remembered, yellow with a long back tongue, a parrot or something similar in garish red and turquoise, a black puma whose eyes glowed with the morning sun as if he was alive . . . Sissie stopped this picture in her head as it struck her, with a shock, that her bedroom at home faced north so that sun seldom came through the curtains and, besides, the curtains had been girlish, decorated with little rosebuds. Yet she knew that she had seen those jungle curtains, often, waking up in her cosy bed to a sensation of excitement and fear.

'Fifteen minutes,' said Sebastien. 'I should pull up the engine now. I can hardly see a thing.' But he did not.

Sissie rummaged in the front of the bow, then at the back. She found life jackets, a bottle of water and, wrapped in a plastic bag, a big torch. Its beam was as powerful as a car headlamp, making them more aware just how dark it had become. Sissie exulted. Light was safety, light kept away wicked beasts. Or was that fire?

'Have you ever read *Swallows and Amazons*?' Sebastien asked. He stopped the engine but the boat continued to drift forward, gradually slowing and weaving to the left. Sissie felt afraid that it would nudge into one of the soft, fudgy banks and they would be under the trees and anyone could come and get them.

'Couldn't we sort of fix ourselves in the middle?'

177

'We'll try.' Sebastien gave Sissie an oar and together they negotiated once more to the centre, but the water was too deep and no suitable stump presented itself. Eventually they found one a metre or two out from the bank to which they tethered the boat.

Sebastien celebrated their arrival by standing at the back of the boat and peeing into the river, making a gilded arc that Sissie wished she could imitate. 'I think they left out these bits in *Swallows and Amazons*,' she said, with her bare backside hanging over the side of the boat.

Although they sat in complete blackness, there was still some light in the sky but it was moving further and further upwards so that they seemed to be sitting in the bottom of an endlessly deep hole.

'Perhaps there'll be stars,' Sissie suggested. But, as she spoke, she found herself splattered by large, ragged drops of water. She watched as Sebastien put up his face and opened his mouth.

'Damn!' Mo's hat tipped off Sebastien's head and fell into the water. Although the current was not very strong, it began to move away. Sebastien grabbed a paddle. 'Direct the torch!' he shouted, standing up so suddenly that the boat rock violently. The hat began to float towards the bank, followed by the brilliant beam of the torch.

Sissie screamed so loudly that Sebastien nearly fell over the side with shock and both their hearts beat so frantically that neither had the breath to speak.

'Eyes,' gasped Sissie eventually. She pointed a trembling red finger. With her other hand she tried to point the torch at the river's edge, low down where the vegetation curled over the water, but she was too weak to hold it up. Sebastien snatched it impatiently.

'There!' There they were, a row of gleaming eyes, crimson in the torchlight, staring at them. Sissie bent double and clutched her chest and then her stomach. She thought she had never felt fear like this, that made your hair stand up and your insides dissolve, and then she thought she had and that this was a repetition of something else she had known before, and that made it worse still.

Sebastien swung the torch slowly along the line. 'Crocodiles,' he said.

'Crocodiles,' whispered Sissie, consoled at least that they were not the eyes of spirits or cannibals. 'Let's go. Let's get out.'

'I don't think they'll attack us,' said Sebastien.

'But we can't stay here, sleep here, with them just a foot or two away staring at us.'

Sebastien switched off the torch. 'They're hypnotized by the torch. It's ironic, really. François was leading us on a cayman hunt – the kind of crocodile round here – this evening from the ship.'

'I wonder if they're searching for us?' Sissie's voice shook.

'They'll think we're safe with Mo.' He paused. In the darkness and silence, save for the continued spattering of rain, it felt like a very long pause. 'I don't think we should move from here.'

'When does it get light?'

'About five.' They each wrapped themselves in a shawl as a protection against insects and lay down in the bottom of the boat. Sebastien thought about François a little longer and then began to recite to himself:

> The forest drips and glows with green.
> The tree-frog croaks his far-off song.
> His voice is stillness, moss and rain
> Drunk from the forest long ago.

The lines made him feel light-hearted and he realized that he wasn't frightened at all. He expected the next day to dawn and the engine to take them back to the ship. François, he knew, often camped out in the rainforest for days at a time.

But Sissie's fear was immense and irrational and growing all the time. It was like a balloon inside her, constricting her breathing where she lay on the bottom of the boat. She knew she must make contact with Sebastien and make him hold her or the balloon would burst, but she was unable to make the small movement necessary and her voice had disappeared too.

She was left with images, the eyes of the puma in that childish bedroom curtain she had imagined, the eyes of the crocodiles, the jagged orange of her scream, which had hung in front of her like lightning in the night. The pressure of these pictures, which spawned

179

others, less intelligible and even more frightening for that, kept her pinned to the bottom of the boat, mostly rigid but occasionally taken by a spasm of trembling.

Above her prone body a circlet of black bats chased mosquitoes for their supper.

Chapter Eighteen

In which Mary makes a Non-feline Friend.

MARY SAT ON her cliff top looking at the sea. It was a beautiful morning, the sun rising behind her into a turquoise blue sky, a flurry of little birds piping around the bushes below, a mist still skimming the surface of the water, while the breeze swirled it into delicate patterns. Soon it would be gone altogether, and the lozenges of sea, sky and headland would be as bright and clear as oil-paint on canvas. As if to celebrate such a unique day, Cleo had followed Mary all the way and now sat beside her, watching attentively the comings and goings of the birds.

'You'll never catch one,' Mary said, startling both of them with the sound of her voice. Cleo rose to her four feet with such a dignified and offended look that Mary burst into laughter. Light and gay, it startled her even more than the sound of her voice. It also seemed to be the last straw for Cleo, who ran off down the path. Laughter had not previously been part of Mary's vocabulary.

She continued to sit on the headland, a hunched and lumpy figure, quite certain that she was alone to think her own thoughts. She did not hear the man until he was within a foot or two and his dark shadow caught her eye.

He began to apologize, although it was Mary who was blocking the path. She was so taken aback – it was before seven o'clock and she had never seen anyone at this hour – that she stared upwards without moving.

'I saw something black and white,' he said. 'I come looking for badgers.' He had a broad, pale, pleasant face, blue eyes, thick grey hair. It was his shadow who had been tall, not him, for he was quite short and stout.

'It was my cat.'

'It follows you all the way here? That's unusual. You've come from the caravans, I suppose.'

Mary stood up slowly. It seemed he was intent on a conversation and, although she would not answer his questions, she was not frightened. 'You want to come out at night for the badgers,' she said.

'Oh, yes?' Somehow they were walking side by side along the narrow path, back the way he'd come. 'I'm from London,' he said. 'Not too knowledgeable about country matters. But I'd like to see a badger.'

'They can be a terrible nuisance,' said Mary, who had already exceeded her daily ration of conversation. The sun warmed her right shoulder, and out of her left eye she could sense the glitter of the water. 'The mist's gone now,' she said. It seemed incredible to be sharing this experience with someone else.

'Yes. When I set out, it was all round me.'

'You must have been low down?'

'Yes.' This time it was he who did not answer her implied question. They stood together and stared out at the sea. A fishing boat appeared round the headland, moving right to left.

'Time for work,' he said.

'Time for breakfast,' she said, and they parted, no names or information exchanged but a perfect morning shared.

Chapter Nineteen

*In which Two Blue Butterflies are found in the Heart of Darkness
and play a very Positive role in the Story.*

SHEET LIGHTNING illuminated part of the rainforest and a handful of its unmapped thousands of lakes and tributaries. It was completely silent, followed by no thunder, no rain, as if a light-switch was being turned on and off, the source to unimaginable power. Sebastien saw it and sat up but Sissie, paralysed in her terror under her blanket, saw nothing.

The tallest trees of the forest, the tropical cedar and the brazil nut, waved their topmost boughs. A sound, but not of thunder, drew nearer. Sebastien opened his eyes again. His bites, which Sissie's creams had subdued, began to itch all together, as an orchestra under a conductor's baton. Again, there was a long-held beam of lightning and in it he saw, beyond and between the trees, black figures running. Scratching furiously without being aware that he was doing so, he screwed up his face and eyes in an attempt to see more clearly. But the switch turned to off and once more he sat in darkness. Now he heard the noise – nothing natural but a man-made engine.

About to signal for help with his torch, his hand slipped back for the light had flooded on again and he could see the crouching figures beyond the tree trunks, setting down something in what appeared to be a clearing. The noise was obviously made by a helicopter.

'I'd rather be eaten by a crocodile than meet that lot,' said Sebastien.

Sissie made an immense effort and turned over, her face sharply white even in the darkness. 'Hold me, Seb. I can't bear it any more!' Her voice, which had begun as a mutter, rose as if she were about to scream.

Sebastien bent so that Sissie thought he was going to hold her but instead he put his hand over her mouth. 'You may not have to if those characters discover us.'

The lightning seemed to have made way for the helicopter and whatever illegal activities – unimaginable perversities, in Sissie's troubled mind – were going on beyond the trees took place under black skies. Rain came for a few minutes, but was hardly heavy enough to penetrate the leaf canopy. In the clearing where the men worked, orange lights were placed on the ground as if for a barbecue party. The helicopter landed, picked up what it had come for and left. The men on the ground left too.

It began to rain more heavily, the water falling like steel rods into the rivers. The crocodiles, attracted by the fresh smells and quiet, glided out from under the banks. In passing, it might have been an accident or curiosity, one nudged the boat where Sissie and Sebastien lay under their shawls. Sissie, huddled tight, shuddered as the boat swung against its moorings. The glowing eyes that had pursued her throughout the night changed again and became the eyes of Sekhmet, Egyptian goddess, lion or cat, male or female. Once more, as she had in the stone chamber, she felt herself on the edge of a discovery but this time her exhaustion was too great and she sank back into a sleep most like unconsciousness.

At about four in the morning, as the palest of pale dawns was rousing the birds into a still sleepy chatter, the arrival of a second helicopter sent them angrily screaming into the air.

'Too late, always too late!' The voice of Texas strove to rise above the noise of the chopper's wings. Howard Howard stood in the clearing, sporting the newest of new junglewear topped by a wide Stetson, which he had to hold down tight with one of his large hands. Around him, some near, some already far, scouting the undergrowth for careless clues (most likely but not most helpful) were at least a dozen men, some in military uniform, all with guns at the ready.

'Did you want a shoot-out, then?' shouted the man nearest to Howard. By now their helicopter had folded its wings, leaving room for a second helicopter to descend, from which sprang at least two dozen men, all soldiers, who at once spread wider and further than the first group.

'What a waste of time it all is!' Howard stared around bitterly. 'Always too late.'

'Like a needle in a haystack,' suggested his companion agreeably. He was dark-skinned and his English was accented. He smiled at his command of the language, which allowed him to use such an apposite simile. Language was such a pleasure.

'Non-sense!' Howard split the word in an insult, American-style, and then walked off on his own. He found a stump on the edge of the forest and, having made a careful inspection for insects, laid a large white handkerchief over it and sat down. Out of the forest, as if searching for him, came a brilliant blue butterfly. As big as his hand, it flew round and round him, dipping and rising, making blue reflections on his clean cream suit. Giving up frustrating observations – whoever had been, had been and gone and that was the way the army wanted it – Howard allowed his heart to flow towards the butterfly and thence, by an easy stage, towards the wonder that was Sissie.

The wonder that was Sissie awoke out of her agony and discovered, to her surprise, that she was alive in the pearly morning light, and, looking about at the trees and the birds and her ex-lover, felt rather keen to bathe her face and hands in the river. She unplaited her hair and shook it round her shoulders.

'Did you hear more helicopters just before it was light?' asked Sebastien.

'I heard nothing but the beat of rain and the beat of my heart.' She paused. 'And some frogs, I think. A great many frogs.'

'They make love very noisily, I'm told.'

'Is that so?' Sissie gazed vaguely into the trees.

'The black night of the soul has passed, I may presume?' Sebastien had put his whole head underwater and then slicked back his hair, giving him a fresh efficient look.

'I guess so.' Sissie nodded. 'I'm taking a walk.'

'Look, no crocodiles.'

'So I see.' Sebastien punted the boat to the bank but, since he showed no inclination to disembark, Sissie clambered over the side and put her long red feet on the soft leafy soil.

'Do you want to borrow my shoes?' called Sebastien.

'I'm fine, thank you.' Although the sun had not yet risen it had been quite bright on the river, but the inside of the forest was filled with mists and shadows. It was noisy enough, however. Sissie felt she walked with a retinue of birds and small animals that fluttered and scuttered and peeped and whistled and chattered and chuntered around her. She walked in an atmosphere of sound but she preferred the butterflies. One, in particular, startled her by its size and blueness. It came down towards her, through an avenue of dark trunks, its blue so brilliant as to be luminous, and then instead of passing on, it circled round, either admiring or looking for admiration, finally fluttering up above her head, remaining and keeping pace with her as she walked.

Howard Howard clamped his Stetson tighter on his head and decided to take a walk. His heavy boots made deep dents in the soft forest floor and his cumbersome presence caused consternation in the wild life in his area, although the blue Morpho butterfly continued to follow him. He did not notice any of this, however, because his eye was turned inwards, looking at Sissie lying on a canopied deck cruising up the great river Amazon. So near and yet so far. He thought and sighed.

Sissie saw Howard approaching as she crouched down for a pee. Rising in excitement and amazement, she bobbed towards him while at the same time frantically hoisting up her jeans. Had she gone completely mad? Was her imagination overstretched by the previous night's tortures, presenting her in ghostly form with what she most desired? He did seem to be advancing unseeingly, like an actor playing the part of Banquo. When he was within twenty yards and

186

quite clearly corporeal (he, too, she noticed, was escorted by a large blue butterfly), she could doubt no longer.

'Howard! Howard Howard!' she cried.

Howard looked outward from within and saw a tall figure, red-gloved hands waving, swathed in mist like a chiffon stole and topped by a living hat, a glimmering blue butterfly. He stopped dead. He stood so heavily that his feet sank another two inches into the ground.

'It's me. Sissie.' Sissie ran towards him, her red feet light as a dancer's.

They met. They clasped in each other's arms. Above their heads the butterflies, less friendly, locked in mortal combat.

'My heart's desire,' whispered Sissie after a few moments, thus abandoning, without any consideration at all, twenty-three years of self-centred independence.

'I am yours for ever,' pledged Howard, the strong protective man. His Stetson had been knocked off by their embrace and his forehead was revealed as high and noble.

Sissy stroked it with awe and a film of red passed in front of Howard's eyes.

'Sugar, why don't you take off your gloves?'

Sissie removed her hand and looked at it with surprise. It was hard not to recall the humiliating event that led to her presence here in the forest but she certainly did not wish to share the story with Howard. His wonderful presence, his arms around her, wiped out all that messy sort of stuff, she told herself and, telling herself, smiled and kissed him on the lips. Howard kissed her back, his blue eyes open but blankly blissful.

At their feet, the two butterflies, still struggling for dominance or death, spiralled downwards into Howard's hat, where they lay quivering in a moment of mutual recuperation.

'We are like Adam and Eve in the garden of Eden,' Sissie breathed into Howard's ear.

'This is, of course, a primeval forest,' agreed Howard. His eyes came into focus a little more. He saw a brave slant of the newly risen sun piercing the trunks and spotlighting their hallowed place of meeting.

'Alone at the beginning of time,' enlarged Sissie. She shifted her red toes in the soft mush of leaves. The sensation was delightful.

Howard cleared his throat. 'Not quite alone, Sugar,' he said.

Ah, Sebastien, thought Sissie, she had quite forgotten him in the ecstasy of finding her heart's ease. He must have followed. She looked round. 'Oh!' she exclaimed, shrinking back into Howard's arms, and 'Oh!' again, as she looked further round.

'Yes.' Howard's voice deepened with masculine authority. 'They are soldiers, real soldiers. Corrupt, as it happens, but that need not concern you. In fact, they need not concern you at all. They are merely part of my job.' Was there patronage in these words? If so, Sissie did not pick it up, she was too busy counting the soldiers. They stood in a circle, each one by a tree, eyes fixed firmly on the central event.

'I guess we should get on with things,' said Howard.

'With our life together,' agreed Sissie lovingly.

'With our life together,' repeated Howard, a little distracted from his lovingness since his previous companion had just stepped out from behind a nearby tree, his somewhat Plumbish face transformed by a comprehensive leer. 'I guess we should move.' Showing efficiency and control he bent down, picked up and put on his hat in one swift movement.

It took but a second for him to wrench it off again, a look of terror on his usually sanguine features. Out of his hair (which stood on end like a cornfield) rose the two blue butterflies still combatant, although now quite ravaged and tattered. Up they went into the darkness of the forest top while the soldiers, corrupt but not without appreciation for good theatre, gave them a spontaneous round of applause.

'Vamos,' commanded Howard's companion, after the clapping had subsided.

'Vamos,' echoed Howard, smoothing down his hair and replacing his hat, which took a certain amount of courage. Sissie, who had gasped at the butterflies, laughed and clapped with the soldiers, which gave her a happy sense of community, then put her arm through Howard's in as proprietorial a way as if they were already married and living in a cottage made for two. Escorted by the army, they walked through the trees, towards the clearing and the helicopter.

In this way, Sissie threw in her lot with a man of her dreams and did not give a green tree frog for Sebastien waiting for her on the bank of a tributary of the river Xeruini, which is where he turned out to be. He would, of course, have searched for Sissie till kingdom come if Mo had not come instead, paddling his canoe with two or three helpmates. He was, incidentally, wearing the hat that had been carried away by the river.

'Good morning,' said Sebastien, pleased, on the whole, that Sissie was not with him. It made good manners, calm politeness, more convincing, he hoped. Nevertheless he did flinch away a little as Mo silently boarded his boat. Must he expect a paddle over his head? No. Mo's face was too impassive.

'We decided to go cayman hunting. That's why we left in such a hurry.' This seemed to Sebastien a stroke of genius, a face-saver all round. 'You should have seen the rows of red eyes gleaming,' he elaborated enthusiastically.

Impassively, Mo cast off from the canoe and said some word of farewell to his companions. He sat at the back of the boat and prepared to start up the engine. This posed a dilemma for Sebastien since they seemed about to abandon Sissie, presumably still wandering among the trees. He looked at Mo and was about to brave a question when Mo spoke.

'She go in the helicopter.'

Just then – indeed, quite on cue – the great trees inside the forest waved their topmost boughs once more and a helicopter lifted off into the bright sky.

'Let's hope they're friendly!' exclaimed Sebastien.

'Friendly,' affirmed Mo, in a dour voice.

'That's all right, then.' As the boat shot briskly into the middle of the river, Sebastien lay back and thought of François.

'You catch no crocodiles?' Mo spoke again after ten or fifteen minutes had passed in uninterrupted progress.

'Er. No. Too big.'

'Too big, too frightening?' Mo's handsome face lightened, brightened.

'Absolutely right,' agreed Sebastien. 'Brazilian crocodiles terrify the English.' This is the limit of my abasement, he thought, but he was quite unprepared for the success of his remark. Mo smiled, and then chuckled and then laughed and then guffawed. And even after the guffaws had subsided, the chuckles reappeared at frequent intervals.

Eventually, just before they reached the ship, Mo took hold of Sebastien's arm so tightly that he shrank nervously. 'She like the pink dolphin. Brazilian crocodile too frightening.' His white teeth gleamed pointedly and off he went into a final paroxysm of what seemed to be self-congratulatory laughter.

Sebastien felt no need to comment.

Chapter Twenty

In which Sissie finds a Spectacular Hat for her Mother.

JANICE AND ROB arrived unexpectedly to visit Mary. Of course, there was no way to visit her expectedly since she had no telephone and no postal address but this was a break from their usual pattern of six-monthly intervals between visits. It was midday, a rainy summer's day without wind when the sky and sea are the same slub grey and the birds are too fed up to sing.

Janice and Rob were not fed up. They had news to impart. They knocked on the caravan door energetically and could hardly wait for Mary to make her usual slow shuffle to open it. In fact, they did not wait but burst in calling, 'Mary! Mary! I hope we're not disturbing you!'

They saw at once that they were, for Mary stood defensively with her back against the table and, at her side, also standing, although not so defensively, was a man. On the table were two mugs and hanging side by side two dripping mackintoshes and two hats, one vaguely Tyrolean with a feather in it. Clearly, they had been for a walk together and were now sharing a cup of coffee.

Janice and Rob, who always meant kindly and were really Mary's only true friends, wished they had waited for her to open the door – she looked so overwhelmed – for they were not only absolutely stunned that she had a caller, a male caller (she had sworn never to speak to a man again), but also delighted. To cover Mary's embarrassment, they made a great play of taking off their mackintoshes and talking of the unseasonable weather.

'This is Ted Mack,' said Mary, finding her voice.

Janice could hardly be blamed for smiling at this somewhat hysterically.

'Ted works in the town,' said Mary which, although an innocuous enough statement, surprised Rob and Janice because they always thought of Mary cast off on a remote headland and nowhere near a town.

'I've come to live here quite recently,' said Ted, who had a gentle voice and a kind face. 'We go for walks together now and again.'

'Ted wants to see a badger,' said Mary.

'No luck yet,' said Ted.

'Oh, Mary!' Janice exclaimed. 'You haven't told Ted who *we* are.' So Mary made the introductions in a perfectly competent way and soon they were all sitting round the table drinking cups of coffee, made perfectly competently by Mary.

After they had talked of this and that for a good twenty minutes, Rob and Janice exchanged a glance, which Ted intercepted and rose at once to his feet. 'I expect you want your sister to yourselves. I should be off anyway.'

Mary went with him to the door while he put on his rain gear and carefully did up every zip, button and press stud. 'I'm on an early shift for the next four days but I might see you one evening.'

'That's right,' said Mary, and she stood, watching him step briskly through the rain for quite a few seconds, before turning inwards.

'We came like this because we had news.' Janice and Rob decided not to beat about the bush. Mary had not sat down again but stood looking at them warily. They both noticed how there was a becoming flush of colour on her skin and Janice, who was more sensitive, also noticed that a way she had had since the tragedy of angling her neck and face to the floor was less marked.

'It's Sissie,' continued Janice. 'To cut a long story short – not that we know much of it – she's married.'

'Married,' repeated Mary. At Sissie's name all her worst characteristics had reappeared and her face was trying to lose itself in her chest.

'Married to an American and living in Manaus.'

'Manaus?' repeated Mary, still without raising her eyes.

'Manaus is in Brazil on the Amazon,' interposed Rob. 'We found it in our atlas.'

'Yes. She sent a letter. In a package. It was a very sweet letter, wasn't it, Rob?'

'Very sweet. Quite surprisingly sweet, considering.'

'She wrote she was so very sorry not to have the family with her on her wedding day, in particular, me – I was most touched by that. And she sent a present. Well, we thought you should have the present. Why don't you read the letter for yourself?'

For a moment it looked as if Mary might refuse. A cloudy tearfulness, which Janice knew well, overtook her face but in the end she accepted the envelope.

'And that's the present.' Janice put a brown parcel on the table and then, because she noticed it had stopped raining, she said that she and Rob would go outside to stretch their legs a little after the long drive.

'We must give her every opportunity,' said Janice, the minute they were clear of the caravan.

'You never give up, do you? Never give up.'

'You're not a mother so you don't understand,' responded Janice firmly, but she smiled at Rob and gave him a kiss because she kept seeing Ted's kind face and feeling there was hope.

Mary picked up the letter at once but the words slipped around the page so confusingly that she decided to open the parcel first. It was large and light and as she unfolded a corner of paper she was suddenly struck by the extraordinary idea that this had come from her daughter, that her daughter's hand had touched it and why, after all, should it be a present for her? She pushed both letter and parcel away from her and would have called for Janice had not Sheba come purring and winding round her legs and asking for lunch.

'Oh, yes. Oh, yes. Be patient.' By the time she could see Sheba contentedly feeding she felt calmer and, even, to her own surprise, curious.

Dear Mum,

This will be a shock to you so I want to tell you at once how happy I am, how gloriously, amazingly happy. I had already met Howard Howard in Paris and London – but when we met on the banks of the Amazon I could only believe Fate meant us to spend our lives together. We were married in a Catholic church, Howard is a cradle Catholic, on Sunday. We are living in a furnished apartment in Manaus because that is his working base. I wish you had been with us on Sunday, you and Dad and Ruth and Adam. We only had Seb, you remember, Seb from Paris, his friend François, and Howard's faceless friends from his office – he works for the American government – did I say he was American? Well, he is and speaks with this wonderful drawl. He wears Stetsons too and cowboy boots, when he's not in disguise like the first time I met him. His friends are faceless because they don't want to be remembered and I've never seen them since the wedding anyway. You will think Howard a perfect son-in-law. I was really sad you weren't all here, particularly you, Mum, a girl should have a mother and, if you remember I promised you a wedding hat. So here it is. I know it seems a little crazy and Howard was furious with me for buying it – in America you're not allowed to import feathers but I felt it was a real celebration hat, a hat for the mother of a crazy girl at her wedding so I sent it to you anyway. Wear it for me, please, at least once. Then you can put it in a jumble sale. Very much love from your joyous ex-super-model, Mrs Howard Sissie Slipper Howard.

Now Mary opened the parcel without hesitation. The letter spoke to her, she could see, not to Janice, who was far too sensible. It became even more obvious why Janice had passed it on to her when she drew out the hat – or rather it popped out because, released from its binding, it sprang open like a conjuror's topper, although it was more of a basin than a chimney.

Mary gasped. Someone had layered every inch with tiny brilliant-coloured feathers, each one lapping over the next so that it was as if a rainbow had been wound round the crown. The brim had been decorated downwards rather than in spirals round so that there was a multitude of stripes ending up in little curling fronds.

Outside the caravan, Janice and Rob debated whether to return. Rather than burst in on an emotional scene, they peered through the window.

Mary stood in front of her little mirror, rapt at the sight of her dull old pudding face transformed by the wonders of Sissie's feathered hat. Behind this glory appeared half each of two straining, curious faces. Mary whipped round, snatched the hat off her head.

'We're so glad you like it!' Janice opened the door, and decided to take the bull by the horns. 'I knew you would and Rob thought you'd be intrigued, at least.'

At least! The patronage of it. Mary wanted to throw back the hat in their faces but instead she clutched it tightly to her ample breasts and stared furiously at the floor.

'Yes,' continued Janice valiantly – but then she had seen worse, so much worse. 'And we are so glad to have met Ted. What did you say he did?' This was a question proposed by Rob because, despite recognizing Ted's kind face, they had a duty to see no one was taking advantage of Mary's nervous condition. ('Nervous condition' was a euphemism that had stood the test of time with Janice and Rob after they had considered 'nervous breakdowns' must have an end.)

'He works in the town prison!' Mary lifted her head and stared defiantly. Her large pale-blue eyes suddenly bore a close resemblance to Sissie's.

Janice, shocked, took a step backwards. 'Oh, Mary,' she murmured and then, because she was on the way out and had Rob at her side and could easily exit in a flash if Mary became violent, she dared even further, 'Does Ted know . . .?' Her question trailed off delicately and she took another step backwards, prepared for the rage.

It did not come. 'He does not know,' answered Mary in dignified tones. 'But I shall wear this hat when we go walking and if he asks I may tell him.'

Tell him what? thought Janice. How much? But she said, 'I see,' and looked at Rob. A picture of her dumpy sister parading along the cliff tops in macintosh and Indian feathered hat presented itself in such vivid terms that she felt a strong urge to laugh and scream with laughter and become quite hysterical with laughter, tears running down her cheeks. And he was called Ted Mack!

Rob spotted the expression on Janice's face and bustled her to the door. 'We're glad, pleased, happy.'

'Very, very happy,' spluttered Janice. And it *was* partly relief and happiness because her sister had someone else in her life (and now she came to think of it, was there not a habitual-looking cat curled up in the corner?) And that someone else was a prison officer. A prison officer!

Bent double with the excuse of renewed rain, Janice just reached the car before exploding. 'Oh, really,' protested Rob mildly. In truth, this uncontrolled laughter made him happy because, lately, Janice had been tired, out of sorts, not her usual positive self. The laughter made her seem young again. He patted her on the back and found a handkerchief to wipe her eyes.

'It's the strain, that's my excuse,' she gulped. 'After twenty years. Do you realize, she kept Sissie's letter?'

'You're a generous woman,' said Rob.

'I only ever held Sissie in trust.'

Inside the caravan, Mary lay on her narrow bunk bed with a blank unfocused expression. Too much had happened and she was frightened about what her mind would do with it. But Sheba jumped on her stomach and began to purr loudly, and beyond that there was the beat of the rain on the roof reminding her, reassuringly, of headland walks. After a while her eyes shut and she fell asleep.

Chapter Twenty-One

In which Sissie realizes that True Love is very different from
Sebastien or Plumb.

IN THE WEEKS and months that followed her marriage, Sissie
often thanked her lucky stars, glittering stars like the flashbulbs
that used to light her catwalk appearances, that she had hurtled from
super-model eminence into the shame of the year that had followed.
How else would she have met Howard Howard, the love of her life?

There had, it is true, been a regrettable blip at the altar rails
when the little leather box extracted from Howard's pocket had
proved to contain a tooth instead of a ring. But any anxiety had been
quickly dismissed by the priest. 'Do you think they have the gold
bands in the favelas?' he had cried. 'It is your holy love that has
brought you together and brought down God's blessing on your
marriage.' Or so Howard had translated his words since Father Pedro
spoke in Portuguese.

A peace had come over Sissie's heart, which lasted still. Soon it
was joined by a physical satisfaction that she had never thought
possible. They were so pleased with each other that the urge to make
love arose out of the simplest caress, causing delightful confusion if
they were out of their apartment.

Hand on her back, big boots clumping, Howard hurried her
along the streets, proud of his ownership, his loving urgency.

'Touch me, hold me, take me for your own!' Howard kissed
Sissie and Sissie kissed Howard and admired his youthfulness, which
felt firm and strong yet had none of the propellant coolness of
Sebastien's. His flesh tasted of honey as she nuzzled and licked and

tried gentle love bites which left no mark. They both agreed that their absolute compatibility was a wondrous miracle, and when Howard admitted that he had never spent more than a couple of nights with the same woman, and that infrequently, Sissie wished she was a virgin pure for him. Only his undeniable knowledge of Sebastien deterred her from attempting a total whitewash of her past. She felt, also, that he deserved the truth.

One of Howard's most attractive traits, to Sissie at least, was his lack of imagination. Better still, he had no sense of humour. Best of all, he did not appear to know what irony meant.

'When I saw you, I saw the most beautiful woman in the world. You made fun of me but I didn't give a hang. I was in love. I will be in love for ever. Love is no short year's sentence.'

'Oh, Howard!' Sissie adored these kind of declarations, even as she wriggled with embarrassment. How could he be so straight-forward? And, of course, he wasn't. Had he not stolen her pearly tooth? Admittedly its loss had contributed to their coming together on the banks of the Amazon, but Sissie had been brought up to believe that the end does not justify the means. That was a deception directed against her but, in truth, his whole life was a deception.

Every morning he went off to work and sometimes returned in the evening. At other times, he was away several days on trips that necessitated him unlocking the cupboard where Sissie pretended not to know his guns were kept. His working life had to be kept secret, Sissie appreciated, although she did advise him against bad disguises as being counter-productive. 'You will never look like a Colombian drug dealer,' she informed him firmly, 'and it would be safest to stop trying.' So why did she consider him straightforward, a clear light in her life, a staunch and steadfast twin soul? It was a mystery. Possibly, it was love.

There was no doubt that Howard's long working hours and frequent absences hampered Sissie's exploration of the country in which she found herself. Unwilling to make friends without Howard, she saw more of Father Pedro than anyone else, tagging along on his day of good works. She was applying herself daily to learning Portuguese but the priest revealed a desire to practise his English which, since she soon suspected it was his principal reason for seeing her, she could not deny him.

They walked beside the river where many of the priest's parishioners had built their wooden shacks on muddy sloping banks. These ramshackle homes were raised on stilts and, since it was half-way through the dry season, they stood high above the ground, which was used as a rubbish dump and through which ran a mostly open sewer. Wooden walkways and verandahs criss-crossed the area but even so it was no fun walking over the foul-smelling filth.

What a catwalk I've come to, thought Sissie fastidiously, but with no regret. She did wish for the first time in her life to be shorter or at least a little less tall, for they were always surrounded by a battalion of children, some hardly more than toddlers, who jumped about her as if they were trying to pull the fairy from the top of the Christmas tree. Several times one or another would fall off the planks into the dripping morass beneath. And yet there was something oddly festive about the scene. The children were so lively and beautiful with their oily brown skin and black eyes (although some, she was surprised to notice, had ginger-gold hair and blue or grey-green eyes). The sky was a clear blue, the sun hot, enough of the houses painted in pastel pink or green to vary the monotony of the brown, and beyond the last run of houses flowed the great river Amazon.

They stopped while Father Pedro talked to a group of women in front of what seemed to be a kind of crèche, judging by the multitude of babies. Sissie waited, poised on a narrow plank, in her shorts, rubber boots (a sensible precaution) and T-shirt looped with a swathe of beads bought for her by Howard – from Indians he told her, encountered during his two-day visits away – and was struck by a sense of déjà vu.

Surrounded by the women the priest turned to her. Sissie put out her hand to him and, as she did so, realized she wasn't suffering from déjà vu at all, but reliving a true memory. Where was it? She had strutted among squalid huts, posed surrounded by children while the photographer commanded, 'Donnez-moi un sourire, Sissie! Pas trop sérieuse, Sissie!' So she had mirthlessly bared her teeth.

Why had she not wanted to smile? The photograph was a tremendous success when it appeared in the magazines. She had been wearing a white silk pret-à-porter dress with a white handbag clasped in front of her and, when the photograph came out, sales of the white handbag exceeded all previous records. Madame B. had crowed at the success: 'Comprenez, Sissie. Women deposit themselves in their handbags and that self is under threat from les muggers, particularly in poor countries where the people are starving and rapacious, even les enfants, particularly les enfants. But the silly woman wants to open her handbag and save the children – except that she is afraid. Now, in this photograph we see a happy, confident woman, white clothes, white handbag, surrounded by children. Unthreatening children, approving children, applauding children. This makes all women feel very good and they want to be like her so they go out and buy the handbag. Voilà, Sissie!'

How much was I paid for that shoot? wondered Sissie, as she stood among the laughing, jumping children – she carried no bag for them to snatch. Ten thousand dollars? More, probably. After the first year or two of her huge earnings, she had taken it all for granted, leaving the details to her agent, not bothering to find out what sums she was earning. Even now, she had no idea of her bank balance.

Pedro turned round and called to Sissie. He wanted to introduce her to the women. Craning down, she shook their hard, warm hands, looked into their curious faces. If she had not been with the priest, what would they have thought of her, this white-skinned woman who teetered uneasily along their catwalks? Would they have looked at her with the same friendliness or set the children to tip the hat off her head, to pull the ring off her finger, the silver hoops out of her ears?

Pedro made a cheerful sign of the cross over the women and took Sissie's arm. 'On we go!' he shouted proudly, using a newly learnt English phrase.

On they went, Sissie thoughtful, Pedro practising irregular English verbs.

'I am, you is, he is.'

'You are,' corrected Sissie automatically.

'Que besteira!'

'What rubbish,' translated Sissie.

'Very good. You go fast, I slow.'

Pedro reverted to Portuguese, too fast for Sissie to catch everything but she understood the message.

'That word is my word for everything that is wrong in Brazil and everything is wrong in Brazil, except the people and the country. You will say I see it from one point of view but that is the point of view of so many millions of people. I am not a good man, I am tempted, I have had a wife . . .'

At this point Sissie assumed she had mistranslated.

'. . . but I have eyes and with my eyes I can see these *favelas*, such a pretty word, like a name for a flower, almost as pretty as you, and I can see they are growing not shrinking, round every city, they are spreading outwards but I do not see them like limpets clinging to the rock, like fungi collecting round the base of a great tree or even like succubus clinging to the branches, sucking and suffocating the main spring. No, I see them like a stain rolling outwards from the blot at the centre, from the rich, the uncaring, the unscrupulous, the weak, the cowardly, the stupid, the insensitive . . .'

What had begun quietly became a tirade, a litany of reproach and abuse, yet Sissie felt none of the black bitterness usually associated with anger. Indeed, every now and again the priest stopped his walk in the breezy sunshine, and the children, who were clustered round them all the time, stopped too and smiled at Sissie, squeezing her hand, peering at her as if to console. It wasn't her fault, they seemed to be saying, that she was big and pallid and rich.

Eventually they arrived at Father Pedro's next destination, a tin hut which housed an ice-cream-making machine, donated by an aid organization to give employment.

Sissie tried to eat an ice-cream but it melted so fast that the children, lying at her feet with their mouths open to catch the drops, got more than she did. She began to feel she was getting heat-stroke and longed to stumble up through this insalubrious wasteland and take a taxi back to her cool apartment. She looked at her hands, sticky from the ice-cream and still showing a reddish tint from Mo's artwork, and saw, under her very eyes, a freckle pop out. It will be there for ever, she felt like crying out, as Pedro argued with a woman who wrung her hands and threw them in the air alternately.

She felt like splashing a tear on the freckle as if that would wash it away, bring her skin back to its former purity. How proud she had been of her white skin when the lights blazed and could not reveal a flaw. How tall and white and special she had been, like a marble-coated minaret of the Taj Mahal. Her neck alone was as long as most of these women's legs. She had always stood out, always.

'On we go!' called Father Pedro. It was two o'clock, early for eating in Brazil, and Sissie pictured hopelessly a little shaded table, crusty bread, a bottle of slightly fizzy wine.

'Now we go to my special friends.' Sissie knew the priest's special friends and her spirits sank still lower. They were physically or mentally handicapped children, looked after in a concrete building with a corrugated iron roof. Really, she could not bear to go there again. Pedro called them the Fortunatos, the lucky ones, and they were lucky, she could see it, with their loving helpers and solid walls and roof, but to her it was all unbearably grotesque.

'Today you will not come with me,' announced Pedro, stepping energetically off a board that ended abruptly and jumping a greenish-silver puddle from which unhygienic horrors protruded. 'You go home by taxi and rest.'

Why did he spoil her like this? Why did he never shout reproaches at her or include her in the stain rolling outwards from the blot at the centre?

Howard had been away the night before and when she arrived back at their apartment, the rooms had a tidy, sterile look. He had been living on the third floor of a concrete block before they married but Sissie had moved them into one floor of a large, crumbling mansion. It had been built during the great rubber boom of the 1880s and shared some of the baroque grandeur of the opera house, which stood, monument to a rich past, at the centre of Manaus.

Sissie liked the height of the three windows in her room, even though they were grimy and cracked. The grime, she had pointed out to Howard, filtered the harshness of the sunlight without need for curtains. She liked, too, the height of the ceilings, the ornate peeling stucco-work, and the marble-lined, gold-tapped bathroom – even if the water came out sporadically in excitable bursts punctuated by long intervals in which the pipes shook and rumbled but ejected nothing. She had, however, invested in new rugs and a new bed, on which she now undressed herself and lay down.

She closed her eyes but the sights she had seen that morning remained vividly before her, and led her on to picture all the other colourful crowd scenes in which she had taken part, not only the photographic shoots but the hundreds of couture shows, until that final deathly one. She saw the streets of Bombay, kaleidoscopic tunnels down which she'd been led by the wilful little Rita, like a Christmas fairy in her pink and tinsel but indomitable at heart. How many shops had she led Sissie into that morning? How many bangles, baubles and beads had Sissie draped about herself, bought with so few rupees, until she had entered the sari bazaar (not that she had wanted a sari; she had wanted a hat for her mother) and there found herself surrounded by a swirling mass of shining colours, pink, orange, crimson, blue, a rainbow of colour, which was admired by her audience, layered and tiered all around her, as if they sat in an amphitheatre and she were the spectacle. And all the time there had been a master of ceremonies, a ringmaster, knocking the handle of his whip on the ground. Knock. Knock. Knock.

Asleep but awake, eyes closed, Sissie tossed and turned so fretfully that she did not hear the bedroom door open or see a man's shoes, white, punch-holed calf, cross her newly acquired Brazilian-Indian weave rug.

'You'll sleep your whole life away. I would be ashamed to sleep so much. Personally, I find more than two or three hours a debilitating bore. By dint of crossing time-zones in well-judged sequence, I once managed to avoid night for a month. I have never felt so energetic, so filled with exuberance.'

Sissie opened her eyes and gazed at the Author. Why did he always come to her when she was at a low ebb? She raised her head but refused to return his smile. 'I'm married,' she said crossly. 'You can't barge in and sit on my bed and start laying down the law.'

'So where's your husband?' asked the Author, a craftily amused look narrowing his eyes. It was not just his shoes that were exquisite. His suit of fine undyed linen was smooth and fashionably crumpled at the same time, his shirt, the coolest of blues, his tie with a motif that suggested macaws in flight was yet too creative to be specific. His silvery hair, although greyer and thinner than before, was styled with a deceptive simplicity that suggested each strand had been individually razor-cut. He presented a remarkable contrast to Sissie, who lay flushed and tangle-haired, her naked body wound in sweat-dampened sheets.

'My husband is in the forest,' she answered defiantly, 'fighting the powers of darkness.'

'What? He leaves you behind? So newly married as you are?'

'He only goes for a few days at a time. Besides, it's dangerous. Not the forest, which, as a matter of fact, I've already been to, but his work. He would not want to put me in the line of fire.' Recognizing with annoyance her tone of defensiveness, near a whine, Sissie roused herself further and was cheered by a useful memory. 'When I was last in the forest, I used that book you so admire, *Magic and Fate*, as lavatory paper.' This came out a little more baldly than Sissie could have wished but nevertheless she was glad to see the Author's smiling expression darken.

'You wiped your bum with the greatest work of philosophical literature written in the twentieth century?'

'I certainly did. Luckily Seb had brought it along. I have to admit, he wasn't too keen. It was entirely my idea.'

The Author stood up, shaking down his trousers so that they aligned neatly across the front of his shoes. 'You have changed,' he told her sternly.

'I told you. I'm married.'

'To that man who wears wigs.'

'I don't know how you dare ridicule Howard,' cried Sissie, getting angrier and hotter every minute. 'He only wears wigs to further his career. When I first met you on the aeroplane you lifted your hair off your head with *pride*!'

'You have misremembered,' said the Author, and he began to walk slowly backwards to the door. 'It was my top teeth.'

'I have not!' screamed Sissie, sitting up on her haunches. 'You are a charlatan!'

'As I was in the area, I thought I should pay you a friendly visit.' The Author slipped backwards over the threshold of the door.

'I'll show you! I'll show you!' screamed Sissie to his shadow, and she bounced up and down on her knees furiously before falling down in an exhausted heap.

'You're so hot.' Howard Howard bent over his wife protectively.

Sissie woke slowly, swam upwards through green water and blue sky. She pursed her lips and kissed Howard thankfully. 'You're back.'

'I hope you haven't caught malaria,' Howard worried. He took off his Stetson, which he hung on the wall as if it were a picture, and eased his sticky feet out of his pointed boots. The mud on the soles smelled rich and musky, as well it might since he had come from the untouched centre of the world.

'I had a visitor,' said Sissie, remembering with a boil of anger. But she had no wish to spoil this joyous moment of Howard's return so she put away the Author's image resolutely.

Sweating and rather smelly as they were, Sissie and Howard lay in bed together and touched each other tenderly in ways they each knew the other liked. After a while this encouraged them to further loving action and they melted deliciously, delightfully in one.

'Heaven!' gasped one or the other – probably Sissie, since Howard was more of the strong and silent type. They shared the same thought. What a miracle it was that they had met, so unlikely, so essential!

'Do you like me being fatter?' asked Sissie lazily.

'Every centimetre.'

'But you wouldn't like me if I grew huge, huge as a mountain.'

'I would love you if you grew as huge as a range of mountains – the Himalayas, for example,' enthused Howard, but it was about then that his face froze, just a tiny freeze yet enough for Sissie to notice.

'What is it? What's wrong?' she whispered anxiously, and it was the sibilants of the whisper that gave her the explanation. She put her fingers to her mouth where her tongue was already wiggling furiously.

'Yes, I'm afraid it's out again.' Howard stroked her arm sympathetically.

'For a temporary tooth, it's done very well,' she said defensively, wondering at what point it had gone and where it was. Howard was wondering the same, burrowing around the murky bed to no effect.

'I suppose you didn't swallow it.'

'Of course I didn't swallow it!' Sissie got out of bed, suddenly certain. 'I know exactly what happened. *He* took it.'

'He?' Howard, still sitting on the bed, looked up at the naked Sissie admiringly. She had grown fatter and it suited her, softening the outlines of the beautiful structure. She would not do on a catwalk now, he told himself with satisfaction.

'He, the Author, who plagues my life.' Sissie wrapped herself in a robe and came over to kiss Howard once more. The happiness of their love-making filled her again. After all, she had the new pearly tooth ready for insertion.

'It sounds to me as if you've been dreaming,' said Howard, without bothering too much, for Sissie's wrap had fallen open and he needed to concentrate on his finger-tips smoothing the swelling flesh, on the pleasure of making the sweet softness gather into hard pointed nipples.

Too tired to make love again, they drifted for a while and then, together, both felt so hungry that they raced each other to the bread. Of course, eating made Sissie unpleasantly aware of her missing tooth. Ever helpful, Howard found the little leather box and held up the perfect tooth to Sissie's obediently open mouth. 'We'll just have to stick it in for tonight's great event.'

Sissie had forgotten about 'tonight's great event', a gala at the Opera House to honour a meeting between two presidents. Luckily, Howard, like many Americans, often kept a stick of chewing-gum handy.

The opera house, newly painted pink for the occasion, as pink as the icing on a birthday cake, as pink as an English baby, was encircled by slow-moving limousines, a herd of shiny black beasts, nose to tail.

Howard and Sissie wore full evening dress, although since none of Sissie's clothes from another life covered her expanding flesh, she was mainly draped in shawls. They hesitated before crossing the road and joining the crowd of guests. Howard's thoughts were, perhaps, of the forest where he fought, as Sissie claimed proudly, the forces of darkness, some of whom were certainly represented in the black limos, or disembarking now, richly clad women on their arms. Sissie, on the other hand, was facing yet another crowd scene, another variation of all those that had made her toss and turn on her bed.

As they crossed the road at last, she fluttering, he striding sturdily in his pointed boots (cleaned up to go with his evening dress) whom should she spot but Father Pedro among the curious citizens pushing to see their president. Nor had he come alone for around him jumped and whistled, stared and grunted, huddled and chortled his Fortunatos, the children with impaired minds or bodies whom he loved so much.

Sissie did not point out Pedro to Howard and they joined the flooding visitors, the men with their thick, slicked-back hair and tanned, handsome faces and the women competing with heavy jewellery, tight, expensively cut dresses and hair that would not have moved if they'd been turned upside down and shaken. But she felt the priest's eyes on her. Even after they had entered the foyer and taken a stately path up the grand staircase, just as grand as the Paris Opera House, she felt his eyes and still heard the curious sounds of celebration made by his children.

'What are we seeing?' she asked Howard.

'A selection, I think. A variety show. An excerpt from a Brazilian opera is the main item.'

'I like the sound of that!'

Howard squeezed his wife's arm and failed to buy a programme. He loved her so much that he could hardly concentrate on practical matters. He had no wish to buy a drink in the bar or talk to anyone he might recognize. It was enough to sit side by side, hand in hand, on their velvet and gold seats while the rest of the opera house filled up round them. The orchestra had just finished tuning up when everybody rose to their feet for the arrival of the visiting president. He came into a box above their heads so they turned and craned to try to see him and Sissie, who was so tall and who had put on platform shoes for the occasion, was the only one who managed it in their part of the amphitheatre.

She cried out, 'But he's Japanese!', which was perfectly true but caused waves of disapproving looks and indrawn breaths very like hisses. Flustered, she sat down again, and Howard kissed her cheek soothingly while the orchestra struck up and the heavy tasselled curtain rose.

Sissie closed her eyes to compose herself. When she opened them again, she found herself staring at the Author, spot-lit, centre stage. He was declaiming to a background of swelling music.

'In the darkness of the night, in the darkness of the forest, we see a beautiful virgin. She is Cecilia, daughter of the Spanish aristocrat Don Antonio. What is she doing so far from home in such a jungly place and who is that standing beside her, with what seem to be orange feathers in his hair? Ah, it is Pery, Il Guarany, the Indian prince, and they are about to sing a great truth to us, which they have come to understand because they know that the delirium of the forest is really within ourselves. They know that, on the eternal pages of fate, all we need is love . . .'

The Author's voice was infinitely cajoling. This was clearly a tragedy that might yet be saved by love and was expected to bring tears rolling down the faces of his audience. As the Author stepped aside and the soprano opened her mouth to sing, Sissie whispered furiously to Howard, 'Why is he here? What has *he* to do with Brazil?'

'Isn't he famous?' whispered Howard vaguely as the soprano began her aria.

Sissie seethed and longed to throw poisoned Indian darts at the shadowy area into which the Author had receded. Why should he come to her in her new-found happiness? Follow her even to the bedroom and wrench the very tooth from her head? If Howard hadn't been an American gum chewer, she would not even have been able to come here tonight – which might, as it turned out, have been a good thing. Ugh. Agh. Grr. Sissie felt childish expressions of rage ready to explode inside her. She heard nothing of Brazil's foremost soprano's sweet tones nor appreciated the lyrical talents of Carlos Gomez, South America's answer to Verdi.

What was all this talk of love? In the Author's mouth the word became desecrated and despoiled. Oozed sentiment, that's what he did. How she hated people who oozed sentiment. She liked people who were simple and direct whom you could judge by their actions and know them to be true. But did she know anyone like that? Once again she was faced by the horrid truth that her beloved Howard was forced by the nature of his business, the terms of his contract, to keep secrets from her. She knew nothing about him beyond the heights of their love. Her whole life, she now saw, had been full of mystery. She had never understood her success as a model. She had never understood any of the principal people in her life: her family, where she had never quite fitted in; Rudolf, a closed book; Sebastien, behind an open book. She had lived all these years as if befogged, shrouded, misted over. She could not explain anything, or anyone or why anything that had happened to her had happened to her.

She had never seen the clear light of day, the clear road ahead, she had never taken one decision for herself. Everything that had happened in her life had happened *to* her. Even Howard, with all his love for her, which she did not doubt for a moment, could not show her the path. Like everyone else, he only showed a part of himself to her. So carried away was Sissie by these important self-revelations that she stopped being cross with the Author and fell back into her seat with a long, noisy, sobbing sigh, which chanced to coincide with the audience's appreciation of the soprano's effortless top A. Amid roaring, clapping, hallooing, whistling, cheering, stamping, sobbing, Sissie made up her mind to take action. If the Author advocated love as the only answer, then there must be something more.

High on her platform feet, off she went, pushing through the crowds, all their eyes turned to the stage where the soprano was fast disappearing under a barrage of bouquets and single stems, which the Author was graciously helping to collect. She was leaving on her own, not even followed by Howard, who was stamping his booted feet with the rest.

Sissie's only worry as she conquered the crowds and flew down the stairs, past surprised groups of black-suited heavies, was that Father Pedro would have left his post. There was a final hold-up as she found the great doors of the opera house locked against the pavement populace, but she discovered a side exit, used all her weight on a bar and was free, outside, being spattered by warm rain.

'Father Pedro!' she implored. And there was Pedro, sturdy guardian to his children and their helpers.

'Father, I have come to cast myself on your mercy. No, that's not right.' The rain was becoming heavier, dragging down Sissie's hair into long rats' tails. Pedro smiled at her. A small child nestled in his arms.

'Was the entertainment so bad?' he asked in Portuguese, but Sissie was only interested in the kindly expression on his face and her decision.

'It's so simple!' she cried.

'Simple,' echoed Pedro.

'Sim, sim, sim,' chorused the bigger children.

'It's so clear!' cried Sissie.

'Claro,' agreed Pedro.

'Ca, ca, ca, ca,' went the children like a flock of macaws.

'Voce beve ter o meu dinhero, o meu dinhero ese pra voce! I shall give you my money. Muito dinhero. You will spend it on these children or whatever you want. I have no idea how much is there but hundreds of thousands of pounds. Doing nothing. Waiting for you. Just waiting. Oh, I'm so happy!'

Sissie threw back her head, so that her pretty chin jutted, and laughed indelicately. 'Now I've shown the Author what's what!'

Chapter Twenty-Two

In which Sissie has Good News, Janice has Bad News and Mary loses her Temper with Ted.

JANICE AND ROB, Adam and Ruth sat round the breakfast table. The black cat, replete with bacon scraps, licked itself conscientiously to prove it was no longer a stray but eligible for polite society. It was raining outside, cold November rain, which was the reason they were all unwilling to move. Adam and Ruth should have been at university but they had come down because Janice had been ill in hospital. Yet here she was, sitting at her usual place and opening a letter from Sissie.

'Another letter?' commented Rob, in a surprised voice.

'It must be two or three months,' said Janice. 'Of course, marriage makes you more responsible.'

'Does it?' Ruth looked at her mother, the most responsible of women. Had she once been irresponsible? It was an impossible idea. In Ruth's view, either you were born responsible or you were not. She had been and was pleased to be so. Sissie never would be. She turned to Adam. 'Do you remember when Sissie dressed you up as a Victorian chimney-sweep and shoved you up the chimney?'

'Sometimes she went too far.' Adam, unlike the rest of his family, did not laugh at other people's jokes. The chimney-sweep episode and others like it had taught him to steer clear of Sissie.

'Well!' exclaimed Janice. She looked up from the letter, her pale, drained face suddenly flushed. 'Well! Sissie is going to have a baby.'

Rob and Ruth could see how pleased this news made Janice and it pleased them. It was just the tonic she needed after the last few weeks and the weeks of treatment that stretched ahead of her.

'So quickly,' she added. 'I *am* surprised!'

'Me too,' commented Adam. 'I wouldn't have thought she had the body to be a mother.'

'Too thin, you mean.' Janice saw his point but her eyes were undimmed. 'Perhaps she's changed. Indeed she must have changed. Such lovely, happy news.' She looked at Rob and he knew who she was thinking about.

Mary walked along the cliff-top in her hat of many feathers. An absurd figure, she held the envelope with her sister's writing on it in her left hand, the hand nearest the cliff edge. There was no sun and the clouds joined the sea in a blank greyness. There was no wind either. If there had been a wind, she could have let the envelope blow out of her fingers and float downwards until it reached the water and joined the other soggy disintegrating remnants of people's lives. Mary was angry with Janice for getting in touch again, for troubling her peace.

But there was no wind and she could not quite convince herself to make the grand gesture needed to throw the envelope into space. In this frame of mind she spotted Ted, still her walking companion, her occasional coffee-time visitor.

Ted continued to be taken aback by Mary's hat but he saw odder things in his prison.

'Not a very kind day,' he said, by way of greeting.

'No.' He was kind, though. Mary felt the familiar lessening of tension in his presence. Should she tell him? But of course he would tell her to open it. He could not understand. They were two private people who met with their secrets untold. Mary stuffed the envelope in her pocket and continued her walk.

'I believe I see the smallest chink of blue,' said Ted, after a while.

The weather was the most active companion to their friendship.

'How are they,' Mary hesitated, 'down there?' This was most unusual from her, a direct question, but she was in a state of indecision about the envelope and therefore more open.

'We had a new Cat A yesterday. A very nasty piece of work. I should say notorious.'

'You don't usually have that sort of offender, do you?'

'Not often. We all went to have a look.'

'Like an animal in a zoo.'

'It's only natural.'

'That's true. Did he mind? You all looking?'

'Well, he didn't have much choice, did he?'

Mary longed to know what this notorious man had done but feared the story would make her emotional and liable to reveal more than she wanted to tell. But their dialogue – all dialogue so strange to her – had lessened the importance of the envelope.

They walked on through the quiet rain, which subdued the roar of the ocean. Water trickled down the hat feathers and ran into Mary's neck. Ted wore his felt hat with its one perky little feather unbowed.

'I guess my chink closed,' said Ted, after a longish pause.

'I had a letter this morning,' said Mary, impulsively pulling it from her pocket.

'Oh, don't,' cried Ted equally urgent, 'the rain will ruin the ink and you won't be able to read it.'

'It's written in biro,' said Mary, before stopping to look at Ted. 'You read it for me.'

'Well,' said Ted. But he could see she was serious. He thought of the letters he had read in the prison, for censorship purposes. As he took the envelope he admitted to himself that he knew Mary had been inside. He could always tell, although he could never quite define what it was about the person. The look of the survivor, perhaps.

'I'll need a cup of tea,' he said.

'"Dear Mary,"' began Ted, over the caravan's table. He looked up. 'This is a covering note. There's another letter inside.'

'One at a time, please, one at a time.' Mary was trying very hard to sound normal.

'"I wanted you to have the pleasure of reading this. I would have come with the news but I haven't been too well. Of course, nothing to worry about. I wanted to say, but I'm glad you have a friend so you don't really need . . ."'

'That's enough,' interrupted Mary. 'What about the other?'

'"Dear Mum,"' read Ted, obediently. She was an odd woman, no doubt.

'That's not for me, that's for Janice,' interrupted Mary again.

'"More good news,"' continued Ted. '"To cut a not very long story short, I'm going to have a baby."'

A baby. The words filled up Mary's head and made her deaf to the rest of the letter. Ted finished reading and looked up with a congratulatory air, 'You'll be a great-aunt, then.'

'I never thought of such a thing,' gasped Mary, 'never thought it possible.'

'People do marry and have children all the time.' Ted eyed the tea-pot longingly. 'Not everyone's like us, you know, confirmed bachelors.'

'Confirmed?' Mary's eyes widened. She realized she had trusted Ted to divine the true state of affairs, that she wanted him to know without her having to tell him.

'Were you ever tempted?' Ted decided to pour himself a cup of tea. 'Don't answer if you don't want. I was once. She was much younger so I never had a chance. Not seriously. She let me spend a bit of my savings on taking her about and then she disappeared for a few weeks and the next thing was a wedding invitation. Perhaps I was broken-hearted, because I didn't go to the wedding and I've never had enough invitations to turn one down. Working in prisons cuts you off, you see. Or it did twenty years ago.'

While Ted talked, Mary became more and more fidgety and finally stood up and went to look out of the window. The chink of blue had reappeared and was speedily splitting open the clouds but for once the view was not enough to quell a growing sense of anger. He was teasing her with all this silly chatter, that's what he was doing. Of course he knew about her. The prison service had a very efficient grapevine. It was probably the only reason he spent time with her, just to take a look at the monster, like that notorious man. What had he said? It was just human nature. Well, she wouldn't stand for it.

Mary whirled round, face red, eyes glaring. 'Stop your chattering. Stop it! This is my caravan! And you don't talk to me like this in my own caravan! You may think you're my friend but I don't! So get out! Get out before I put you out!'

Ted put down his tea-cup and looked with amazement but not as much amazement as if he'd been a bank clerk. In his profession he saw anger daily and then saw the day that followed it. He was not frightened but, because it was Mary, he was distressed.

'I shall go at once,' he said, suiting action to words, 'but just remember, I had no intention of offending you.'

Mary's anger had hold of her but she registered the words as he hoped. Meanwhile she snatched the letter off the table, tore it into tiny fragments and threw the fragments after Ted's fast retreating figure. He had not even stopped to collect his hat and coat, which hung beside the stove.

Mary saw them and flung them out of the door too and then saw her hat with its delicate trail of feathers. At that her passion left her and she sat down exhausted. He should have known what she was thinking, she told herself incoherently, and now everything was spoiled, everything.

Chapter Twenty-Three

In which Sissie goes to Rio with High Hopes.

HOWARD AND SISSIE lay naked in bed. Howard, ever hopeful, had been trying on a new disguise, a moustache and beard kit that lay rather oddly between them. Outside it was raining as it had been every day for the last six weeks. Howard described how the waters of the great rivers had risen so high inside the forest that fishes put their mouths out of the water to eat fruit off the trees. He said that three of the clearings where they had used to put down their helicopter were now submerged. They found drowned baby monkeys regularly and quite a cat's cradle of dead and tangled snakes.

Even inside their bedroom there was a good deal of water. It trickled down the cracked window-panes and through unseen crevices in the roof and walls. Everything in the room felt damp including Sissie's hair, which had grown longer than ever and lay about her like seaweed. Howard had tried without success to persuade her back into a concrete block. 'I am happy here,' she told him. 'Besides, damp is good for my skin and essential for my plants.'

These days Sissie's plants took up most of her time. She had found an admirer at the Manaus Botanical Garden, who gave her interesting specimens in pots. She was nursing a rare climbing palm, which had only recently been discovered to science although, as the curator pointed out proudly, this was hardly unusual in the Amazon basin where, it is estimated, there are far more plants undiscovered than discovered.

216

At the thought of Sissie's love for her plants, Howard kissed her tenderly. He knew the plants were a substitute for him during his frequent absences. It was extremely bad luck that he should meet the love of his life – and what a love, he kissed her again – when years of preparatory work were rising to a dramatic and dangerous conclusion.

'Sissie, honey, did you have to give Father Pedro quite all your money?'

'It arrived in his bank today.' She sighed and rolled alongside Howard's body so she could kiss him without moving. 'Did I tell you how happy I am?'

She was always telling him about her happiness. It was a mantra that was beginning to make him uneasy. 'My salary is scarcely as generous as I would like.'

'Salary?' Sissie pronounced the word as if it were new to her and it very nearly was. In her years as a model she never heard of anyone on a salary, unless perhaps the dressers, and when she tried to cast her mind back it all seemed unbelievably long ago and quite unreal.

'There's another thing.' Howard turned his face from Sissie's kisses. 'Everyone assumes Texans have money but I think I should make it clear I am not that sort of Texan. Dime Box just about sums up my assets.'

'Darling Howard, you made a joke. Just let me be clear, I did not marry you for your money.' Sissie laughed at his serious face and began to tickle him.

'And now there's the baby—'

'The baby,' Sissie interrupted. 'I did marry you for the baby. Oh, I certainly did.' She put her head on his chest and then began to lick his skin moving slowly downwards. 'I am a tapir,' she said, making guzzling noises. 'I am the largest mammal in Amazonia and I'm going to eat you right up.'

Howard thought he had captured a comet in his bed, not an ugly long-nosed tapir, but he was certainly not strong enough to withstand the tapir's assault.

'Oh, Sissie,' he gulped, 'you give me such pleasure. I thank God for the eight hundred and ninetieth time – which makes ten times a day on average – that I had kept myself free to marry such a planet among women!'

217

'Be careful,' warned Sissie. 'I do believe you're beginning to show signs of a sense of humour and an imagination.'

It was unusual for Sissie to be up as early as Howard, particularly on the days when he was going on one of his trips. On those days she liked to cuddle under the bedclothes until he'd gone and then for as long as possible after that before she became resolute and took on life once more. But this Monday was different. When Howard's helicopter took off for the forest – he never revealed his exact location – Sissie's aeroplane would leave for Rio de Janeiro. There, she would see a dentist and an obstetrician, have her tooth fixed in securely, for it popped out only too regularly, and have her baby checked as sound and safe. If she had time, she also planned to see the Sugar Loaf mountain, Our Lord of Sorrows and the Copacabana beach, where traditionally the most beautiful flesh in the world was displayed without disguise.

How sweetly Howard and Sissie said goodbye! Young lovers, young marrieds, soon to be parents. But Howard was pale and there was a stern frown between his eyes. He had not wanted to make love that morning and the lines of his body were tense.

'Don't worry.' Sissie touched his eyelids with her fingertips, ghostly pale in the dawn light. 'It'll be a new adventure for me.'

Howard was glad she thought his anxiety entirely for her and congratulated himself on keeping from her the frightening nature of his work, the black adventures. He was struck suddenly by a happy thought. 'You stay where you are, in your comfortable hotel, and I'll come to meet you there when I'm finished. We'll do the sights together.'

Doing the sights together! The very idea made them fall into each other's arms again and agree that what was so extraordinary was that they had not had such an obviously good idea before.

As if on cue, plans more than satisfactory, Howard's mobile phone began to emit impatient bleeps and whistles. Off Howard went, down the three flights of stairs and out into the street where, as usual, it was raining.

For the first time, Sissie watched him get into the black car, which already seemed over-full with large men, and the car depart.

Naturally he did not turn and wave since he did not imagine Sissie was watching. But perhaps he wouldn't have anyway, given the brutal company he was keeping.

Warmed still by the prospect of their hotel assignment – thick white towels, she imagined, and champagne in the fridge – Sissie went among her plants, watering and reassuring them of her return before too long. Then she zipped up her little bag.

Sissie, in her aeroplane, looked down on the wedding of the black waters of the river Negro and the golden flow of the river Soleindero. Her heart (and her womb) was full of Howard.

The sun was hot in Rio and there was a beach in front of the hotel. Sissie decided to go for a swim but the sand was crowded with young men running and jumping and tussling and kicking a football with passionate intensity. Despite picking her way as carefully as possible and keeping her eye on the game, she suddenly found herself in the middle of a race to win the ball and three or four players turned on her, shouting, with what felt like hatred, 'Gringo! Gringo! Move, gringo!' So she retreated, heart thudding, to the hotel pool.

The obstetrician was quite old and very kind. He assured Sissie that she looked far too well for any serious examination to be necessary. 'I trained at St Thomas's, Waterloo,' he told her, 'and when you go back I shall recommend a colleague to look after you.'

'But this is an Amazon baby!' cried Sissie. 'If it's a girl I may call her Amazonia.'

The doctor looked unimpressed and, as Sissie shared with him a description of her plants, it soon became clear that he had never visited the northern area of his country and considered it a backward sort of place that was best left to Indians or the poor in search of land. Although he was so kind, Sissie eventually noticed his lack of enthusiasm and took away her prescription for iron pills, which he thought a good idea despite her assurances that she was less pale than usual, feeling a little subdued.

The taxi driver who drove her back to the hotel hardly raised her spirits by dwelling on the dangers of his native city. 'I see you're wearing the rings,' he noted disapprovingly, in harsh accents. 'If you plan to walk and live, I recommend you take them off at once but, even without them, a taxi is essential for the shortest distance.'

'My husband will escort me.' Sissie's voice was so haughty that he didn't dare address her further but muttered imprecations under his breath.

That evening Sissie ate in a chilli joint by the side of the hotel pool. It was decorated with swagging of highly coloured plastic vegetables, which rattled against each other in the breeze. A sickness, which was not due to her pregnancy, came over her and she longed for her dripping room in Manaus, her plants, which she could hear breathing in and out. Of course she longed for Howard too, but he had gone where she couldn't follow, even in her thoughts.

The sickness – perhaps it was the same form of homesickness, loneliness by another name, that she had once felt on a sidewalk café in Paris – persisted throughout the night. Finding it impossible to sleep, Sissie lay awake and listened to the sounds of international revelry that floated up from the poolside.

At dawn she stepped through the window to her balcony and looked out to sea. The sky was murky, perhaps because it was so early, but she could still just make out the heights of Corcovado with the silhouette of the open-armed Christ on top. 'In two days I shall see Howard,' she said aloud. Comforted, she returned to her bed and slept for an hour or two. When she woke, her tooth had fallen out again and lay on the pillow like a tear.

That morning the sky was still murky, the air clammy without turning into rain and, since Sissie's appointment with the dentist was not till one o'clock, she did not bother to leave her room. When she did eventually, around midday, she took on the world as flamboyantly as only she knew how, in her faithful platform sandals, a rainbow-coloured knife-pleated mini-skirt (held together over her fattening stomach by a chain of safety-pins), a white stretch T-shirt, which showed off her now magnificent breasts, and her long hair tied up in a pony-tail that cascaded from the top of her head. Silver hoop earrings and black Egyptian-style eye make-up completed an ensemble that caused the entire foyer of the hotel to gasp at her entrance.

Sissie swagger-walked across to the desk – bravura is as bravura does – and asked the receptionist to order her a taxi.

'What name?' gulped the young man, whose eyes were on a level with her thighs.

'Howard,' said Sissie.

'Ah.' The young man swallowed his gulp. 'I was just calling your room. The manager requires your presence.'

'But I have to see my dentist.'

'This way, please.' The receptionist, all in black, came out from behind his desk and escorted Sissie tenderly by the elbow. 'I shall inform you of your taxi.'

Four female librarians from Texas, also waiting for a taxi, watched her go, as did everyone else in the foyer although without the benefit of knowing who she was.

'That was that super-model,' said one librarian to another. 'I'd know her anywhere. Sissie, she's called. I once stuck a picture of her on my ice-box door to stop me eating.'

'That girl wasn't skinny at all,' objected a second librarian.

The manager's office was rather grand. It had an enormous mahogany desk, which must have caused quite a clearing in the rainforest, leather-studded chairs, a sofa and a very springy carpet.

The manager went red and began to sweat when he saw Sissie. He looked longingly at the door closing behind his receptionist.

'Is it about payment?' asked Sissie. Her attention, perhaps purposefully, was concentrated on her tooth, which she had only just managed to stick in and which was likely to fall into the thick pile of cream-coloured carpet and be lost for ever.

'Please sit,' implored the manager, who was heavy-set and handsome. Normally he would have behaved in a quite different way with a girl of Sissie's appearance.

'No, thank you,' said Sissie. 'I'm in a hurry.'

The manager looked at the spectacular figure, impatiently swinging her little sling-bag in front of him, and only just managed to avoid the temptation to cross himself. He cleared his throat. Delay would not improve matters. 'I have received a secret telephone call, of high priority, on my personal line, not known to many.' He paused, and his fat, handsome fingers played anxiously with a gold bracelet on his wrist.

It was the word 'secret' that told Sissie. She knew everything at once, without another word. The knowledge of Howard Howard's death swept through her head and her heart and her body, numbing sensation, stopping the flow of her blood and causing her to fall on the carpet in a swoon-like trance.

The manager was aghast. His real sympathy for this young woman's tragic situation was tempered by the fear that, since he had been sworn to secrecy over this telling, anyone he summoned to help was very likely to misconstrue the situation. He had been known to have beautiful young women in his office in jollier circumstances. If only she were wearing less dramatic clothes or if her breasts had been less prominent. The manager chewed his lips and prayed to the Virgin Mary that she would arise. But she did not.

So then he came round from his desk and felt her pulse. At least she wasn't dead.

At this moment there was a knock at the door, but before he could take action a pleasant woman's face appeared. 'I need to speak to the manager about our check.'

An American woman! It was the happiest of arrivals. The manager snatched her inside and since she seemed to be attached to three other similar women in lightweight macintoshes, they were soon all in the room and crouched around Sissie.

The manager allowed himself to make the sign of the cross and promised the Virgin Mary ten dollars for providing him with not one but four pure-minded women (possibly even virgins) who were also American and would understand the need for security.

Although in a swoon, Sissie was not unconscious and she heard the conversation around her. When the manager explained that her husband had been shot last night, the word 'shot' had a horrible potency as she imagined a bullet plunging into Howard's sweet skin, which she had so recently caressed. The blankness into which she had entered became more profound.

Sissie was transported to her room by the staff elevator to avoid upsetting the guests. It was littered with cigarette butts and smelt disgusting but she was tended by four guardian angels, who had

222

cancelled their flight to Salvador to look after a compatriot by marriage. They would have done it for anyone, but it was a bit of a bonus that she was famous or had been famous not so long ago.

A doctor was called, a very old man who liked being summoned to the hotel because he was usually given a lavish meal. He was, in fact, the manager's uncle and therefore could be trusted to keep his mouth shut. Sissie only had two guardian librarians now, one on either side of the bed, because the other two had gone to search for her tooth. As predicted it had fallen out and the good women spent a long time crawling on their hands and knees across the manager's carpet – which was a total waste of time as the tooth lay among the cigarette stubs in the staff elevator where they never thought of looking.

'She's pregnant,' announced the doctor, pleased to make a positive input. 'Three or four months, I'd say.'

'Oh dear,' said the librarian who had first recognized Sissie. 'This is so sad.' Her eyes filled with tears.

'And who is to deal with the things that need to be dealt with?' said the second librarian, who enjoyed filling in forms.

No one answered her question for Sissie was still not talking and the manager, who might have known, had retreated. Sissie was also in retreat although tears seeped from under her closed eyelids, making the Egyptian black make-up dissolve into panda smudges.

'Even a super-model must have a family,' said the first librarian, who was called Maureen and was the eldest of six brothers and sisters, which had somehow used up any urge for motherhood in herself, although she remained very motherly.

'She's perfectly conscious or, rather, as conscious as she prefers to be and I can see nothing amiss,' said the doctor, packing his bag. 'I'll be in the dining room for an hour or so if you need me further.'

Maureen and her team kept vigil at Sissie's bedside. One of them took down the high pony-tail to make her more comfortable and another undid the chain of safety-pins holding her skirt together and slipped it gently off.

The clouds dispersed and a fierce evening sun glittered off the sea and through the drawn curtains.

Sissie rose suddenly from her bed. It had just struck her that the manager had lied, or perhaps he didn't even exist, and that all these hours had been a bad dream and that Howard would arrive any minute. She looked at Maureen with surprise but smiled politely. 'My husband will be here soon so I'll just go into the bathroom and prepare myself.'

The manager sat waiting for her when she reappeared, freshly washed with brushed hair and reapplied make-up, although, of course, still toothless. He told her again what he had told her before, which was not very much, and then added, so that even Maureen winced in pain, 'I understand there'll be no body.'

Sissie returned to the bathroom where she vomited.

The manager defended himself to Maureen. 'It is security, you understand. Her husband was on a secret assignment for your country. They will manage everything.'

'So there is nothing to be dealt with, after all,' whispered the librarian who was good at filling in forms.

'But how can the poor girl cope with such an unnatural thing?' Maureen whispered back.

Sissie had now decided that Howard was waiting for her in their apartment in Manaus, that his disappearance was simply a ruse to deceive the forces of darkness. She quietly packed her bag and prepared to leave the room.

Since the manager had left again, she turned to Maureen. 'I have things to do back home. Back home in Manaus,' she added, in order to be clear. She spoke quietly in a rational manner but Maureen saw that she was distraught.

'I'll come with you,' she said.

'Thank you,' Sissie responded, but as if she did not care either way. Which indeed she did not. Despite the steps she was taking, merciful blankness still filled her heart.

All four librarians accompanied Sissie to the airport and to Manaus. 'After all, we had planned to see it,' they told each other. 'There's a nineteenth-century opera house there, left over from the famous rubber boom.' They pretended there was another reason but really they were kind-hearted, shocked witnesses to Sissie's suffering.

When Howard was not in the apartment where it was still raining outside and in, Sissie waited for him there for two days, neither eating nor sleeping, although she closed her eyes often. Her only action was to tend her plants, picking off dead leaves, wiping them shiny clean, carefully regulating the right level of moisture.

Then one afternoon when the sun had come out for an hour or two and the librarians had gone for a tour of the opera house, Sissie went out to find Father Pedro.

He welcomed her more warmly than ever. 'But I have so much to show you! Your money is working a stream of miracles. Come, we will go at once!'

She had found him, as usual, where the poorest people lived on the river banks. But the scene was quite transformed. Weeks of continual rain had pushed the waters up to the doors of the shacks and the plank walks no longer bridged mud and filth but water in which the filth floated until it slowly dispersed.

So keen was Pedro on the good news he had to show Sissie that it took him some time to notice the change in her. 'But you are white, like a spirito. You have been ill? Malaria, perhaps? And your tooth. Why no tooth?'

'No malaria,' said Sissie.

'The rain, then. Rain makes people ill.'

'Not the rain. Will you take me to see the Fortunatos?'

'That is where we are going, if we are not dead first by drowning. I shall show you what your dollars are already buying.'

The priest was speaking fast and furiously in Portuguese and Sissie found, to her surprise, that she was following it with no difficulty, as if the shock of the last few days had broken through some barrier of understanding.

They stood in the concrete hut and already a wall had been knocked through and land flattened beyond. The children, some of whom should have been having lessons, stopped everything and followed them round. They uttered their strange calls and grunts which Sissie had previously thought so tragic but which now seemed the music of happiness compared to what she heard in her heart.

'It is folly, of course, to build in the rainy season, but the dispossessed cannot wait for the sun. Besides, look, the sun!'

The sun indeed shone brightly on the workers' yellow helmets, but not for many more seconds as the massed ranks of black clouds prepared for another deluge. 'Depressa rapido! Under cover.' Pedro pulled Sissie into a rickety construction composed of plywood, cardboard and corrugated iron.

The rain hit the corrugated-iron roof like gunfire. Sissie clutched the priest and cried, 'He's been shot!' And, although the noise drowned her words, he understood her anguish and leant closer so that his wiry, grey-black hair scraped her cheek. 'Howard's dead!' Sissie shrieked. 'He's been shot!' The need to raise her voice was a great release and she felt like screaming without stop. But Pedro took her arm and made her sit down on the wet floor. She noticed then how badly she was shaking.

Instead of screaming, she began to cry, water, leaking from the roof, mingling with her tears.

A woman carrying a child came in through the doorway. The priest pointed to Sissie and said a sentence that ended with the heavy word, 'morto'.

The woman, who was young and strong, gave her baby to the priest and crouched down beside Sissie. She held her close, rocking her slightly as she might her baby. She seemed so practised in this comforting that Sissie, in all her desperation, became curious and looked up into her face. The woman smiled, a humble, gentle smile, and then she passed her hands lightly over Sissie's swelling breasts and stomach, 'Bebe,' she murmured, still smiling. She turned her face to where her baby sucked on one of the priest's fingers. 'Bebe,' she repeated, black eyes glowing, as she conjured for Sissie the magic of a future.

Chapter Twenty-Four

In which Mary sees the Worst.

MARY CURVED protectively round the child. It was her fourth birthday and she had a pink satin ribbon in her hair and some crumbs of sugar round her mouth. She faced away from her mother, looking at *him*, but Mary could imagine her eyes wide with terror and she could feel her heart fluttering like a clock without the pendulum.

'You're a little greedy monster! Do you hear that! Mother's spoilt little greedy monster! Nothing left over for Dad, is there! Nothing ever of anything for Dad, not ever, not ever fucking ever!'

His voice was distorted, mocking, loud, drunk. He was working himself into a passion. She must get the child out before he lost control. But it was the child he was fixed on. Her birthday. He was jealous of her birthday, of her cake, her ribbon, her happiness, of the love she, Mary, gave her. The child felt as fragile as a bird in her arms. Why had she not predicted this, guessed he would return, guessed he would be drunk?

His voice became louder, more dangerous, particularly when Mary tried to edge a little in the direction of the door.

'I've got something more to say to you, little greedy monster birthday girl! I want you right there in front of me.'

He was tall, very very tall, six foot five, but now he crouched down and assumed a macabre, high-pitched wheedling tone. 'Wouldn't you give your dad one little crumb of your birthday cake?' He stood up again as the child tried to lose herself in her mother's body. 'Your fucking dad, mind you, not just anyone. But no, you had to eat it all, didn't you? You and your fucking mother. I might as well not be your dad at all, might I? But you're stuffed with cake, cake and Mummy's love, Mummy's love and cake, aren't you? So what can I do about that? What can I do about that when I want a bit of birthday cake? When it's all inside your fucking tummy. All the pretty icing sugar and cream fucking filling.'

It was when he picked up the knife that Mary had used earlier to cut the cake that this nightmare usually ended. She had dreamed it often over the last twenty years, although less frequently lately. But on this black night in early December, the nightmare continued further and she saw the eyes of her other little daughter, barely two years old staring at her from under the table. The dream did stop then, before he had lunged with the knife and the child had screamed and screamed and she had taken the knife where he had thrown it and gone towards him.

Sweating in the freezing caravan, Mary crawled out of her sleeping-bag and stood shaking in the middle of the room. She could still hear screaming but gradually it changed until she recognized the high-pitched shrieks of a cat. Holding onto the table, she tottered the few steps to the door and opened it.

'Cleo! Cleo!'

There was a small scuffle nearby, a paler shadow shot round the corner of the caravan and Cleo slunk in, tail down by her legs. Although her black fur made her invisible, Mary followed her progress as she went to her corner and began to lick herself.

Mary got back into her sleeping-bag and prepared to wait for morning. But after half an hour or so, when Cleo had settled down into a warm ball, she got off her bed again and felt her way to the corner where her hat and coat hung. Feeling upwards, her fingers found the layers of silky feathers. Tenderly, she stroked them, her fingertips feeling the outline of each feather and smoothing it over its neighbour until there was not a ruffled one on the whole hat.

Chapter Twenty-Five

In which Death predominates.

A SHORT PROCESSION of long cars passed slowly through an avenue of pampas grass. The tall white feathered flowers were not cheerful and probably were not supposed to be since this was a crematorium. In fact, they were last year's growth and pretty knocked about. It was April, a cool blustery day nearer winter than spring.

The coffin was in the first car, piled high with pink and white flowers, so very many that the funeral attendants were squeezed off their seats. There were more on the roof of the car, too, shaped like a graceful hat, with dome and wide, curved brim.

In the second car, Rob, Ruth and Adam sat, knees close, faces stern with the need to contain their grief. Other cars, other people waited at the chapel.

The service was brief, the coffin consigned to the flames, and the mourners gathered outside to admire the flowers.

'I've never seen a funeral wreath shaped like a hat before,' said one lady to another, when the family were not in earshot. 'But why couldn't she come herself? I mean, she may be famous but she was her eldest daughter.'

'She's pregnant, I understand,' said a more sympathetic lady. 'And then her husband disappeared without trace not so long ago.'

'I still think she should be here,' insisted the first lady.

Her husband joined her. He had worked in Janice's office and was truly upset. 'Time to move on.'

'And not a drink or a sandwich.'

'I suppose the family are too upset. Five months from beginning to end.'

'Sissie always was different, and by that I mean difficult. I remember as a little girl . . .' But she was given no time to finish for the gentleman took an elbow in each hand and walked both ladies off to their cars. Personally, he would miss Janice very much and that was all there was to it.

Rob, Ruth and Adam drove back to the house and there was Sissie sitting in the lounge, pale as a ghost and thin, were it not for her huge swelling tummy.

No one could reproach her, not even Adam who suspected she had never had a husband and that his death last year – without a body, mind you – had all been an invention. She was just another unmarried mother, in his view, or single parent, if you preferred. Ruth, too, had harboured critical thoughts when Sissie had not come back to be with her mother, although she had to admit that in the end Janice had gone down so suddenly that it had been impossible for her to be there in time.

Only Rob regarded her with total affection – more than before, in fact – because he knew that that was what Janice would have wanted. Besides, it was now he and he alone who held Sissie's history. He had not yet found the courage to write to Mary of her sister's death.

'Now you are in England, you must stay for the baby,' he said, touching her shoulder.

'Yes,' agreed Ruth, trying to be kind to this large pale, almost ugly person. Surely she could have found a better front tooth than that prominent lump of concrete? 'Once we're back at university, there'll be plenty of room.' Where was her schoolgirl heroine, the super-model, as beautiful as sin, as rich as Croesus?

'Thank you.' Sissie looked at each of their faces with a strange enquiring expression. 'I'm sorry I didn't come to the service. I just couldn't.' She had sat in the house thinking of the mass Father Pedro had said for Howard, although he had made a point of assuring her that without a body there was always hope. That was why she had not returned when she heard her mother was ill. She did not want to be on the other side of the world when Howard came back. She also had been unable to believe that Janice was seriously ill. There was never anything wrong with Janice that she couldn't manage.

The mass had been held in one of the few pretty old churches remaining, whitewashed and with an ornamental bell tower although the bell had gone missing. A boy had banged a gong in the front porch instead. The Fortunatos filled the front benches and kept up their usual cacophony of noises, despite all attempts to quieten them. Sissie had not minded at all.

It was at this service that Sissie introduced Maureen, the librarian, to Father Pedro. She was in Manaus still, left behind by the three other librarians, living in Sissie's apartment, and helping to organize Pedro's ambitious plans to spend Sissie's money. If Howard should reappear, Maureen would be there to greet him. Maureen was determined that at last she had found her true vocation. 'I shall start a Help-the-Children-of-Manaus Club back home,' she told Sissie. 'If they can give for the rainforest then they can certainly give to the children of the rainforest.'

'But these children haven't come from the rainforest,' Sissie had pointed out.

'They're in it now.' Maureen had been undeterred but, then, she was that sort of person.

Once again Sissie had taken an aeroplane at short notice, with only the smallest of bags to keep her company. As they rose into the sky, the baby inside her lurched upwards also. She had thought of Janice in snatches of happy memories and regrets that were too blurred for her to understand.

'I'm sorry I didn't come to the service,' she repeated. She supposed it was unhappiness that made it impossible for her to perform in the way a daughter should. Perhaps she was having a breakdown.

In the middle of the night Sissie and Rob woke up one after the other and went down to the kitchen for a drink.

Rob, who had never wanted Sissie to know the truth of her

background, felt a terrible temptation to reveal all. He remembered how Janice had wanted to tell and how he had stopped her. Guiltily, he remembered how he had torn apart and thrown away the hat that Sissie had tried to give Janice and how Janice had insisted on sending the weird feathered object to Mary. In the last months he had realized that the secret had weighed heavily on Janice and that she had felt instinctively that it was wrong to keep it from the adult Sissie. Of course he did not blame Janice's cancer on it, but he knew this anxiety had been gnawing away at her heart.

He looked at Sissie's clear pale face, the concrete tooth, her unhappy dark-rimmed eyes, the black hair drawn back tightly. She did not seem ugly to him but utterly desolate. He would not be the one to give her deranged Mary as a mother, to give her such a terrible past. Not now. Let her become a mother first. He would do nothing till after that. Janice may have intended to bring Mary and Sissie together eventually, but she had been doing it slowly and carefully.

'One step at a time,' he said to Sissie. 'That's the way to deal with pain. Or so they say.' He believed she had had a husband and he had died, been shot, vanished. Anyone whose life had started the way hers had was sure to attract drama and tragedy.

'I'll have the baby in England,' said Sissie, making up her mind. 'He won't come back now.'

'Near her bed she kept a photograph of you on the catwalk,' said Rob. 'She was so very proud of you.'

Chapter Twenty-Six

*In which Cleo proves a Cat can be a Mummy too and Mary
discovers a Storm is best kept in a Tea-pot.*

A SPRING GALE had been blowing in from the sea for twenty-four
hours. The waves wound themselves higher and higher until
the spray burst like pale flying petals over the cliff-top. Mary had
never seen such a sight in all the years she had walked along the
headland. On the whole she found it exhilarating, even when the
gusts threatened to rock her caravan off its stand.

But they both survived the night and at first light, not that it was
light, Mary put on her coat and went outside again. To her surprise
Cleo followed her.

'Go in. Go back!'

Cleo had been restless all night, twisting about in her corner and
letting out little mews, but Mary had supposed it was fear of the
storm and couldn't think why the cat would want to follow her
outside. It was not raining but the wind was as strong as ever.

'Don't be so stupid!' she cried, in the teeth of the gale, but Cleo
ignored her and came all the same.

It was an occasion when Mary would have liked a companion,
someone to exclaim at the force and violence of Nature's attack. It
was terrifying and wonderful. If only Ted would appear along the
track and they could shout about it together. But Ted was avoiding
her path – she knew he was still in the area because she had seen him
once in the distance – so she must make do with Cleo, black fur
parted by the wind.

Stumpy woman bent double, small cat blown against her legs

and then away again, they made their way into the face of the storm. Mary put her face up for a moment and felt the skin rippled backwards by the strength of the wind and she thought of turning back, the air in her lungs emptied and the air all round her too fierce to catch, but then she bent her head once more and took a gulping breath.

By now she had forgotten the cat. Cleo must fight her own battles. She reached the cliff edge and stood there leaning her weight against the wind, smiling. Out at sea, the sky was still dark, churning up the waves into more and more frantic assaults on the land. But we're withstanding it, thought Mary. The sea may boil itself up into a cauldron of foam, a heavy, crashing, battering rain of water, a lashing, whipping whirl of waves . . .

Mary had to step back quickly as a cascade of something wetter than petals or confetti or all the light-hearted celebration froth of white hit the top of the cliff and burst round her head.

Mary gallumphed backwards laughing, soaked, her expression like a small child who dares the sea by running near the waves and then is caught out by one wave bolder than all the rest.

Cleo, also wet, crawled under brambles and furze by the path. Her usually sure instinct was not working as well as usual and she crept nearer and nearer the cliff edge.

It began to rain or, at least, the wind that was already carrying water from the sea began to pick up the water from the clouds – breaking open now. It swept above Mary, much of it too high for her to notice, although it gave another layer of sound to the whistling wind and crashing sea. She crouched down lower and saw Cleo, eyes bright under the furze.

'Here, Cleo! Come here!' she shouted, ridiculously for the cat could never have heard her. Besides, Cleo felt she had found suitable shelter just in time and was busy.

It took Mary several minutes to realize that her cat was giving birth. Little squirming things became visible – at any rate, the white on their fur showed up. Nothing else, as Cleo coiled deeper and deeper into the undergrowth.

Mary was nervous of going much closer. The path had been made slippery by the rain and, although the wind generally blew inwards, it occasionally changed direction in vicious spurts. The dark mass of clouds on the horizon had broken and moved closer and an eerie white light shone on the furthest stretch of sea.

Cleo mewed piteously and Mary took one tentative step forward and then another more daring. Her foot hit a patch of shiny mud over grass and took her with it in a sweeping, legs-first chute. Before she knew what had happened, she was over the edge, hands grabbing ineffectually at the brambles in which Cleo crouched.

I'm going to die, thought Mary, in that split second as she flew out into light sky, wind, rain, seaspray, and she felt the peace of farewell.

Ted was a man of habit and stumped up from the town whatever the weather. In the last few months he had taken care to avoid Mary – she would summon him when she wanted, he wasn't one to look for trouble – but on this morning the weather did affect him in one way because he decided he wouldn't bother thinking about whether he saw Mary or not but go where he wanted freely, up to the top and along, suss out what was happening at the sharpest point, the one nearest the sea, jutting out like a prow of a ship, where he and Mary used to stand and talk. Hat with perky feather exchanged for a sou'wester, he battled upwards from the town, enjoying the struggle as Mary had earlier.

If he had been honest he would have admitted to himself that he expected to see Mary on the headland, if not waiting for him, prepared to continue their dialogue. After all, this was real weather and that was their common interest. He was surprised, therefore, still unacknowledged to himself, when he could not spot Mary up there – disappointed, too. But he went on nonetheless, admiring the advance of the black clouds, the shining white behind.

By the time he reached the headland, the wind had become less consistently powerful. For several seconds at a time it relaxed, as if in need of a rest. During one of these calms (although the sea boomed and thundered as loud as ever) he heard a little feline squeak, a squeal, a mini miaow. The very smallness of it made him pay attention. He thought he had stumbled on a bird's nest. Why would he think of a cat?

However, he looked around and found nothing – Cleo and her

kittens were securely tucked in by now and still not over the cliff, as Mary had feared. Nevertheless, he continued to listen and look, and, as the wind dropped further, it became easier for him to stand straight and peer and prod and even approach the cliff's edge.

'Help!' cried Mary, thinking she was making a considerable sound. That moment of joyous farewell had been brief. A tumbling, scraping fall, a bump and she had landed on a rocky ledge, the pain in her leg curiously reassuring, so quickly is the desire for easeful death turned into a passion for life.

The 'Help!' was pathetic, a smaller squeak than the kitten's. Although alive and conscious, the shock of her falling and the pain from one leg, which stuck out at a most peculiar angle, drained her voice of power. She did not know that Ted was above her so there seemed no point in making greater effort. Hers was a little plea to show herself that she wasn't planning to fall into the nastily close and turbulent sea.

So Ted, hand firmly holding a bush, did not lean over the cliff because of a call from Mary, he did it instinctively, for no reason he could ever explain afterwards.

Rescuing a person caught half-way down a cliff with the tail end of a gale still blowing is not easy. Ted was a realist so he called in the professionals. The helicopter rescue service came but it was too windy so the climbers followed and the ambulance – its wheels stuck in the mud so that it had to be rescued by a tractor. Ted stayed calm and eventually he sat in hospital beside Mary, who had broken one leg and her collar-bone and was bruised all over.

'Cleo,' she whispered. A young lady medic had given her such a nice injection as she lay on the ledge that she had not managed to mention the cat before.

Ted was glad he could rescue something all on his own so, after Mary had been wheeled off to have her leg set, he returned to the cliff with a cardboard box. The wind had almost completely died away and a strange sun, artificial in its brilliance, streaked the still rolling sea. He took out the four mewing kittens one by one and, with Cleo following anxiously, carried them back to Mary's caravan. There he made himself at home, put on the kettle, lit the stove.

He took his cup of tea to the table but found himself obstructed by an open drawer so full of photographs and newspaper clippings that he couldn't close it. Prison had made him used to poking into other people's business but he knew how sensitive Mary was about her privacy. Nevertheless, as it was impossible to shut the drawer without re-ordering it, he could hardly avoid seeing that all the pictures were of the same girl, a beautiful young model, professional, 'top class', as Ted put it to himself. He couldn't believe she had anything to do with his friend, the recluse who lived in a caravan. He did not, for a moment, link such a splendid, incomprehensible creature with the niece who was going to have a baby, but he couldn't resist spreading them over the table, sorting out the full length into one pile and the close-up faces into another and separating the black and white from the colour and the newspaper from the glossy.

When he had covered the whole table-top in patterns of elegance of one sort or another, he stacked them all back neatly into the drawer, looked at his watch and smiled. Mary would be safely back in bed by now.

Chapter Twenty-Seven

In which Petra arrives bringing Bliss to Sissie
but not Happiness.

S ISSIE SWEPT along the hillside. Her hair was cut in short, black feathered layers to her head. On her broad back a baby in a papoose bounced and hiccuped, its gnome-like face peering slit-eyed over her shoulders. She looked straight ahead, glad to feel the cropped turf under her swinging stride, to see the blue and cloudy sky so close and all around, to hear the sparrows flittering in the low hedge to her right and to spot a buzzard, suspended in quivering concentration above its prey.

'Drat and killer bees!' A trickle of warm milk was running down her neck. The baby, who was a girl, changed her hiccups to appreciative gurgles and smiles as Sissie took her off her back and laid her on the grass. She was long like Sissie with the heavy bones of Howard Howard, and his big feet which she used to kick off her papoose.

'Oh, Petra!' Sissie gave up and sat down on the grass beside her daughter. She had fed her early, and jammed her straight away into the carrier, determined to get in a walk on such a sprightly summer morning. But it was really as nice to sit high and patronize the world below. She could see clearly the village in which she was living, safe and tamed, her rented cottage a red-brick dot on the outskirts.

She had found the village during a bicycle ride before Petra's birth. Pedalling on an old upright model suited her stomach and gave her a sense of freedom. This village, only six or seven miles from where Sissie had grown up, ridden her pony, gone to school, seemed part of another world which she had never entered. The twenty or so houses, the church and the pub were strung, web-like, among the wooded slopes on one side of a valley on whose other side Sissie now sat in contemplation. The valley was like a private kingdom, she thought, its one narrow road, following the course of a winding stream, unused by anyone except the villagers. Mostly, they seemed keen to keep the secret, although the owner of the pub tried to encourage visitors from outside and even had a couple of rooms to rent.

It was the right place to be – Sissie had recognized that at once – and it had seemed a miracle to discover that the ugly modern bungalow was for rent that summer. To Sissie, it was beautiful. The owner, a retired school-mistress, had gone to stay with her sister in Canada. Sissie loved the well-washed lino flooring, the ironed floral curtains, the ordinary bedroom with pink candlewick bedspread and brown chest of drawers. She loved the oval mock-Chinese rugs in the living room, the suite of matching sofa and chairs, the ornaments collected from the school-mistress's annual foreign holiday. It was the least stylish place Sissie had ever entered but the water ran smoothly into the lemon yellow bath, the linen cupboard smelled of lavender, pots of scented geraniums stood at the kitchen window, and the overhead lights shone brightly into every neat corner. It was security and order. Sissie thought of those children living in the stilted shacks of Manaus, and the floral curtains assumed the beauty of Versace's most intricate brocades.

Sissie squeezed a reluctant Petra back into the papoose and headed downwards. As she straightened up from the grass, the sun behind her head gleamed on the two top windows of the pub and, in one flash, a spark of something almost caught her eye but then Petra began to blow mum-mum-mum bubbles and Sissie was diverted.

Sebastien was coming. That was why she had taken her walk early. Seb – urban dweller when he wasn't following François – whose imagination used to live in the poetic landscape of a Jesuit priest, was coming to see the real English landscape.

Sissie hastened down the track shaded by the high-banked hedge and topped by wild saplings of sycamore and beech. As always, at this point, she sniffed the delicious smell of wild garlic and wondered where the plants hid themselves. Would Sebastien appreciate well-washed lino and candlewick bedspreads?

Sissie sat on her bed feeding her baby and the clouds gathered together over the little valley. Rain made Sissie feel like crying. At first it had been linked with the dank bedroom in Manaus where she had been so happy with Howard, but lately she had been haunted by an image of his corpse, pierced by bullets, lying forgotten on the mushy forest floor while the rain dripped down onto him, through layer after layer of dark, funereal leaves.

It seemed that death would not let her look him in the face. Both Howard and Janice had bowed out in her absence, without a farewell. Unconsciously, Sissie had been listening to a noise that she assumed to be thunder, but now it became sharper and louder and accompanied by shouting. Feeling foolish, Sissie recognized Sebastien's voice, put Petra in her cot and ran downstairs.

'Fort Knox, thy spirit lives on in a secluded corner of old England.' He stopped thundering on the door as Sissie drew back bolts at top and bottom and turned the key in the middle.

'I live here a woman on my own.' They embraced and Sissie looked beyond Sebastien's bony shoulders to the unchanging reassurance of hill and sky.

'That's not what I've heard.'

'Oh, village gossip.' Sissie saw it might actually be fun to have him here, not just as a painful witness to her past. 'Tea and cake?'

'"Tea and cake",' Sebastien mocked her again. 'I see you've found the only charmless house in a radius of thirty miles.'

Sissie laughed. 'Why are you wearing a suit, Seb? Do sit down. I can tell you three-piece suites are very comfortable, particularly when covered in washable Dralon. And what are you doing here, anyway? I thought you hated England, except in books. And where is François?'

'All is shame and failure!' Sebastien put his fist to his head theatrically but then sat down and crossed his legs like a man without a care in the world. 'So where is it?'

Tears came into Sissie's eyes. He had remembered she had a baby. This was far more than she had expected. She looked at Sebastien seriously. 'Are you sure you've not contracted a fatal illness?'

'I told you all is shame and failure. Nothing fatal.'

Sissie brought down Petra who was asleep, large head lolling. Sebastien studied her enthusiastically. 'But where's the cowboy hat and boots?'

'Oh, Seb!' Would she cry? Would she flood the room with tears so that they ran down the sides of the wall like the water in the Manaus apartment? Was Sebastien a bony shoulder to cry on? He hadn't been before in that first death by stiletto. It was too dangerous to let go. Sissie laid Petra on one of the armchairs. 'How is Paris?'

'Paris? My dear, but I've come from London. I have a job.'

Sebastien had a job. Sebastien the spoilt, the cool, the irresponsible had a job for which he wore a suit. 'I suppose it is Saturday,' said Sissie vaguely.

'I have weekends off.'

'So you've come to stay for a country weekend.' There was a meaning here that escaped Sissie. The ordinariness of it was a deception, this new Sebastien a man in fancy dress not to be trusted. 'How did you get here?' she asked suspiciously.

'I'll show you.' He took her outside round the corner of the house and there stood an enormously large black motor-cycle with gleaming chrome mirror and spoke wheels and mudguards. Nearby was a black visored helmet and a small leather suitcase. 'I should bring them further in out of the rain.'

'Not the bike!' exclaimed Sissie, taken aback.

The little house was beginning to fill up and Petra woke up and began to cry.

'As soon as it's stopped raining, I'll take you to see the church.' Petra was still crying as Sissie stuffed her into the papoose, and she continued a depressed whimpering as they started along the narrow road.

Sebastien sniffed the air. 'Heady stuff. Fresh as a nun's wimple.' He looked up at the still dripping trees, the clouds scurrying away from the horizon. 'I bought the bike, it's 1970, you know, when François left me for another. That's why I've come. Vraiment. For consolation.'

'I'm sorry.' Sissie was still distracted. Petra was still crying. 'I'm glad to see you, Seb. I see no one here. But I'm afraid I may not be too good on consolation.'

'Entendu. Why don't you leave me to forage around in the church myself and take Petra home?'

They stood in the porch of the squat stone church. 'It's Anglo-Saxon,' said Sissie, making an effort.

'Well. I must say. That puts my bike in its place.'

Sissie left him there, standing back to admire the solid tower with the weathercock on the top. Petra stopped crying almost at once and the birds started to sing again and the wind rustled through the trees. 'So lovely now!' she said to a woman who always walked her dog at this time of the afternoon.

'And aren't we enjoying it!' answered the woman cheeringly, and her dog, sniffing, nose down for water rats, ran along the banks of the stream.

Sebastien did not return until the cottage was washed with a dusky blue and Petra had gone to bed. Sissie drank a glass of red wine in slow sips. She waited and listened.

'I've been drinking in the pub,' Sebastien announced. Sissie noticed that his pale face was flushed. 'Yes. I decided it would be easier for you if I stayed there. They have two rooms. The landlord, or rather the landlady, is full of ideas for expansion but I don't expect you'd be very keen on that. Spoil your country idyll, I wouldn't be surprised.'

Sissie feared she had failed him but could not find the enthusiasm to do much about it. 'Would you like ham and bread and cheese?'

'Quite the little housewife.'

'I'll never be little.' Sissie led the way to the kitchen.

'You do have a large presence, that's true. That is a compliment, I hope you realize. I like people with large presences. Staying in the other room at the pub is a man with a very large presence. Huge. Gigantic. A Viking among men.'

Sissie realized that Sebastien had been doing some serious drinking. It put them out of tune, which was perhaps what he had planned. She continued her slow, careful sips of the red wine. 'Was François not the love of your life, after all?'

'I am working in the City. In the City we are above such things. We couldn't tell a pink dolphin from a Red Howler Monkey.'

Sissie felt her heart take a slide and a lurch. Had he meant that to happen? She put out a hand to him but he did not seem to notice.

'How are *you* living then?'

'You see how I am living.'

'Financially. How are you living financially? We in the City think financially. We put financial matters high on the agenda.'

'Oh, I see.' Sissie decided to believe that this was a real question expecting a real answer. 'A letter arrived with a cheque when I was still in Manaus. It was my widow's pension or something like that.'

'So you are independent, I may assume, comfortable, even.' Sebastien poured himself a tumblerful of red wine. 'I heard somewhere you have given away all your money.'

Such concern. What did it mean?

'We can't all make money our central consideration, that's certainly true.' Sebastien stood up suddenly, knocking the wine in a fierce crimson stream across the table and onto the floor. He stared at it frowning. 'I think I would like to stay here with you, after all, if that's OK.'

Sissie decided she did not want to know what was going on inside Sebastien's head or what adventures he had found at the pub with the Viking. 'You might at least clear up the wine.'

This seemed to strike him as a pleasurable invitation, for he rolled up the sleeves of his City shirt, found a pail and cloth and, as he swabbed, recited:

> 'Western wind when wilt thou blow
> the small rain down can rain
> Christ if my love were in my arms
> and I in my bed again.

Sissie left him and stood outside her front door under the soft night air and the stars, which shone from a smooth, ebony sky. After a while her sadness made it necessary to move so she took a few steps down the lane and then decided to circle the village. If Petra did wake, which she wouldn't for another hour when her next feed was due, Sebastien was there. It was a heady feeling to be relieved of responsibility and that must have been why Sissie found her heart beating faster as she reached the pub. She looked in through the open window and, sure enough, there was an immense blond man sitting with his back to her, drinking, it seemed, with the regulars, mostly farm-workers but also a doctor who owned horses and a young couple who had just moved into the village.

It was an ordinary enough scene but Sissie felt a sense of panic rising. Her half-formed intention had been to collect Sebastien's suitcase and inform the landlady of his change of plan but instead she turned and fled back down the lane, arriving out of breath, just as Sebastien stepped outside the cottage with Petra in his arms.

'What are you doing?' shrieked Sissie. She snatched the baby, who was yawning and blinking lazily.

'She woke up. I picked her up. Right or wrong?' He didn't seem to be drunk any more. He stood straight and looked at mother and baby with a clear conscience. 'Did you see him, then?'

'Did I see *who*?' Irritated, Sissie went inside to change and feed Petra. 'You use the bathroom first. I'll be about half an hour.'

But Sebastien ignored her command and came and sat admiringly on the end of Sissie's bed. 'However often do you feed her?'

'All the time. Whenever she wants.'

'And you're happy?'

'Seb, whatever is the matter with you? Happy? What do you mean?' Even he could not forget the deaths in her life.

'You *seem* happy. Although that monstrous tooth is a bad sign.'

'I am what I have to be.'

'I should think that's a definition of happiness. Call no man happy till he dies, he is at best but fortunate.'

Sissie smiled, not at anything Sebastien was saying but because Petra was sucking so sweetly at her breast and because she could see her round head with its soft cap of pale hair and her fingers opening and shutting in time with her sucking and her bare toes curled up in concentrated bliss. Bliss, thought Sissie, vaguely, eyes closing, not happiness. Just a few moments of bliss.

When Sissie opened her eyes again, Petra had stopped sucking and had fallen asleep across her lap. Sebastien had gone. She was too sleepy to wonder why and, on the whole, relieved to put off further communication until the following day. If it came to that, when had they ever talked?

Sissie fed her baby once more at four o'clock in the morning. A moon had risen bright enough to shed light through her floral

curtains and the house, as usual, was absolutely silent. But when she
went to the bathroom she saw a yellow line under Sebastien's door.
Holding her breath, she tiptoed back to bed. She always slept most
deeply for the next two or three hours.

Sebastien pushed his motor-cycle carefully down the lane. He already
wore his helmet and his dark suit jacket was fully buttoned against
the early-morning cool. When he reached the pub a man was
waiting, wearing a padded anorak that made him seem even bigger
than he was already. He got on the back of the bike as Sebastien
started the engine with a monstrous roar. Off they shot, sending up
a dozen or more sparrows from the hedgerows, two baby rabbits
from the grassy verge and three Canada geese who'd spent the night
on the stream.

Sven, who wasn't wearing a helmet because he believed his head
was as hard as any helmet and because he did not believe in following
the rule of law, gave a menacing Nordic chuckle which, translated,
meant, 'I couldn't resist the ride but I will return.'

Sissie luxuriated in bed for quite a few minutes (Petra still slept,
which was a miracle) before she remembered Sebastien. She went
out to the landing and there lay a note. She took it down to the
kitchen where the linoleum felt sticky under her bare feet.

> Carissima Sissie,
> Your maternal beauty is beyond compare, beyond penetration,
> beyond me. Your world is so bright it hurts my eyes. Your skin
> is phosphorescent, luminous, transparent and so is your baby's.
> I expect I've invented you both. You are in my imagination. If
> anyone told me you were real, I'd knock him down. I dreamt
> of you so hard all night I didn't sleep a wink. So at six I crept
> away. Oh, darling Sissie, benedictus benedicta, farewell from
> your ever-loving Seb.
>
> P.S. Your little valley brought me consolation, after all. But
> sometimes I wonder if it is all worth more than a Blue-footed
> Booby.

Sissie went up to the narrow room where Sebastien had slept or not slept and drew back the curtains. The window faced east and a belligerent young sun filled the room. It glared with particular ferocity at the lilac candlewick bedspread on which a book lay open, face downwards. Sissie sprang on it with ferocity to outdo that of the sun. *Magic and Fate*. That must have been what he was quoting last night when she so sensibly fell asleep. She picked up the book by the scruff of the spine, as a triumphant policeman might arrest a villain, and became even crosser when two or three pages dropped out. Clearly it was the very same copy that she had boasted to the Author of desecrating. How could Seb have claimed it back from Madame Didi when her horrible son, Mo, had so nearly ravished her? How dare he bring it into her home! Sissie was just contemplating ten ways, each more vicious than the last, of ending *Magic and Fate*'s active life for ever when she heard Petra's most indignant and tragic wails from next door.

Normally it took the baby some minutes to reach such a climax, which indicated she had been screaming unheard by her mother. Another black mark to *Magic and Fate*. Abandoning the book, Sissie ran to her bedroom.

Owing to feeding, bathing Petra, breakfasting, dressing herself, it was nearly two hours before Sissie found the right time to resume her act of vengeance. The sun had turned the corner of the cottage and the little room was dim. But there it was, a book on the floor by the bed where she must have thrown it, although, as a matter of fact, she thought she had dropped it on the bed.

Sissie picked up the book, from which no loose pages fluttered, and saw it was *Wives and Daughters* by Mrs Gaskell. It was typical of *Magic and Fate* to transform itself into something else in order to avoid capital punishment. More rationally she supposed it had dropped behind the bed. Let it lie there in darkness and disgrace, a life sentence if not death.

Chapter Twenty-Eight

In which Mary finds there is more than one sort of Crutch.

'I DON'T THINK there's room in this caravan for you, your broken leg, your crutches, Cleo, her four kittens and me visiting now and again,' said Ted Mack with assurance.

Mary, who was sitting on one of the two chairs with her leg up on the other, looked round the little room while Ted waited for a response. 'I like the view out,' she murmured defensively.

'If you ask me, it's no better than a prison cell and, as you know, I am not being theoretical.'

Mary did not like this reference one bit but she hid her annoyance from Ted because she never again wanted to risk driving him away as she had before.

'Your sister and brother-in-law looked as if they had a few pennies to rub together,' began Ted thoughtfully, but then caught such a horrified expression on Mary's face that he added quickly, 'or you could put yourself on the council list.'

Mary's expression had been more reflex than a true reflection of her feelings. Not that she would ever take a penny of Rob's or Janice's money – she was far too indebted to them already – but she had been becoming more and more aware of a real wish to see her sister. Over all these years, more than twenty now, she had only tolerated Janice's visits, never invited her and, until recently, done her best to stop her coming. Janice, with her mission to inform her of Sissie's life, had brought nothing except pain. Mary had had nothing to tell Janice, because she was only living because she was too cowardly to die. But now, if she were to be honest, she would have to admit that she wanted to tell her sister about the morning of the storm, Cleo's kittens, her extraordinary rescue, her days in hospital, the nurses' brisk chatter, the noise of the town in which she found herself, the girl in the bed next door who had fallen off the back of her boyfriend's motor bicycle and had two broken legs. Ted was, well, Ted, but he wasn't her sister, he wasn't a woman, and he still didn't know the truth of her life.

'So you don't agree?' said Ted, without rancour. He was always without rancour. That was his most attractive attribute, at least to Mary.

'It is small,' she said, eventually remembering what he had been talking about. 'I think I'll write to Janice.'

'You know what I think about that.'

'Yes. Yes.' Ted had endlessly pressed for Janice's address when she was in hospital. But it was too soon then, too much happening. Besides, she had thought her sister would visit in the normal course of events.

'Dear Janice,' Mary began in her head. 'I have had a little accident . . .'

Rob was shocked by the sight of the envelope for he thought he recognized his wife's handwriting. As Mary had never written to him before, it did not occur to him that sisters' writing is often similar. It was even more disturbing that the envelope was addressed to Janice, as if her ghost were writing to the person she had once been, his wife, Mrs Rob Slipper.

Rob took the envelope to the kitchen table and calmed himself with the thought of their happiness together, which had even survived the difficulties of her sister and her sister's daughter. How Janice would have enjoyed Sissie's baby! And then he opened the envelope.

Dear Janice,
    I have had a little accident. In fact it was very nearly the Big End as I fell down the cliff! I had gone to rescue Cleo who was having kittens but as it turned out she was safe and I was in danger. A storm was blowing up, you see, I expect you

remember that spell of bad weather. The gales killed quite a few, I heard afterwards, and without Ted's help they would have killed me.

By now Rob understood who was his correspondent, and his shock turned to guilt. Mary believed her sister was still alive. Mary was making an unprecedented overture to someone who had died. Rob continued to read the letter with the uneasy feelings of an eavesdropper. Why could not Mary have communicated earlier when it would have made Janice so happy? He skipped through to the end of the letter and found a postscript:

Did Sissie have her baby? I wonder sometimes.

She wondered sometimes! Rob thought of Sissie, encapsulated with her baby in her village idyll, surviving by sheer willpower, husband's death by disappearance and mother's death by cancer. This was not the moment for an invasion, if that's indeed what Mary was planning and there was an invasive feel to her letter. All this detail of her accident, her kittens, her friend, what was it supposed to mean? How would Janice have reacted?

Shocked, guilty, and in a thorough panic, Rob tore up the letter and drove off to work.

Sissie was making a daisy chain on the patch of lawn at the back of her cottage. Petra sat beside her, naked and sun-tanned. 'No, Petra. Wait!' As fast as she linked the flowers, pushing each feathery head through a hole in a delicate stem, Petra's chubby fingers tore them apart. 'If you wait, I'll make you a bracelet and a necklace and maybe even a tiara.'

Petra wasn't just a vandal. Admittedly, most often she threw away the flowers with gleeful triumph but sometimes she held up a single daisy and studied it as if she were a botanist. Her round blue eyes crossed with concentration and it seemed like a bid to under-stand its magic powers further – or even assume them for herself when she popped it into her mouth.

'No. Petra. No.' Sissie felt round Petra's slippery tongue and pulled out the flower. 'I'll find you something you'll like even more.' Sissie went into the house, baby on one hip, and reappeared with a bowl of water on the other hip. Now that Petra was diverted, dabbling and splashing, Sissie worked with dedication and soon she had a necklace long enough to slip over Petra's head, a couple of bracelets and a tiara to place among her fair curls. Surprisingly, Petra sat quite still while Sissie decorated her, with a pleased, self-conscious look on her face.

'Well,' Sissie stood back to admire her handiwork, 'you're the Spirit of Summer.' But that was a bad idea, a depressing thought, for these hot days belonged to autumn, not summer, and in less than a week the retired school-mistress would reclaim her home.

Petra, taking advantage of her mother's inattention, used both hands to tear off all her adornments and throw them into the bowl. There, to her delight, they floated, delicate circlets moving on the swell of the water.

Mary expected that Janice would answer her letter in person. Each morning of those hot days she rose early and made sure not to be out of the caravan after eleven when her sister might have arrived. One particularly hot Sunday Ted came at midday carrying sand-wiches and beer in a plastic bag.

'We're going for a picnic,' he said. 'I've borrowed a car so your leg can come too. There's a beach no one knows about. Well, let's be honest, only about a hundred people know about.'

Mary looked round for an escape. Sunday was the most likely day for Janice and Rob to visit. 'My leg itches,' she said. 'It itches inside the plaster.'

'It'll be cooler on the beach,' responded Ted, and took Mary's crutches to her as a dog picks up its lead when it wants to go for a walk. 'In fact, if you stay here you'll probably be found crisp and toasted at the end of the day.' He put up his hand and touched the ceiling. 'Ouch! Hotter than gas mark nine.'

She went with him. She could never resist his thoughtful, good-humoured bullying.

*

Mary sat on the pebbles, back against a slice of cliff indistinguishable from the one she had fallen down, since it was only a mile or two further along the coast. The sun was behind her so she sat in the shade and watched the illuminated sea and the strip of beach before it as a spectator watches the stage. There was a cast of at least the hundred promised by Ted: teenage boys with too-long legs playing frisbee, their younger brothers swimming and digging and eating, tired mothers flat out, hoping their husbands were coping with the children, lively mothers splashing their babies so they screamed with pleasure or surprise, proud fathers pedal-boating their family on a horizontal trail, going in and out of Mary's view. There were young girls, camped in a group, passing round sun-lotion numbers like a mantra, an old man with a dog taking a serious walk, a couple of hitch-hikers, who also moved in and out of Mary's picture. It was a vivid scene that changed continually as if she had a kaleidoscope to her eye.

Very comfortable, more than half asleep, Mary tried to pick out Ted. He was going for a swim, he had said, but he hadn't changed into a costume anywhere near her. Mary looked into the brightness and saw him just entering the water, his figure not softly plump, as she had vaguely suspected, but stocky and hard. He looked strong. As she watched he put on goggles, waded a foot or two into the water, which became quickly deep, and dived into it, a curve of which a dolphin would have been proud. She lost sight of him among the splashes and the ball throwers and then he emerged again, striking out in an energetic crawl through the emerald water.

Mary sighed, and something happened to her in that instant. Unacknowledged, she allowed herself to love.

Ted stood in front of Mary, drying his middle-aged body with a thin, greyish towel. 'Didn't I tell you you'd feel good?'

'I didn't know you were such a strong swimmer.'

'I swim in the town baths every day.'

Ted laid his towel on the sand and sat beside Mary. His feet were calloused, his legs undeniably too short for his body. His face and hands were sunburnt, the rest of his body whitish, the chest sparsely haired, and when he leant forward his stomach protruded. But for Mary he was transformed and she would never again see him objectively.

251

'Here we are. Cheese sandwiches. I thought they'd be safe.'

Mary put out her hand to take the sandwich and her hand touched Ted's. Their eyes met. Frankly, they looked at each other, and then Mary looked down and, in need of a diversion, took a large bite of sandwich. She had remembered her past, her age, her ugly body, the dead and withering skin that itched under her plaster cast. The shining knight into which Ted had been transformed by her loving gaze could not conceivably be interested in someone like her.

'I've been given another house,' said Ted abruptly. 'It's too big for one.' His meaning was clear.

Mary began to cry, huge drops that made the pebbles shine.

Ted was dignified and did not try to comfort her. 'I know what you're thinking. You're right to see the truth of it. I'll never be more than a prison officer.'

As Mary understood that he had interpreted her tears as rejection, she stopped crying and turned on him fiercely. 'You're more than that! Much, much more. You're more important to me than anyone in the whole world!' She hesitated and her eyes slid past him to where the blue sky met the green sea. 'More important than everybody except one,' she corrected herself quietly.

Seeing Mary's face become gentle, Ted, so keen to be close to her and understand, suddenly saw all those photographs of that girl, the big blue eyes of her, and he did understand. 'Except your daughter,' he said.

Mary couldn't cry again because she had already, so she took his hand, a plain hand with short fingers and nails in need of a cut, and kissed the palm. It seemed to her that by pronouncing those words he had given her back her daughter.

Chapter Twenty-Nine

In which Sissie finds a Fire-eater and Someone less Welcome at the Last of the Summer Sun.

THE AUTHOR strode about the stage impatiently. He knew he was wrong to peddle his talent in such humble and out of the way circumstances. Obscurity was, he had to admit, in some sense his métier, but the humbleness, the mean size of the stage, the lack of polish on the hastily erected planks, was galling. He could not be insulted because he had elected to come to this outdoor venue, this stage in a forgotten east-coast castle, a sixth port never counted. But that made him even crosser, because he must blame himself. He would be surprised if half showed up of the three hundred upwards fervently promised by the organizers.

The Author was now white-haired, his handsome face sallow and lined as if too much world travel had speeded up his rate of ageing. The change in appearance had lessened his dramatic charisma and enhanced his guru tendency, as age gives the patina of wisdom. He felt he should have been sharing his genius with thousands. There were people out there whose lives could be changed by listening to a few of his magical words. He feared that his white hairs were not to be given the respect they deserved and, worse still, it might rain.

Sissie had moved out of the cottage into one of the rooms of the public house. It looked out across almost the same view of the hillside but she was conscious that more timidly conventional people like her father might not approve of bringing up a child in a room

253

filled with the smell of beer and smoke, which seeped up, in friendly fashion, through the floorboards. For that reason she had not told him. For another reason, too – that she had very little money left and, if he knew that, he would feel obliged, for Petra's sake, to offer them a place in his house. Under no circumstances would she return to the house that she had abandoned, particularly after her mother's death and her poor showing as a mourner (she did mourn, however). Far better that he should think she was still rich beyond his wildest dreams and that her way of living was whimsical self-indulgence rather than necessity.

Sissie, large and long and rosy with sun, lay on her narrow bed reading a letter from Maureen. Maureen was happy: every word glowed with fulfilment. She told Sissie of the little triumphs as she, with Father Pedro, created an oasis of order out of chaos and need. 'Maria walks,' she wrote excitedly. 'The floor is so smooth and clean, she's never known a floor like it so she dared to get up and walk. No one thought she was capable of taking a step. Four years old and never walked before. Just think of it! And all, all thanks to you . . .'

Reluctantly, Sissie sat up and put one foot after the other onto the ugly orange carpet. She was earning pocket money by serving in the pub at lunch-time – at least, cutting bread and cheese and carrying it into the lounge. Petra sat in an old pram, used for carting potatoes, set in the backyard among the beer barrels. Her fingers opened and shut as she tried to catch the sparrows that flickered around her provocatively.

'There're six walkers in,' said Sissie's landlady, 'so make the bread thick.' Walkers were always ravenous, gobbling gobbets of anything they were given, pickled onions squelching between their teeth, every tired lettuce leaf and trace of chutney scraped from their plate, all grist, presumably, to their muscle and stringy sinew for they were never fat. Sissie, if not exactly fat, had more than adequate flesh to cover her splendid bones. Combined with her generous bosom – she was still feeding Petra – she was a striking, monumental presence, not someone whom even the most beer-laden dared take lightly. No one now guessed her famous past.

Sissie carried through the first two hunky slices of bread and cheese and her eye was caught by the same large sticker adorning each of six backpacks lined up neatly along the floor. It showed a stone circle in a wedge of hills, the stones standing up like giant ill-spaced teeth, and behind them a grassy plateau on which a sun, composed of dashing hexagonals, presided nobly. 'The Last of the Summer Sun,' she read. 'A spectacle for all the family.'

Plonking down a plate in front of a leather-faced man in shorts, Sissie asked, 'What's the Last of the Summer Sun?'

'The end of our trail. Two hundred and fifty miles walking from Newark, New Jersey. A meeting. A celebration. Theatre.'

'But what if it rains?' Sissie was taken aback to find that these were American walkers (their East-Coast voices quite unlike Howard's Southern drawl) but she persevered nonetheless.

'It usually does,' said the man with a cheerful grin.

'Think of the sun as a mythic symbol,' added his female companion helpfully.

The 'spectacle for all the family' would take place only seven miles from the village, hardly further than her childhood home. The celebration was an annual event, she was told, held at this landmark place of mystery, a minor Stonehenge. Yet, like the village itself, Sissie had no recollection of having seen the stone circle before, as if the world she had inhabited as a child had provided its own alternative geography. Her parents' house, the road, the small town where she went to school, a few friends' houses, so little to remember from sixteen years of growing up.

Later that evening, Sissie found clothes for Petra and her to wear, old material, held together with the usual safety-pins, a necklace she had bought in India and which had survived where all else had disappeared, a couture mini-dress, which seemed to fit Petra. Petra was a heavy baby, no longer able to fit into the papoose, so Sissie borrowed the old pram from her landlady. 'Don't forget your rent,' the landlady said. 'You're a week behind.'

During the night the room next door to Sissie's heaved with the weight of the six walkers who, presumably, were taking turns to sleep in the two beds. Sissie might have wondered if they were doing something more interesting than climbing in and out of the beds, except that their bodies had seemed too dedicated to the pursuit of mileage to make sex feasible. She thought of how she and Howard had met, the honey sweetness of his body – or was it hers? She could not tell the difference. She looked for Petra, sleeping in the darkness, and forced herself to smile. As soon as it was light, the walkers dragged their backpacks about the floor for a while and then left, their boots making determined sounds down the wooden stairs.

After feeding Petra, Sissie dressed them both in their finery and put nappies and a few more clothes into a sling-bag. Then she took an envelope with money and went to the landlady.

'I'm sure you'll get a lift back,' said the landlady, offering them a picnic of cheese sandwiches left over from the night before.

'I'm sure we will.' Sissie looked out of the window at the hillside.

'Anyway, it's a lovely day for an outing. The last nice day, if the weather forecast's anything to go by. I always say you should get out more.'

'Oh, I've loved being here,' replied Sissie. Which later made the landlady think.

Petra enjoyed riding along in the deep old pram; she did not care that it smelt of earth and that the springs had uncoiled. She bounced about on her bottom and babbled nearly comprehensible words. Sissie felt sure she knew they were on a proper journey and that she was displaying enthusiastic encouragement. She began to sing, a song she didn't even know she knew, about a lass on Richmond Hill, more sweet than Mayday morn. To her surprise, this song was followed by another and then another, as if a key to a distant memory had turned in her head. She sang them in a special way, too, with emphasis intact, as if she knew all this without even trying.

It was weird, but wonderful, in keeping with the day, and Sissie trudged along behind the pram with an eager spirit. This lasted for as long as they held to the lanes and narrow roads around the village where the banks were heavy with the uncut grass of early autumn and butterflies and other less charming insects made halos above their heads. But after an hour or two they had to enter a bigger road where cars came in noisy trails of six or seven and, if there was another in opposition, shaved so close that the exhaust fumes filled their noses. Eventually, at the top of a steepish hill, Sissie decided she had had enough.

Grabbing Petra, she bundled both of them over a fence and landed, as in another country, in a field of corn stubble. Through the middle of it, like a parting through a crew-cut, led a straight path, about a metre wide, which went to the horizon but on its way passed a small tree bounded by grass. Just the place for their picnic.

Sissie took a few steps and then saw that the ground was so hard and flattened – beaten down, she presumed, by the feet of countless walkers – that she could easily push the pram along it. She sat Petra – who immediately began to eat grass – at the edge of the field, and returned for the pram.

The songs came back again as they rattled their way towards the tree. One man and his dog went to mow a meadow . . . ten men, nine men, eight men, seven men, six men, five men, four men, three men, two men, one man and his dog went to mow a meadow. Why could she not remember Janice teaching her this, she and Ruth singing it together?

Sissie sat under the tree, feeding Petra and eating her sandwich. The sky to which she had been advancing was clear blue but, now facing the other way, she saw, at some distance, rolls of clouds curling over like waves in their eagerness to advance.

Petra seldom cried. Her large healthy body and her doting, ever-present mother combined to make hers a thoroughly satisfactory life. So when the first blobs of rain fell, she laughed rather than cried and tried to catch them as she did everything, bees, butterflies, thistle-down, sunbeams, pieces of fluff that floated on the air-streams and were invisible to adult eyes. Sissie looked at her trusting pink cheeks and decided she didn't mind rain either, although as it grew heavier she drew the leaky hood over Petra's head and pushed more quickly towards a group of sycamores growing in a hedge.

This particular roll of clouds passed by quickly and once again the sky cleared. However, the track, which seemed to continue through field after field, had become soft and it was harder to push the pram.

Despite the bumpings and rattlings, Petra fell forward and went to sleep, her bottom stuck in the air. Left on her own, Sissie began to sing for the third time.

> 'Golden slumbers kiss your eyes
> Smiles awake you when you rise
> Sleep, my darling, do not cry
> And I will sing a lullaby.'

She sang it over and over again until the lyrical rhythms had been flattened out and the repetition turned it into a dirge-like marching song.

It was then that a face came to join the song, a woman's face, rather smooth, rather round with pale eyes and fairish hair. She was not unlike Janice but not Janice: the nose was shorter, the face broader, the brow higher, the hair the same colour but curlier. This face, like the song, seemed to be remembered rather than imagined. It stayed with her for some time, for as long as the sun stayed out, in fact, an unthreatening, even comforting presence. But as the skies darkened and another roll of clouds banked overhead, this time with a hint of thunder, she felt that the song and the face hid something more menacing.

Petra woke up with the rain. The air had cooled with the first deluge and now it cooled still further. The path became more and more inhospitable, passing through the scrubby remains of a mostly cleared wood, and Petra began to grizzle. Sissie was now truly tired and probably lost. It would be tea-time, she thought nostalgically, in the village in the little valley. She stopped under the half-hearted shelter of a holly tree, standing alone like a pariah, and took Petra out of the pram for a feed. This seemed to be one of the longest days of her life and, as water still dripped onto her feet however much she tried to draw them in under her prickly umbrella, she yearned for the warm rain of the Amazon. But yearning was a dangerous business.

Under such unpromising circumstances, Sissie felt disinclined to move even when Petra was full up and patted away her breasts – unattractively covered with goose pimples, she noticed. Mother and baby lolled together and after a while the sun came out yet again. But still Sissie didn't move. Quite apart from the tired muscles of her arms and legs, the pram would need bailing out before she could continue.

Some time later when Petra had half fallen asleep, Sissie thought she heard music. Leaving the baby, she made her way to the other side of the ravaged wood where she could hear that the music, of a sweeping filmic nature, was interspersed by an amplified male voice but she could still see nothing. There was no longer a path to be followed but a wide, short-cropped grassy field, sloping upwards. At

258

the top Sissie was sure she would be able to see the source of music and voice, with any luck her destination, but dare she leave Petra alone? The delightful freedom from pushing the pram had given her new energy and she was sure her long legs would get her up and back before Petra woke. Sissie bounded, springing off the damp grass, a vague headache disappearing at once.

She reached the crest of the hill and there, spread out over the next hillside was the spectacle, giant stone teeth, grassy stage, cars, flags, tents, stalls, crowds and all. She only glanced for a second and then flew back down the slope and through the scrub to where the holly stood as a dark marker.

'Petra! Petra! We've arrived! Nearly arrived!' she called from afar.

And there was the tree and there was the pram. 'Petra! Petra!' It was impossible she had gone. Sissie had left her at the base of the tree and she could not crawl. Images of wild beasts, lions, tigers, pumas who slunk out of the forest and snatched away desirably chubby babies made her scream even more loudly. 'Petra! Petra! Where are you? Petra!'

She began to run in circles, round and round the tree, for there was nowhere the baby could be hidden, no scrub thick enough – unless, unless . . . Then Sissie began to think of human kidnappers and murderers and she thought she would choke with terror and her eyes swirled about and her suntan sat on top of skin drained of all colour. She tried to calm herself, control this frantic useless searching and she heard again the music and the voice that the horror had blotted out and she thought she must run to them and get help.

'The Last of the Summer Sun' was still not fully under way when Sissie arrived but there were all kinds of improvised sideshows and unscheduled entertainments. A young woman, for example, wearing yellow gauntlets was swallowing flames from a blow-torch for an admiring crowd while a little further on a man who would have convinced Elvis Presley's mother that her son had risen whole, sang 'Are You Lonesome Tonight'. There was some order in the meeting, however: marshals with armbands and a few strolling policemen.

Sissie ran up to one and gasped, 'Lost! Lost!' The policeman took her by the shoulders good-naturedly and, as no words followed, pointed her in the direction of a small tent such as if for a painted medieval scene of jousting.

'That way,' he told her. 'They'll help you. Make an announcement.'

Incapable of explaining the seriousness, Sissie stumbled away, crying in frustration, added to fear, as the greater crowd of people in this area blocked her progress.

At last she fell through the flap in the tent and screamed into the dimness, 'I've lost my baby!'

A jolly woman's voice said, 'That wasn't too long, then.'

Not too long? Sissie peered wildly round and there sitting in the comfortable lap of a dark-uniformed woman was Petra.

'Sometimes we have them for hours. Yours is such a good baby that I'll be sorry to lose her. Some of them screech at you as if you're trying to murder them instead of look after them.'

Sissie was too taken aback to be anything sensible: relieved, enquiring, thankful. She just stood there, panting and staring, and eventually muttered, 'I only left her for a minute.'

'They all say that, dear. Not that I'm saying it's not true. But an awful lot can happen in a baby's life in a minute. What feels like a minute, anyway.' She held out Petra to Sissie.

Now Sissie hugged her and clasped her and promised herself never to lose sight of her for one *second*, ever again. And only then she thought of asking, 'But where did you find her?'

'Oh, I didn't find her.' The woman stood up and picked up a clipboard from a trestle table. 'A man found her. He brought her in.'

'A man!' gasped Sissie.

'Men are far more responsible about children than women give them credit for. Notice my badge.' She tapped her shoulder, 'St John.'

'But why should he have been in that w—' began Sissie and then stopped, confused. She had, after all, left her baby unguarded, open to the elements and worse.

'He was a man with almost white hair. Usually I take their names in case the owner wants to thank them but he said his in such a rumble and he was in such a hurry to leave that I'm afraid I didn't get it down. He was a very big man.'

'Thank you, anyway,' said Sissie, who didn't hear the last sentence because she, too, felt in a hurry to leave. She could not work out what it meant, this almost white-haired kidnapper, but she knew she didn't want to stay any longer in his footprints.

When she came out of the tent, the crowd was moving in one direction towards the jutting stones and the grassy stage beyond. It was obvious that the main event of the evening was about to begin. She followed, giving money to enter an enclosure where officials removed illegal substances from some pockets and bags in a random sort of way.

Sissie, still dazed by her experiences, offered them her pockets but she had none under her baby and they waved her through laughing. She was the last in a line of stragglers, finding space among the audience who squatted expectantly in the middle of a circle of upright boulders. Above them the grassy plateau, which looked so like a stage, had a sternly old-fashioned look because the low sun glowed from directly behind so that instead of lighting the actors, as in a normal stage, it turned them into dark silhouettes edged with gold. A choir was in full voice. When Sissie had settled herself and Petra, she saw uncountable numbers, rows beyond her range of vision, singing, in six or eight or ten parts, what sounded like the king of all madrigals. The amplification system, black boxes nearly as large as the stones, stood sentinel round the gathering and, since they were not co-ordinated, they added to the amount of parts in the song. It was as if battalions of sound were marching in every direction. The audience were excited, bemused, heads turning from side to side.

Sissie, already discomposed, hugged Petra to her and tried to concentrate on the stage. But the sun had dropped still lower and turned so fiery a colour that it was too bright for her eyes. She leant forward over Petra's downy head while around her the audience thrilled and rocked to climactic noise. Then silence. Total, absolute. Sissie peered up.

As the Author had told Sissie so long ago, he believed in spectacle to accompany his great words, but he liked someone else to provide the spectacle. He had used Sissie for this purpose in Bombay and she had done very well, although she had not been as exciting as the time he had featured two giant turtles half-way

261

through the act of love. However, he had been taken by surprise by the enormous size of this respectably hippie gathering, and had prepared no drama. It must be him alone, taking the stage between the waves of receding white-robed singers.

So, he started up the back of the little grass knoll, ready to throw up his arms as he arrived at the top and, indeed, he did so but no one had told him about the wire trailing from the microphone, hidden in the grass, taut across his feet.

The Author took his several great strides, threw up his arms in a gesture of victory and – down he crashed.

Sissie looked up at exactly this moment and stared with horror to see a black creature, rimmed in fire, crawling along towards her. Its mouth gaped wide but no sound issued from it. Black puma, panther or mythic beast, a sacrifice to the descending gods of night, or god itself, it rolled and hunched its way to the front of the stage.

'Look!' cried Petra, although they were a way back and a baby's vision is supposed to be poor. Probably she didn't say, 'Look!' at all since it would have been her first identifiable word, but Sissie thought she did and that her beloved child had not only faced kidnap and abandonment but, hardly an hour later, had identified a monstrous threat, as if risen from primordial subterra.

The Author, tripped and fallen, attempted to rise. The audience, roaring in appreciation, encouraged him to make the effort, but as he staggered onto his hind legs, something snapped, a tendon, his will, a link from brain to leg, and he collapsed more thoroughly than before. Oh, what a spectacle was there.

'Look!' screamed Petra, her newborn voice more piercing than all the rest – even if she were truly saying 'ook!' or 'ooo!' or making another meaningless expression of surprise and, in fact, although Sissie was too shaken to realize it, delight.

Once more, the Author, always the professional, struggled to rise to the occasion. In Sissie's eyes this ugly, writhing thing was more threatening still. Yet all around there were people enthralled, having a really lovely evening. Doubtless, they knew he was a man who at some point or other they hoped would balance himself upright and shout or sing (whatever was his hiring) an uplifting word or two or three. Some cheered, some began to sing themselves and the fire-eating lady relit her torch but lost heart when she discovered she'd mislaid her yellow rubber gloves. It was an interval of expectancy just made for popping a pill or lighting a fag of various denominations, and this duly took place.

Only Sissie stared aghast and it was she who, entirely without the aid of Ecstasy, saw a vision. A man in flames coming from hell to greet her, on the ground, crawling, half dead, red blood trailing, but still coming to greet her, get her. Or if not her, her baby. She recognized him now. She had seen him before. Unable to move, Sissie opened her mouth to scream.

At that moment, a further spectacle, better than any *son et lumière*, burst over all their heads. Sissie had forgotten the rolls of cloud chasing up behind but they had not forgotten her. Because the sun was still ahead (glowing in a last recklessness before disappearing behind the horizon) no one had noticed the blackness trekking so stealthily from the east. The first they knew was lightning that split the sky above their heads and then used the space to whistle down to earth. Like a silver spear thrown by a greater master and accompanied by a magnificent thundercrack, the lightning headed for the Author and, doubtless, would have made short work of him, a burnt ember at best, had not a wild figure burst the audience asunder and catapulted towards him with such fury that he was stimulated to rise at last to his feet and hurl himself out of its path and, as it happened, the path of the lightning.

'No! No! No!' screamed Sissie. And then, as if there was nothing more to say, 'No! No! No!'

The lightning, foiled of its rightful prey, sizzled down between the two of them, causing a large black hole in the grassy mound. Sissie teetered on the edge of it and the Author, still not recognizing his aggressor (hardly surprising as she was three stone heavier than when he'd last seen her and had a baby tucked under her arm), wriggled backwards agitatedly. The audience, meanwhile, was far too excited by the lightning, the hole and the storm effects in general – which did not yet include rain – to take much notice of either. Only a band of walkers, identifiable by their boots, sinews and weatherbeaten skin, who sat near the front, watched with interest as a tall form climbed up onto the mound.

'Surely that's the giantess with the concrete tooth who brought us stale bread and cheese in the pub last night?' asked one of the other.

Sissie progressed, weather no interest. The Author hobbled on his crumpled legs. He had been chased by viragos round the world and knew what to expect but there was no escaping this one in her seven-league boots.

'Got you!' Sissie, tears of rage and exertion flying from her eyes, held him triumphantly by the lapels of his black silk suit. Although he had nowhere to go but a dive off the back edge of the mound which, in his present crippled state, he was unlikely to attempt. And then she saw who she had got. No nightmare figure from the past but the man who dogged her life, her evil demon. All the more reason, then, to hold onto his collar and shake him without mercy, white hair a flapping flag of guilt.

'Thief! Kidnapper! Seducer! Con-man! Charlatan! False friend!' A final ray of sun, giving an even fiercer glow to his antagonist's countenance than her (mostly) righteous anger, brought recognition and, with it, hope. The Author turned on a somewhat desperate charm. 'Sissie! Divine Sissie! Sissie the magnificent! Sissie the mummy!'

'Don't you dare talk about motherhood. You, who—'

'But you dressed yourself as a mummy. On the ship—' The Author was plaintive and his voice came in jerks because Sissie was still shaking him backwards and forwards (old age had not only whitened his hair but reduced his weight). Sissie, however, had no intention of listening to him so he might as well have saved his breath.

'You follow me to my private bed of joy and then steal my tooth! You sully with your presence what should have been a joyful evening with my late husband. And then – and then – when I'm as far from the world as I could possibly be, when I have found a nook or, more likely, a cranny, where I can enjoy my baby, my beautiful innocent baby, the only person I love in the world, you come sneaking along . . .' Sissie's voice rose to a scream, 'and steal her!'

At this Petra, who had so far been exceptionally good-tempered about the manhandling by her mother, decided to scream too. With the strength of ten, Sissie pulled down the Author to sit beside her and, almost with the same movement, opened her dress and gave Petra a breast.

The Author watched in wonderment. Sissie caught his expression and said in a bossy, school-mistressy tone, which actually hid a little embarrassment, 'Have you never seen a mother feeding before?'

'Not in these circumstances,' he replied, passing a weary hand over his brow.

'Why . . .' began Sissie on the attack again, but she had to lower her tone or Petra stopped sucking, 'why did you want to steal my baby?'

'But I didn't.' The Author pressed home his advantage while Sissie was surprised into silence. 'I have never stolen a baby in my life. In fact, I don't believe I've even looked at a baby before now. Moreover, it's going to rain.'

It was or, rather, did. Huge round balls of rain that exploded on their heads and all about them.

'Come on,' suggested the Author. 'We can sit in my car.'

Even Sissie saw that this was too good an offer to miss. 'It's been chasing me all day,' she said, clutching Petra as they hurried along. 'The rain, I mean.' An image of the dripping walls in Manaus passed before she had time to suppress it.

The Author, gallant now, took off his beautiful jacket and tried to hold it over mother and child's heads. It would have been a charming gesture, turning them into a conventional family unit, protective man, with his woman and baby, but unfortunately Sissie's head was way beyond the range of his still wobbly legs so she batted him away irritably. 'I'm not afraid of being recognized you know.'

The car was splendid – stretched almost to infinity, it seemed to Sissie as she bent her head thankfully to enter. The Author got in beside her and in front sat the impervious back view of a chauffeur.

'I did not kidnap that darling little baby,' said the Author, oozing charm.

'You are grand,' said Sissie, so happy to be feeding Petra on soft leather while the elements warred away outside that she was inclined to believe him. 'The lady from the St John said it was a man with white hair – when did that happen, incidentally? – and even if she hadn't, I'd have suspected you. When things go wrong, you're always near at hand.'

'White hair, you say? Perhaps this lady meant white blond. That Nordic fairness that is almost white.' He patted her hand. 'But how did anyone manage to get so close to your baby? You seem like one being.'

Sissie blushed and even in the dimness caught a knowing sheen from the chauffeur's eyes in the rear-view mirror. 'We were temporarily parted,' she admitted. She paused. The rain beat overhead. 'There are problems.'

'Problems. Problems. My dear, I am so sorry. I remember the last time a young woman said that to me, a knife thudded into her back hardly ten seconds later. Luckily, we were already in Poughkeepsie hospital where the trauma unit had a knowledge of knife wounds unequalled anywhere except in ill-run restaurants and—'

'Please,' interrupted Sissie.

'Let her speak,' the chauffeur also intervened in a superb bass voice.

'Speak!' commanded the Author.

'It's money,' muttered Sissie.

'Money!' exclaimed the Author, looking utterly amazed. 'You are talking to me about money.' He spaced each word with heavy emphasis.

'I know. I know.' Sissie bent shamefacedly over Petra's head and a tear trickled from each eye. 'I never thought about money before I gave it all away. And I wouldn't even worry about it now, were it not for Petra.' She gathered energy. 'And, as a matter of fact, I gave it away because I was so cross with the rubbish you were spouting in Manaus, sullying the purity of a great opera house, a great country—'

'Brazil? A great country?'

'Yes. Of course. And I'm glad I gave it all away and I wouldn't – I won't take a penny back but I can't have Petra kidnapped in a forest, even if there was only one miserable tree left standing.' The trickle of tears turned to a flow.

'There, there,' said the Author. 'We'll work something out.'

Sissie buttoned up her dress for Petra had fallen asleep, head drooping deliciously, and looked up. Much to her amazement, she saw they were no longer stationary in the field but speeding along a wide road. 'Wherever are you taking me?' she cried.

'Not to worry.' The Author, giving in to wicked pleasure, laid his hand on Sissie's breasts, which were heaving with the constant shocks to her system. 'At least you've stopped spouting. Let us agree, it's all a question of making ends meet.'

The chauffeur, who had such a light touch on the wheel, now removed a hand in order to remove his hat and thus revealed his thick hair, which was almost luminous in its pale blondness.

Sissie, thinking over the Author's remark, took no notice. 'There's only one sure way to make ends meet,' she said, in a determined voice, and put the Author's age-freckled hand back where it belonged.

Chapter Thirty

*In which Mary goes on a Wild Goose Chase and is shown a
Perambulator full of Orchids.*

THE DOCTOR split open the casing on Mary's leg. 'It may not
look too beautiful,' he told her, his nose wrinkling at the sight
and aroma of withered, flaking skin, 'but I can assure you the bones
have healed very nicely.'

Ted was waiting for her outside the hospital. He still wore his
prison-officer uniform, which produced much the same reaction in
Mary as her leg had in the doctor. In all the world she had one
friend and that friend was a screw. Oh, the wicked tricks of fate!

'I'm taking you to see my house,' said Ted. 'Summer is over,
autumn at least half-way through and soon it will be winter. You
don't want to spend another winter in that caravan.'

'I like winter. There're fewer people around.'

'Last winter, maybe, not this one. You have changed. You don't
want to be alone all the time.'

Mary was not sure she agreed with this analysis but his firmness
made her smile and she allowed him to lead her along the pavement,
even if it did make her feel like one of his prisoners. Surely that
couldn't be why she liked him?

The house was two storeys high, as square and comfortable as
Ted himself. 'It's not as near the jail as most of them,' said Ted, after
he had showed her the neat sitting room and the main bedroom,
which was furnished with two single beds, 'and it's too big for one.'

He looked at her, then, straight in the eyes, so that Mary turned
bright red like a child and scuttled downstairs as if she were chased

by a mad axeman. Returning once more to the safety of the living room, they stood nervously apart. 'Well, there's not much wrong with your leg if you can rattle down like that,' commented Ted eventually.

'It does ache.' Mary sat down, feeling it sensible to resume the patient's role. It was best not to think of what went on in beds – not with the memories she had collected during her marriage. 'I would need a separate bedroom,' she said impulsively.

'There are two bedrooms,' replied Ted, on the defensive because, after all, she had run away or he could have showed her the nice spare room.

'Oh, yes!' cried Mary, trying to look as if she thought he had meant the spare bedroom for her all along.

'Tea,' suggested Ted, before things became too strained. He had no bad memories of sex or what went with sex. In fact, he had very few memories of sex since it had never been high on his list of priorities. What he wanted from Mary was an extension of what he already had, companionship, and he was not waiting eagerly to tear the clothes from her body. It was not a matter of age but of temperament.

Mary's blushes subsided as she realized there was no sexual charge coming from Ted and it was her own past that had disturbed her. It seemed possible they might live in harmony.

It was easy leaving the caravan. Mary just shut the door on it without removing anything except one small suitcase of clothes, the cat and the one remaining kitten for which Ted had not found a home. She even left her feathered hat, telling Ted, 'It'll be a place for us to stop off at on our walks.' It was a declaration of independence of which they were both aware and it was made more telling when Cleo refused to live in the house and led her daughter on the road to the cliffs. It was clear she was not going to submit to town life.

'I'll just leave a window open in the caravan,' said Mary, 'and then I can feed her on our walks.' It did not seem a very tidy solution to Ted but there were more important things to deal with in Mary's life. It had begun to dawn on him that it was not enough to know that she had a staggeringly beautiful daughter who had been a model: he also had to discover the whole story of their separation, and why and when Mary had spent time inside. This was a difficult matter, he understood – her fragility constantly amazed his unimaginative solidity. He had not even dared to organize the marriage, although he was sure it would take place at some point, for fear of making her feel trapped. He still continued in most of his bachelor ways, swimming each morning, ironing his own white shirts, doing most of the shopping and, of course, sleeping separately in the main bedroom. Mary was an honoured guest, that's what he wanted her to feel.

One Saturday morning, a day on which he liked to lie in if he was off duty, he came down to the kitchen to find Mary wearing a coat with a bag on the table. He suddenly noticed how much weight she had lost since her accident and that she no longer looked like a dumpy old lady.

'I'm going to find my brother-in-law,' she explained, with an air of defiance, 'since he doesn't answer my letters.'

Ted felt the edge of his unshaven chin. He heard the milkman put a bottle on the step. It was very early. 'That's a long journey without a car.'

'I've looked up the trains. There's one to London in half an hour. And then change stations and not too long a wait for another.'

Ted thought he had time to shave and asked, with utmost delicacy, 'And would you like an escort?'

Neither of them thought of this as a 'prison escort' since unexpected relief made Mary look at Ted with a rare smile, as pure and heart-warming as a baby's. For the first time Ted felt an impulse to kiss this mysterious creature who had put herself in his care.

The day had started bright and cool, the leaves on the chestnut tree avenue on the way to the station so dry they looked like marbled paper. One fell on Mary's foot as if to nudge her into response. She dropped behind Ted and quickly and guiltily popped it into her bag. A talisman against evil spirits.

It was raining in London, cold water sliding down the windows of first one train and then, after they had scuttled through tube lines from one station to another, down the sides of another.

'Your sister will be pleased to see you,' suggested Ted tentatively as Mary stared at the moving, partly rain-curtained world. 'I expect you've been to her house before.'

'Only once. A long time ago. When I first,' she hesitated, 'came out.' Ted looked down tactfully. 'Then I found the caravan,' continued Mary, 'and after a while she and Rob began to visit me twice a year.' Again she turned to the window.

'And now you want to know about your daughter's baby?' Ted prompted her, understanding that this rain-enveloped no-man's land was releasing her into an unusual freedom of speech. But this time Mary was brief.

'Yes.' This subject was still taboo.

Their journey ended after an hour but it was still drizzling as they waited outside the station for a taxi.

'Our train back is at 5.30 p.m.,' said Ted, thinking Mary needed this life-line of return. The rain was flattening and darkening the hair round her high unlined forehead.

The taxi passed through the main street of the town which, despite the weather, was crowded with shoppers.

'Of course, they don't know we're coming,' said Ted, suddenly.

'I wrote to Janice.'

'Not to tell her you were visiting.'

'That's her fault. She didn't answer my letter.'

'But they might not be there!' Ted felt a little desperate at Mary's lack of realism. He blamed himself for failing to protect her from this possibility but she had thrown the plan at him so suddenly.

They moved into a country road on the outskirts of town and their driver waited for instructions. He was a suspicious Sussex man, doubting that this odd couple knew where they were going. His radio squawked on and off.

'Look! Look!' Mary interrupted it shrilly. There was Rob driving along in front of them. 'Just follow that car.'

Rob missed Janice particularly when he did the Saturday shop. He thought, What is the point of working all your life for your family, for your wife, your two children and one extra, if you found yourself all on your own unloading the groceries and then for the rest of the day ahead?

The taxi shot behind him into his driveway just as he opened the boot of his car. At least it had stopped raining. Mary lost her nerve at the last minute so Rob saw Ted peering out of the window of the taxi, a total stranger as far as he knew, although the face seemed vaguely familiar. Ted was silent, just not up to explaining who he was. Mary huddled in the back seat.

'Are you looking for someone?' called Rob.

But by then Ted had thought of paying off the driver. Rob marched up to the taxi and said crossly, 'I think you've come to the wrong house.' Mary's round blue eyes stared up at him. Rob felt a terrible pallor and leant against the side of the house.

'Janice didn't answer my letters.' Mary was unblinking, steady, although her heart galloped and pounded. Rob's face was a blur to her but she knew why she was there. 'You see, I wanted to know about Sissie's baby.'

Rob's brain whirled in confusion. He was trying to make himself tell her the tragedy of Janice's death and she had come to hear about the birth of Sissie's child. Sissie had a baby. He could tell her that. Why did Mary remind him so strongly of Janice now? She never had before; before, she had been a dull, featureless mass.

'I've got another job, you know.' The driver turned impatiently.

Rob opened the car door so that Mary could stumble out. Her bad leg had stiffened so much on the journey she could hardly stand. She clutched onto Rob for support but to him it felt like the clawing hand of emotion. He should have answered her letters. Anything was better than this visit. Oh, how he hated the pull and muddle of misery! They had done their duty by Mary, more than their duty.

'Was the baby born?' pleaded Mary, catching his pain. 'Was it all right?'

Ted stood at a respectful distance. He had watched such scenes played out in prison often enough but now he suffered for Mary.

'Come in.' Rob led the way, abandoning the groceries, the still open car. For a methodical man this was near a breakdown.

The first thing Mary noticed about the house was the black cat. 'So like mine!' she exclaimed.

'She was a stray,' Rob said, looking down as if he didn't really see her although she was rubbing herself against his legs.

'So was mine!' Mary was even more excited. 'You know, Janice and I always had a black cat when we were children. We said it brought us luck. Where is Janice?'

Rob began to cry, not quietly but loud, frame-shaking sobs. Mary stared in horror. Ted came and took her arm. Rob sat on the floor, where they were in the hallway. He had never cried like this since her death. It was the thought of her childhood that had done for him and Mary looking so like her now.

Mary sat down beside him and eventually he managed to say that word 'cancer' and at last Mary knew she must turn her mind round from happy thoughts of a granddaughter to the unexpected loss of a sister. The possibility of happiness had appeared so recently and so tentatively that it did not take much effort to enter into Rob's grief. She looked up at Ted for reassurance and there he was, serious but as solid as ever. She must not be swallowed up by grief because this time she would not blame herself, not even as undeserving survivor.

She held Rob – it was so odd to feel someone else's pain – and she told him she was so very, very sorry. As often as he told her, sobbingly, about the suddenness of the illness, of the speed with which death had followed, she told him how very, very sorry she was. But still she waited to be told about Sissie's baby.

Ted found his way to the kitchen and made tea for them all and then he found Rob's whisky bottle ready to hand and put a drop of that in. He fed the cat too and waited for Rob and Mary.

Rob felt light-headed after all his crying. He staggered into the kitchen like someone already drunk and wiped his eyes on a kitchen towel. He looked twenty years younger than the man who had approached his groceries. He felt both ashamed of his outburst and proud. He felt shaky, released and, after he had had a sip of his tea, just about giggly.

'It's the relief, I suppose,' he apologized. 'I had to stay strong in front of the children and I've been on my own so much.'

'I am Janice's sister.' Mary sipped her own tea. Now she had to ask. 'And Sissie? Did she have her baby?'

'Oh, yes! A little girl, called Petra after a priest she knew in Brazil.' Rob was enthusiastic, fast entering a high. Janice was dead. Now he had taken on the great black beast. Now he would look beyond it.

'She must like Brazil very much to give up Paris for it,' Mary probed.

'Brazil?' Rob looked at her, puzzled. But did she not know?

'Ted and I looked up Manaus in his atlas.'

'But she isn't in Manaus. She lives only half an hour's drive away. They live—' Rob stopped abruptly. Of course, Mary knew nothing about Sissie's circumstances and he was not going to go through another death with her, even if neither of them knew the man. He would drive her to visit Sissie and the baby. In his new spirit of openness he would say, this is the moment to introduce mother to daughter and granddaughter. He would play an all-powerful God and make right what was wrong. How pleased Janice should be with him! He could feel her approval now, making the sun come through the windows, the cat purr, her sister and her friend – he just about remembered Ted now – smile.

'I'll take you to see them!' he shouted, as if announcing victory.

Groceries still not unloaded, the three drove along narrow lanes, up hills so steep and through villages that insisted they were real and not part of commuter belt (which they were). The fields, trees, hedges, verges, refreshed by the rain and now dried by the sun, also played a game of pretence, that winter was not breathing down their necks.

Mary crouched in the back of the car while the men, Rob still exhilarated, renewed their acquaintance. They liked each other at once – both practical men fighting for order against the randomness of destiny. Or so they thought. They would also have agreed, if they had been capable of such a discussion, which they weren't, analysis running counter to their nature, that women were the cause of it all – destiny, that is. All, all. If Mary had been part of such a discussion, quite impossible, and if she had pointed out that a man, her husband, had started the chain of events that led to them sitting in this car, defrosting groceries spilling wantonly about her, both men would have neither denied nor accepted. Sympathy they could give but deeper layers of emotion told them that women were at the heart of the matter.

'Nearly there!' announced Rob, jovially. 'Let's hope we don't meet an oncoming coal lorry.'

Mary put her head between her knees, not because she feared

the oncoming coal lorry – to end her days under a layer of black dust held no terrors for her – but because she felt sick. Then she was sick, luckily into one of the grocery bags.

His mood somewhat deflated, Rob stopped the car. They all stood outside, already in the valley Sissie loved, with the sun turning the bracken on one flank a fiery orange. 'I'm sorry. I'm so nervous.' She paused, lowered her voice to a whisper. 'Are you going to tell? Who I am?'

Rob looked taken aback. Somehow he had felt that revelation, truth, was part of the deal, that without any action on his side, any difficult passing of information, all would be gloriously, even magically clear. Somewhere, in the uncoiled tails of his mind, was the sense that this strike to right the course of perverted fate would make more sense of Janice's death.

Mary being sick over his frozen, actually, soggy, peas – she had not noticed them still at the bottom of the bag – did not quite fit into this uplifting scenario. Neither did the nitty-grittiness of her question. He could not answer it. 'The bungalow's on the edge of the village. Why don't we walk?'

They walked, Mary hobbling on her bad leg. Ted held the bag of vomit until they could find a place to dump it without despoiling the countryside. It has to be admitted that the day was becoming rather too much for him.

Thus they arrived at the cottage. 'Of course, Sissie likes to lead her own life.' Outside the small front door with its ugly glass panels, Rob's optimistic pink gauze began to curl up at the edges. 'I suppose it's a couple of months or more since I last saw her.'

A face swam, magnified and distorted, behind the thick glass. Mary clutched Ted's hand, unfortunately the one fingertip holding the plastic bag which then dropped to the ground. The door opened. An old woman with grey hair, a petal-soft wrinkled face and sharp eyes stared at them in astonishment.

Rob gaped, Mary cried out, Ted tried to kick the bag behind him.

'We're looking for – for my daughter,' Rob managed eventually.

The woman smiled understandingly, rose with school-teacher's confidence above the oddness of their appearance. 'Sissie, dear Sissie. And such a lovely baby. Well done!'

'Well done,' repeated Mary wonderingly.

'But I'm afraid she's not here any more. Last I heard she was down at the pub . . .' She stopped. Mary, shaking visibly, had turned and was hobbling fast down the path. Abandoning the bag, Ted hastened after her. Rob was left to make his apologies and reject kindly offers of tea.

'I'm so sorry.' Mary stood in the road. 'I thought she, Sissie,' she pronounced the name with difficulty, 'was going to open the door.'

'We all did,' said Ted soothingly.

Rob caught them up, definitely subdued, and they set off again along the lane. The sun was still bright on the hillside but it was dark and cold where they walked. Sunlight glinted off the top of the pub, however, and although it was not open it looked welcoming enough. For a moment, all three of them, catching each other's image, saw Sissie smiling and waving from an upper window. Simultaneously they watched her change into the moving shadow of leaves from an overhanging tree.

Rob knocked at the door. Mary frowned in concentration, took a step backwards and then her brow cleared. She had understood that Sissie was not there for her. Not today.

This time they did accept the landlady's invitation to tea, generous enough as they'd interrupted her afternoon nap. They sat in the dim lounge, which smelled of centuries of beer-quaffing, and drank tea that seemed to have a beery flavour.

'She went quite suddenly a few weeks ago.' The landlady was used to chatting in a group with people she had never met before. She made quite a story of it. Lovely Sissie, ex-super model, 'although you'd never think it now, except for her height – quite a giant actually. And that dear little baby. (Petra, she called her. Petra Amazonia Howard. Quite a mouthful.) I certainly took to that baby. Otherwise I'd never have had them staying here. Babies and pubs don't mix. My own children are long grown up. But Sissie loved this village and I was sorry for her having no husband. My own left me, you know, when my two were three and four. If I hadn't inherited a bit of money I don't know where I'd be.'

At this point Rob, as father, could hardly help feeling a reproach aimed his way. He glanced at Mary to see her reaction but she seemed calm, unmoved by the story, as if she were hardly listening.

'She worked a bit for me too. Helped out when I was busy.'

Rob tried and failed to see Sissie behind a bar.

'So I have to admit I was surprised when she upped and offed, just like that. No goodbyes. She didn't confide in me but we got on well enough. She took my pram, too.'

'Your pram?' Rob looked interested and Mary gave the word her attention.

'Just my old potato pram I'd lent her. She was going off for an outing, you see, and I wanted to encourage her. "You can't be a hermit all your life, I told her."'

Rob looked serious. 'So I owe you for a pram.'

'Oh, no. The pram came back.'

'Came back?'

'It was brought back. Come and see. It's in the yard. Quite an attraction.'

The landlady, an imposing figure in tightly corseting jeans, took them through to the yard. They trailed behind, like tourists who'd already seen too much.

'There!' The landlady pointed, not that there was any need. The pram, painted dark blue and decorated with silver stars, shone out among the dingy piles of kegs and crates. In it, banked in a fabulous array of subtle pallor, were flowers that must and could only be orchids.

'Wow!' said Ted, impressed.

'Quite,' agreed the landlady. 'It arrived on a lorry a few days after she left. A sort of thank you, I suppose.'

'But not a word from Sissie herself?' Rob enquired again to make certain.

'Not a word.'

Mary cleared her throat, 'So Sissie has disappeared?'

The landlady, who was more awake than ever now, shook her head decisively. 'Disappeared? Oh, no. I wouldn't say that. Not at all. If I'd thought that, I'd have called the police. No. She's just somewhere else, isn't she? My worry is how to look after these orchids. They're nearly as much trouble as children, you know. One of my regulars suggested I put them up for raffle. So I expect that's what I'll do. For the church roof fund. I'm sure Sissie wouldn't mind. It's Anglo-Saxon.'

Chapter Thirty-One

In which Sissie is a Supplicant in Paris and Bianca suggests a Role for a Motherly Model.

T HE AUTHOR had risen in Sissie's estimation for not only had he whispered, 'Paris,' in her ear at the right moment (admittedly for the price of his age-speckled hand being laid on her lactating bosom) but he had also given her a purseful of cash, just like in a fairy story. 'Americans never look after their widows generously,' he had said, inspiring a sad tear in one eye and an angry tear in the other because it wasn't poor Howard's fault that she had decided to give away her money. She did not at all mind taking the Author's ill-gotten gains, however, and tucked the notes in her bosom as she thrust his hand back where it belonged. She would transfer them to her little sling-bag – the same she had worn through all her adventures.

Sissie went through the Tunnel to France. Petra and she, with their cash funding, boarded the train in that station greenhouse at Waterloo and arrived at another station in Paris. They were aligned, so Sissie vaguely imagined, with Dick Whittington and his cat and all the generations of young and hopefuls who set off for The or A Capital assuming the streets to be paved with gold. It was an odd alignment for a woman who had been queen of Paris, or at least a part of it, for over four years.

The difference, so simple, was that then her fame had happened to her. Others had had the will and she had been their magnificent puppet. Now it was her will, and she and Petra would survive or not by the choices she made. The immediate step was to call her agent.

278

'Non! Non! Non, non! Madame est occupée. C'est Sissie? Pas possible. Sissie est morte.'

This was the assistant assistant secretary to Sissie's agent, Madame B., who had marketed her for stardom, spun gold out of her remarkably lengthy looks and pursued her greedily when Rudolf's death seemed to have turned her off public performance. Letters from her still arrived, unknown to Sissie, at the horse-filled flat, now occupied by a minor academic, female, of the Sorbonne, who felt threatened by even such tenuous proximity with a super-model and made no attempt at returning to sender.

Such rejection was so unusual in Madame B.'s life that it was no wonder that her staff eventually received the impression that Sissie was not merely errant but dead. There was no other sensible explanation for her dereliction to the duty of making Madame B. more and more millions of francs.

'I'm not dead!' cried Sissie, in English because her French was a little rusty and she knew that all Madame B.'s assistants spoke several European languages – such was the pull of glamour for even the best educated. 'I'm so alive I arrived on the train from London just a few minutes ago.'

But Madame B.'s assistant assistant secretary merely assumed she was dealing with a nutter and put down the telephone. It was only two or three days later that she jokingly mentioned to the assistant secretary that someone calling herself Sissie had rung and the assistant secretary casually passed on this faintly amusing fact to the top assistant, who chanced to mention it to Madame B. as they sat in the bar of the Ritz, waiting for the repair of a fused lighting system during the pret-à-porter shows.

'Sissie?' Her eyes glittered savagely, in the way they did when a particularly large cheque came into the office.

'Sissie, super-model,' elaborated the top assistant, who was called Bianca.

'Sissie was unique.' Madame held up her martini glass as if in homage. 'For four years, she was at the top of her profession. Our profession. She made more money for me than all the other girls put together. She was magic. But now she is dead. You hear? Dead.'

'Magic?' queried the assistant, who was Greek and built like a statue.

Sissie, meanwhile, was saving her wads by renting a mean apartment in Rue Mouffetard, which might have seemed attractively bohemian with its little iron-railed balcony and its surround of winding medieval streets were it not for Petra's presence, which demanded all sorts of unsightly objects, such as potties, nappies, bottles, tins of filthy-smelling nourishing messes and – this a new acquisition – a push-chair. Having a baby seemed to be a full-time job, which it had not been in the larger confines of her country cottage or even her room in the pub. Besides, every day was colder, wetter and windier than the last and, if Petra did not go out regularly, she cried. So did Sissie.

In calmer moments, she tried to recall all the grand people who had courted her in her great days but all she could remember was trying to avoid them and going back to her strangely secluded life with Sebastien. She did not yet admit the fear that the Sissie whose body she now inhabited was not very like the one so admired previously. This thought she put from her, the day-to-day living enough to occupy her, her ambition focused solely on getting through to Madame B. It was only at night, between sleeping and waking, that an image of her final, fatal catwalk came to trouble her.

Sissie pushed Petra down the Avenue Montaigne. They were both dressed to kill in gleaming black – particularly striking, Sissie thought, on a rose-cheeked Anglo-American baby. It was a gesture towards widowhood and also reflected a first intimation that her shape had undergone a real change. Of course, she had hardly ever – more probably, never – bought off-the-peg in Paris, having been offered haute couture samples as a walking advertisement, so she was not at all clear about regular sizing, but it seemed that she was being shown towards a rail in the far reaches of the shop and that even then nothing very much would close round her bosom. Bravely, she reminded herself that the French were meagrely formed waist up and that bosoms were 'in', or so she had read in magazines conscientiously bought for research. Black lacing, she decided, rather than safety-pins, was the answer to far-reaching gaps.

There were no obvious guards to Madame B.'s sanctum, no growling mastiffs at the bottom of the stone steps that rose from an elegant courtyard where the urns were watered by the disappointed tears of young hopefuls. Madame was a power, dispensing success or failure. At the top of the steps was the heavy door and beyond that the row of rooms full of secretaries, and they did snarl through their sharp faces: terrier-like they sapped the confidence of visitors and few were strong enough to blow over the little rooms like a pack of cards.

In her prime, Sissie had done just that, without even knowing what she was about. Rooms and secretaries folded up before her platform-shoed progress. But times had changed, and she knew to be wary. Shutting up the push-chair and propping it behind a stone cupid, Sissie crept round the back of the courtyard until she reached a small door, known to hardly any, a service staircase that led up to a corridor and thence, via the toilettes, to a back door and Madame B.'s inner sanctum. Sissie knew it because this was the way she had been bustled out (and then through the dustbins onto the street) in the heyday of her fame, when photographers could keep their children in private education by snapping a revealing shot of the agency's star.

Then she had not noticed the dank odour, the murky greenness, the insalubrious dripping and scurrying. Now she could only sympathize as Petra began to snivel, her nose running as if she had caught an instant cold. 'Ssh, darling, ssh.'

Through the not-very-clean-either toilets they went, the crop-haired black giant with the yellowish face – her sunburn was fading – and her black-clad baby with a runny nose.

'Merde! Shit! Merde!' Madame B., surreptitiously snaffling soft-centred Belgian chocolates, fell back in her dominating leather chair and nearly choked at the ghastly apparition.

'I have returned!' cried Sissie in English, head hitting the jamb of the little side door from which she was making her entrance.

'Wah!' cried Petra, in an internationally recognized language of outrage.

Madame B., diverted by the need to conceal the silver-spangled box in a locked drawer, could hardly take in what she was seeing. She certainly did not identify her former money-spinner.

'I do not allow les enfants ici!' she squelched, mouth still clogged with delicious goo. She pressed a button, which would summon two or three secretaries, believing that either a madman intent on non-erotic strangulation had climbed in through her window or that she was having a heart attack and hallucinating monsters.

'But, Madame, it is Sissie!'

'Sissie!' Madame snorted in powerful disbelief. 'Sissie est morte! Sissie is dead!' She pulled on her trademark white gloves over sticky fingers. Except for her height, this ogre with squalling baby had nothing in common with the fine wondrousness of Sissie. 'I know your type,' she snarled scornfully. 'You are the sort of sad creature who arises in the wake of the tragic death of the famous. Do you know how many Anastasias there have been since her murder at the hands of revolutionary anti-royalists?'

Sissie felt confused. It *is* confusing to be accused of pretending to be yourself. Petra was beginning to feel heavy so she put her down on a softly padded sofa where, in years gone by, she had often entwined her length of legs while Madame threw her honey-basted encomiums. 'There you are, my sweet.' She took off the baby's black plastic coat and felt pleased to see her regain her usual good humour.

This settling in enraged Madame further. 'Do you know what Sissie was like? Mais non. Mais non, mais non! You have studied a few bad photographs – although it is true she *never* took a bad photograph. But in life, ah, she had a swan's neck, a gazelle's legs, a lion's head, a cat's hips, a . . . a . . . Eh bien, she was a composite of all that is most beautiful and elegant and natural in the animal kingdom while you . . . you . . .' Again words temporarily failed her.

So far the unreality of the situation had given Sissie a certain armour but this personalized venom was harder to sustain. Meanwhile, Bianca had arrived at the door. However, seeing Madame in full flow, she hesitated. It was Madame's prerogative not to be interrupted.

'Mais vous . . . vous . . . vous êtes dégoutante, disgusting, vulgar, your peau is like cow's 'ide, your cheveux like wiry wool, vos yeux commes les petits pois, et votre poitrine – your bosom is monstrous, malformé, the poitrine of a rhinoceros, a hippopotamus, and where there should be the sinuosities of youth, of a waist fit to be girdled like the great goddess Atalanta, you have nothing, or rather everything, an expanding roll of mountainous' – her voice rose to a shriek, expressing deep-felt horror and revulsion – 'FLESH!'

Now Bianca and the other assistants did rush forward because Madame's usually beige complexion had turned purple and her eyes bulged alarmingly. Pustules of sweat glared from her excitedly open pores. She was not a nice sight.

'De l'eau,' commanded one.

'Du vin,' suggested another.

Sissie sank down beside Petra, who was entertaining herself by chewing the braided corner of a Louis XV cushion. She was far too shocked to do anything but sit because she realized that Madame, monstrous and vile as she was (but she had always been that, even when exuding adulation), was also right. She was not that Super-model Sissie. She could barely remember her, dim, slim, smooth, cold creature from the past.

Sissie gathered up Petra and rose. They all stared and for a second the accretions of the last years disappeared and in her graceful dignity they saw Sissie the Super-model. Bianca, in particular, stared, and her pale olive cheeks deepened to rose. Then Madame, held up on either side, dispelled the magic. 'And your teeth,' she growled. 'Vos dents sont dégueulasses!'

As Sissie and Petra walked back along the Rue St Honoré it started to rain. Sissie pushed energetically, enjoying, with masochistic satisfaction, the water dripping off her feathered hair and down her neck. She suspected that her tawdry black garment, on becoming wet, would stain her skin. Certainly her mascara would ooze familiarly about her cheeks. Looking down, she saw that her breasts were as hard as twin warheads which reminded her that she hadn't fed Petra for hours. Yet she had fallen asleep, securely sheltered under the hood of the push-chair.

Sissie made her way to the river and watched the rain bounce on its shiny surface like water off a duck's back. Water, always water. Should she take the hysterical rejection of her interview as the final chapter in the autobiography of a super-model? With wet, cold fingers, she extracted her little bag and counted the money. Why was she fooling herself that she had a choice in the matter?

Baby bottles had joined nappies in the not-so-romantic garret. To Sissie's mortification Petra took to the Lait Bébé at once, greedily slurping at the rubber nozzle which allowed her so much more milk at a time and soon learning to hold the container with her fat little hands. Sissie, weak from lack of food, breasts aching from unwanted milk (although they were already beginning to soften round the edges like balloons losing air), skin plastered with purifying masks and creams, lay on the bed and watched her. Such vitality! Such contentment! There was a knock at the door.

This was a unique happening. No one visited them; they visited no one. Perhaps a complaint from one of the flats below. Sissie opened the door. A well-turned-out young woman, in Parisian style with the good handbag, good shoes of a matron and the neatly clasped waist of a schoolgirl, stood with an expectant smile.

'Je suis Bianca.' She spoke as if confident of recognition.

Sissie frowned, which cracked her white face mask like railway lines in snow. Did she know a Bianca? Had she ever known a Bianca? The girl had straight, camel-coloured hair, as fine and glossy as a paintbrush.

'I work for Madame Bertrand. In the past, I was nothing. Now I am her assistant.' She hesitated. Once more her pale face glowed as if a lamp had been put on under the skin. 'I was there the night, la nuit tragique, la nuit de mort . . .'

Oh, that old night, thought Sissie, closing her eyes, for, after all, there had been other tragedies since. And that Bianca: now she remembered her, cowering somewhere under the wisps of chiffon as she snatched them from the rails and used them to staunch her wounds.

'Entrez,' said Sissie graciously. 'I remember you.'

Swinging her paintbrush head deferentially, Bianca entered the tiny room. Her manners were good, Sissie saw, because she showed no signs of dismay at the squalid surroundings, Sissie's own unaesthetic appearance or at greedy Petra who, having emptied her bottle, flung it to the floor with a howl of rage and disbelief.

'It was I who picked up the heel when it fell from Rudolf's lifeless hand and rolled under the chair.' She made a move as if to open her handbag.

'I don't think I want to hear about this.' Sissie turned away from her visitor and gazed out of the window.

'It is understood. I am silent.' Bianca sat on a corner of Petra's chair and dangled a bracelet in front of the baby so that she stopped crying and began to chew it instead. 'I was in Madame B.'s when you came a few days ago.'

'I hope your employer had a heart-attack and died.' Sissie lay back on her bed. 'I may presume you're not carrying a message of shame and apology.'

'Mais non! Madame est encore furieuse! She calls you an imposter. But today she has flown to the States and she will forget.'

'So why did you come?'

'Because I believe in you.'

'Moi? Me?' Sissie began to laugh and more of her face mask cracked till she looked like the bottom of a dried-up oasis.

'You are too large, certainly, but now you are real!' In her excitement Bianca jumped up and, shedding her formality, fixed Sissie with a passionate glare. 'More important is the information que je suis arrivée pour vous dire.'

'What have you come to tell me?' Sissie was kindly, not least because humiliation tends to make people kinder (if they have kindness in them – the truly nasty get nastier still) and because this dialogue made a change from her soliloquies with Petra.

'Waldo Walenska,' Bianca's symmetrical features bunched together as she named one of the half-dozen most successful designers (his musky scent had hit the market last year like a Dyno-rod, carrying all before it), 'is looking for a number-one more-mature model. I knew at once you were the one. And I knew it even more when I visited my mother and mentioned your reappearance and she, herself, without any prompting declaimed, "Ah, *that one* is who Waldo searches. We must yank them together."'

In a flash of past times Sissie now remembered that Bianca, so humble and unimportant, had also been the daughter of a Greek shipping magnate who financed his wife's principal occupation of buying haute couture with the exact equivalent of what he spent on his mistresses. He had many very expensive mistresses.

'And does your mother buy at Waldo Walenska?'

'Bien sûr. She is besotted. She spends more than a fortune. But she detests and despises these spindly young models. She calls them pin girls and stick insects, and says she will not attend another show if Waldo cannot find better. By better, she means bigger.'

Sissie longed to be convinced. She looked at her feet on which she had just used a grater to pare callouses as you would deal with the disobliging bits of a carrot or a potato. 'Do you remember Jerry Hall? How we young ones laughed at her thickening waist and wrinkled elbows! And she a great beauty. No, I must be as skinny as the youngest.'

'You are wrong, Sissie. You have been away. Times have changed. Money commands the world now. The world must listen when my father's money speaks. Rappelez-vous que je vous apporte l'espoir!'

Sissie studied Bianca with new attention. She saw that something powerful shone about her, not the aura of a giant like Father Pedro but the sparkling confidence of a fairy godmother.

'And remember,' Bianca pointed to where Petra, bracelet round her own little wrist, slept contentedly, 'your baby is your passport to maturity. I must go now – I have an appointment with my tutor.'

'With your tutor?' Sissie was surprised enough to question.

'He is teaching me about Blue-footed Boobies.'

'But? But . . .' But before Sissie could produce Sebastien's name, Bianca had click-clacked out of the apartment on her matronly shoes and shut the door. Sissie was left to ask herself how many people in her life could be interested in Blue-footed Boobies without being in touch with each other.

Well. Well. Sissie rose from the bed and went to assess herself in the mirror. She received a nasty shock for the mobility of her mask had led her to forget its presence and she found herself staring at a shattered window in which one feature stood out, a lumpy, yellowish, prominent and imperfectly angled tooth. Tears sprang out of her eyes causing new decorative squiggles to her face. Somehow she, unlike Madame B., had overlooked the tooth of the matter, the fact that this quick-fill lump of concrete was nowhere near as good as the temporary one and not a patch on the pearly wonder so lovingly cast and ordered by Plumb.

Plumb! That, of course, was the answer. He must make her another. Her father would order it with emergency stickers and, unlike previously, she would have it inserted here in Paris. Sissie consulted a calendar taped to the wall. The haute-couture shows, in which she hoped to display her remade self, were early the following year. It was a race, she saw, picking up a celery stick and demolishing it as if she were a sink-disposal unit.

Bianca might be only a little rich girl playing games in the fashion industry, she thought, as she washed off her mask so that her little basin ran white, but that was what the industry was all about.

Chapter Thirty-Two

In which Ted is Hopeful and Mary is Doubtful.

'THE WORLD is your oyster!' Ted cried, and passed over his savings account to Mary. 'I have been waiting all these years to spend it on someone I loved, and our honeymoon is a most fitting occasion.' His face became almost handsome with the pleasure of generosity.

'An oyster,' repeated Mary, and she pictured a pearl nestling in an oyster shell like a baby in a womb and then she thought of Paris. 'Perhaps we should go to Paris,' she suggested, with due timidity. For too many years she had dreamed (or rather suppressed her dreams) of that radiant city which had made Sissie, her daughter, Sissie – now she would say it – fashion queen, queen of beauty.

'Paris is the place for a honeymoon par excellence,' announced Ted solemnly.

Each dark evening they made their plans. First, Ted had to throw off the dull look that came from his work in prison. 'They want me to be a gaoler, Mary, and I cannot be that any more,' he confided in her. She knew that she was the reason he could no longer be a gaoler, something no man should be, and she was pleased. Then they ate, for Mary, much to Ted's surprise and delight, had begun to cook tasty little meals. Eventually they settled side by side on a sofa and they looked at travel brochures – such brochures, promising such unimaginable entertainments! Like a double-act Rip Van Winkle, asleep for twenty years and re-entering the world with gusto, they pored over 'Candlelit dinner for two with real French escargots, steak flambé and soufflé aux fraises des bois'. They agreed that top priority would be the 'Starlit Drive for two in a horse-drawn cabriolet'. They deliberated but came to no conclusion about 'The Alternative Folies Bergères – two hundred years of tradition goes one hundred per cent better!' They spread photographs of hotels across the table as Mary had once spread photographs of Sissie, and thought perhaps the two nicest and not too pricey either were the Hôtel Angleterre, which had balconies, and the Hôtel Napoleon Bonaparte, which boasted an elegantly carved roof. When they caught each other's eye, they smiled and made extra cups of tea to calm themselves. Mary even bought a *Teach Yourself French* book and mocked Ted with his terrible pronunciation, for at least she had learnt it at school.

The only fly in the ointment was the reason for all this celebration: their marriage. It was not even the marriage itself. Mary could not imagine that a legal document would change their comfortable togetherness. She had total trust in Ted. But she knew there would be need before for the Confession. She must lay her nightmare before him and test how lenient his loving made him.

Yet, instead, she laughed over brochures, and agreed that their first dinner out should be at the Café Toulouse-Lautrec where 'the artist's famous paintings come to life with the colourful clientele'. She laughed, and at the end of one evening she found that she was holding hands with Ted and that she wanted to be closer to him. So they put off the light with slow rather solemn movements, hiding the excitement underneath, and went up the stairs together, hand in hand, like Adam and Eve in Paradise.

Except it wasn't like that. For one thing, a woman of over fifty who hasn't slept with a man for over twenty years hardly feels able to cast off her clothes and jump into bed. Which was probably just as well or Ted would have fled in terror. So they both remained sober and put on their cosy night clothes separately. But all the same, they did get into bed together and Ted stroked Mary's face.

'You're beautiful,' he said.

And Mary realized she was, or rather she had been, and now, under Ted's gentle attention, was getting a little of it back again. However, the associations of being beautiful were not altogether good. Her husband had thought her beautiful. Although not very sensitive himself, he had seen her beauty reflected in other men's eyes of admiration. He had become jealous of her and his jealousy had spread to the girls.

'I'd rather not be beautiful,' Mary said, secure in Ted's arms.

Mary was still too much of a mystery for Ted to mind about that. He tried to kiss her cheek but their noses got in the way. 'I'm a bit rusty at this sort of thing.'

'You sound like the Tin Man.' Mary was languid and happy again now she had sorted out that point about beauty. She could feel Ted's heart beating, his warm dry skin, his breath, his solid love.

'I always liked that show, *The Wizard of Oz.*'

'My girls loved—' Mary gasped, aghast at what she was saying. That was before time had stopped. She didn't look at those happier times. That would be unbearable.

Ted held her. Knowing so little, he held her. How could there be a better moment for a confession? Perhaps on the cliffs, standing apart, the wind blowing half her words away. Confessions led to intimacy. Did she want intimacy with this man, this man's body? Anyone's body, if it came to that. Hadn't she wanted to cast off even the weight of her own body often enough over the last twenty years?

Ted nuzzled against her neck. Humbly. There was no black fierceness in him as there had been in her husband. At first she had liked it, been excited by the dark hairs on his body, the sharp angles of his bones so little covered with flesh, his passion for her softness, his need to be inside her, forcing her down on the bed. Not rape but something she should have been frightened of, wary. She should have known how bad it would turn. She did eventually, but by then it was too late. She had felt trapped, helpless, hopeless. He had still felt that need for her. She had felt sorry for him and she had felt excited too. That was the true confession.

Why had she not taken the girls and abandoned him? Protected them from him and him from himself? She had not been crazy like him. Instead there had been two deaths. How could she ever lose the burden of that guilt, try to shuffle some off on this kindly man?

Violently, Mary flung aside the bedclothes and stood trembling by the bed. She must go at once, back to her caravan, live alone with her cats like the witch she was.

'What's the matter?' Ted sat up and stared at her in the darkness. He had known these moments before when people, women, had left

290

him. But he had felt more secure this time, expecting so little, proceeding with such caution.

'I can't! I can't!'

'That's all right. I didn't mean anything. I just wanted to hold you.'

He didn't understand. He thought it was sex she was frightened of. Well, perhaps she was but that was only a tiny thing beside the great mountain of her guilt, her despair.

'You don't understand!'

'Tell me.' Ted sat up straight and still. All along he had approached her quietly, waiting.

'I can't!' she still screamed. And then whispered, 'It's too bad.'

'Tell me. Sit down.'

'I can't.' It was true. Her body was too rigid to bend.

'I know you were in prison. I'm not frightened of that. I see prisoners every day. Some are bad, some have bad luck.'

'Far worse.'

'I know you have a beautiful daughter.'

There was a long silence. 'I had two beautiful daughters.'

A terrible fear made Ted's body chill. Had she killed her own daughter? No one could recover from that. 'What happened?'

Words rushed through Mary's mouth, gushed and tumbled. 'Ever since that day it's all pretence, any happiness, that is. At least I made sure she never knew, never saw me again, my little one, my little darling, my sweet Sissie who watched it – watched it, do you hear? I should have died too. I knew it. I tried often but they stopped me. Why? I don't know and then I was too tired to do it. For a long time they gave me pills. Pills. Pills. Pills. In one prison, hospital, prison, I don't know the difference and then they let me out and by then I couldn't do it, so I removed myself, that was the very best thing and she, Sissie, didn't know me, she knew Janice. I was never even tempted to see her, I tried to stop Jan telling me about her and then . . . and then . . .'

'What happened?' Ted asked again, the chill still at his heart.

'What happened?' Mary was gasping, bewildered with her thoughts.

'What happened the day your other daughter died?'

291

Mary stared but could only see the pallor of Ted's pyjamas. 'He killed Lou and I killed him.' She sat then, collapsed on the bed. The nightmare was out, never spoken before.

Ted breathed very slowly, trying not to make it sound like relief. He mustn't do that to her. 'There,' he said. 'There you are.' But he didn't try to touch her. There was a long silence.

Mary's confessional rush changed to a string of staccato sentences, sometimes with long, painful intervals between them. 'He wasn't so evil as all that. He was unbalanced. He loved me too much. He began to hate Lou because I loved her. Sissie hid under the table. He was evil. Sissie was good at hiding. She grew up hiding. But it worked. He hardly noticed her. He didn't care about her. That was a bit of luck for her. That night, though, I thought he might go for her. There were her big eyes watching from under the table and when she screamed I thought he might turn his attentions to her.'

'You were defending her. A mother has to defend her children.'

'It was too late for Lou. I was covered with her blood. My own daughter's. I can never forget. Not for one instant. It's not true I was defending Sissie when I picked up the knife. I wanted to kill him. I hated him. I am a murderer too. I was determined to kill him. I wanted him dead.' She stopped again as if she could not go on. A new confession.

Ted was not going to think of her as a murderer. 'You were defending your child, yourself. He was a madman. You're not a murderer.'

'He'd dropped the knife. I picked it up.'

'He might have picked it up again.'

'Sissie watched her mother kill her father. She wasn't too young to know what she was seeing.'

'She was only little. Little girls forget.'

'No. I've seen it in those photographs. In her eyes. So big. Great empty holes, frightened to see. She hasn't forgotten.'

Ted could think of nothing to say. Mary was so certain. Did a little child remember such a horror or was it too much for memory?

'Janice wanted her to know about me but I wouldn't let her.'

'But, Mary, we went looking for Sissie only a few weeks ago.'

'I hadn't decided what I would tell her. I just wanted to see her.

292

I owed it to Janice. No. I just wanted to see her. I wanted to see if she knew, if she recognized it was me. Her mother.'

'We'll find her.' Ted was pleased to discover something positive he could help with. He could see Mary slumping exhaustedly on the edge of the bed.

'I don't think so. I don't know.'

'Come to bed now.'

She was so tired it was easy to lie in his arms now. Easy even to fall asleep.

Chapter Thirty-Three

*In which Plumb re-enters the story, Sebastien studies the
Blue-footed Booby and Bianca sends a Fax.*

R OB PICKED up his post. There was very much less of it since
Janice's death, sometimes none at all. She had been the one
with friends and contacts and things in train. Soon Ruth would finish
university and, if she could find a job nearby, she would come and
live with him. If not, at least she'd be there at the weekends. Rob
opened the top letter without noticing it.

Dear Dad. I need a bit of help, just a little but I'm afraid you
won't like it. I want you to go to Plumb, yes, wicked Mr Plumb,
the dentist, seducer of young women and anyone else available,
and get him to send the mould of my front tooth to the above
address. I'd do it myself but that harridan housekeeper he's
taken up with won't let me through to him on the telephone.
Petra and I are very well but I need the tooth mould urgently
as I'm returning to my old profession and just occasionally I am
forced to smile. I hope you are well and not too lonely. I
suppose you see a lot of Ruth and Adam. My apologies for
giving you such an unenviable task. Your ever loving Sissie.

Rob telephoned Plumb but when he gave his name the harridan
housekeeper put down the telephone. So he went round one evening
after work. It was the week before Christmas and the high street was
decorated with plastic Christmas trees, which jutted out of the wall

294

above each shop window like a figurehead juts from the prow of a ship. Rob, cold, icy inside and out, rang the surgery bell.

Plumb, in at-home gear, a cardigan and slacks, opened the door and showed him into the waiting room whose central dried flower decoration was hung with gleaming red balls.

'I have come for Sissie's mould,' announced Rob, wanting the whole affair over as quickly as possible.

'Sissie's mould?' Oh, what a mould! Of lips and cheeks and buttocks and breasts and . . . Plumb's eyes glazed as he remembered that almost unbelievable time. He thought such swelling lewdness had been scourged from his body by the formidable Mrs Patterson but those two words, 'Sissie's mould', were enough for his lust to gleam as red, as shiny, as those balls . . .

'Yes. Her front tooth. She is in Paris. I shall send it.'

'You have an address for her?' In matters of lust Plumb made up his mind quickly, although he cast an anxious look over his shoulder as he spoke. 'Because I shall need to get it out from my files. Just give me the address and I'll send it on.'

Rob was surprised by Plumb's coolness. He had expected the man to be cowed and confused in the presence of Sissie's father but he could not appreciate the power of Plumb's longing.

'I've only her letter.'

'Tear the heading off.'

'I need it.'

'Copy it on the bottom.' Steps were approaching, giving greater urgency to Plumb's manner.

'I could send—'

'No. No. Now.' He was panting. Soon there would be that voice: 'Eddie, dear, where are you?'

Rob gave in. He wanted to be away from this lascivious monster. Plumb snatched the paper and stuffed it deep into his pocket.

'You!' said Mrs Patterson, arriving at the door.

Rob deigned no words but dashed past with the most scornful of looks. But, at the last, he turned. 'She's married,' he shouted, 'and with a lovely baby!'

*

Rob wrote to Mary. He now had the address where she lived with that strange prison officer – life is so odd, but then Janice had said that it was not so odd because it was like all patients wanting to marry their doctors. But to find him on a cliff-side!

Dear Mary,
In case you are interested, I have an address for Sissie. She is resuming her old career and she and her baby are well but I know nothing further. As ever, Rob.

Sebastien, on a remote island called Punta Pitt, in an archipelago in the Pacific, paused in writing up notes about Blue-footed Boobies. Why was he trying to please François when he was no longer part of his life? Pushing aside his pad, he began to think about the Greek shipping magnate's daughter he had met in Paris. First Sissie and then Bianca. What was it about rich women that attracted him? Must they possess money to make up for their female sex? The men he liked never had money. He had been brought up by wealthy parents so maybe he was looking for the comfort they no longer gave him.

His efforts to enter the City world of money had been disappointing. His boss had seemed to believe that he should not only do his job industriously and efficiently, which he did, but also behave and talk as if it were important, which he could not.

'Earnest, earthless, equal, attunable, vaulty, voluminous . . .'

Too much reading of a Jesuit poet, perhaps. There had also been the question of what to do with the Viking . . . He had fled to the loneliness of a Booby bonanza – there was the Masked Booby too. But now he dreamt of this Greek girl, her light, swinging hair, her black eyes, her trim figure, controlled at the waist as if a potter had held his finger at the clay just a little longer than usual.

Sebastien left his table set up under an awning of thatch as if he were a modern Robinson Crusoe and headed out along the beach. There was one stretch of shore and sea where you were as likely to see a Greek shipping magnate's daughter as a Booby. It had taken some trial and error to find it – the beastly creatures would pop out just as he felt safe – but at last he could be sure of a Booby-free swim.

Bianca sent a fax. The family ship will be cruising near Punta Pitt towards the end of December. We will send a boat to pick you up for Christmas lunch.

Chapter Thirty-Four

*In which Plumb is spurned once more and Waldo Walenska makes
Sissie and Boudicca the inspiration for his collection.*

S ISSIE WAS thinner. She pulled the tape measure tight round her
waist and gave a self-satisfied nod. Then she stood on her newly
bought weighing machine. That, too, produced a good result.
Tomorrow was Christmas Day and she would let up a little, allow
herself to share Petra's delicious chocolate yoghurt, sip the tiniest
bottle of champagne she had bought in the supermarché on the
corner. In her days of low-grade anorexia (although she had been
starving herself for a purpose rather than self immolation – had she?
hadn't she?), she would have paid heavily in self-disgust for such
indulgences.

Sissie looked at Petra sitting like a complacent Buddha, and
thought that as she became slimmer her daughter grew fatter. She
must be careful not to become one of those elegantly drawn mothers
with large ungainly daughters. Single mothers, they were most often
with no balancing male presence. A weakness, doubtless due to
starvation as she told herself, caused her to stumble towards her bed
and lie down. It would pass. She must be strong.

Snowflakes, shaped like tiny fluted bowls, floated about the dome of
Sacré Coeur, touched lightly on the Seine, sometimes dissolving in
its mass, trailed past steamed-up café windows and picked up speed
over rooftops.

Sissie was staring out of the window and a taxi drew up below her eyes. Noisy, sharp-edged, shiny, it seemed a natural enemy to the dreamy snowflakes and Sissie didn't like the look of it from the start.

Plumb got out. Plumb! Sissie rushed from the window and, with instinctive self-defence, placed a chair against her door plus weighing machine to give it substance, before it struck her that he might be transporting her mould in person.

Plumb climbed the stairs to Sissie's garret with a heart that raced and boomed, although this might have been partly due to the seventy-eight steep steps. Certainly he could not speak when he reached the top. But this might have been Sissie's appearance. No longer (but not shorter) the etiolated nymphette he had made his own, sexually speaking, here stood a woman in all the magnificence of maturity.

Overwhelmed, but again it might have been the stairs, the flight, the early rise, he tripped and fell at her feet.

'Come in, come in,' cried Sissie, impatient for her mould.

At floor level, Plumb found himself meeting the curious gaze of a large baby, sitting upright in the middle of the small room. She smiled, displaying two white teeth and a happy nature.

'I know you are married and have a baby,' mumbled Plumb, attempting to rise. 'But, oh, where is your husband?'

'Overseas,' replied Sissie, disdain outbalancing charm. She was certainly not going to tell him the truth. 'I presume you are the bearer of my mould?'

'Oh, yes. Oh, yes.' Plumb now got himself upright. 'But far, far better than that.'

'Impossible.' Sissie held out her hand.

'Between Christmas and New Year . . .' Plumb began to revive, the glow in his loins as he looked at Sissie giving a flush to his cheeks and a sheen to his dark eyes. He knew this woman's secret parts and was fool enough to let the knowledge give him confidence. '. . . New Year, I achieved the impossible. I dominated the laboratory, bullied the technicians, terrorized the secretarial staff and have produced for you, for love of you,' Plumb's voice deepened huskily, 'a new pearly white tooth!'

It came from behind his back with a flourish, rabbit out of the hat, cat out of the bag, Jack out of its box.

'I cannot thank you enough. I cannot! I cannot!' Sissie pounced on it joyfully, and almost tearfully. This was the finishing touch to her nearly made old self.

Petra, hearing her happy cry, clapped her hands and shouted, inappropriately, 'Da-da, Dada!'

'So can you pop it in?' enquired Sissie confidentially. So much easier (and cheaper) to have a dentist in her own garret than in the Avenue Kléber where she had her appointment.

'It just so happens I have Superglue and my heavy-duty removal equipment.'

'Oh, you won't need that. This old thing falls out all the time.' Sissie nonchalantly fished out the tooth, although it hardly deserved the name, and flung it into a bin.

Plumb bent over Sissie in lover's tender stance. The fact that he was inserting a false tooth did not deter a man as proud of his profession as Plumb. Besides, what delights he might be rewarded with!

'There! In a matter of minutes, it will be there for a matter of months or even years. I have a patient who did a temporary do-it-yourself job with Superglue, and three years—'

'Wonderful. Wonderful,' Sissie murmured at her reflection in the glass. At last, at very very long last. 'Plumb!' She whirled on him.

'Oh, yes.'

'Are you rich?'

'All dentists are rich. They may pretend—'

'So can you take me out to a very expensive lunch?'

'You don't understand, Sissie. I have fled Mrs Patterson, the harridan housekeeper, for you, I have driven to Heathrow Airport, I have put my car in the short-term car park, which costs twice as much as a night in the Ritz. I have burnt all sorts of boats, I am flinging myself on your mercy . . .'

Seeing he was about to fall to his knees again, Sissie became alarmed and interrupted, with a kind of practicality that Plumb did not associate with her, 'So I'll ring a taxi, as they're hardly on demand in Paris and, perhaps, book a table since my French may be less rusty than yours.'

Sissie had seen that here was an escort to take her back into the Paris she had denied. Well, life, or rather Rudolf's death, had denied her for she had been passive. She fixed on Le Télégraphe, near the

Musée d'Orsay and the most glamorous of locations because there she would be seen by those who were most fashionable, editors, designers, photographers. How she had fled those goggle-eyed wolves in the past!

Plumb, sidelined onto the bed, watched as Sissie prepared herself and Petra for the fray. All the old arts of dress and make-up were performed so that he found himself climbing into the taxi with a restored public persona.

'You did say you've got pots of money?' enquired Sissie who reeked of Jicky – a Guerlain fragrance to inform the cognoscenti that she was independent of any designer.

'Oh, yes!' But Plumb's heart was quivering nervously and when Petra was plonked on his lap in order to preserve a sheath of black satin that enclosed Sissie's middle areas – her thigh-high boots left two inches of shiny maroon-tighted leg visible – he sagged just a fraction.

Sissie's entrance caused quite a sensation. A Channel Four film unit, picking up a snatch of Parisian high life in order to attack it, was able to film her restored beauty – if significantly more of it. Her name, so ridiculous and therefore memorable, hissed about the restaurant and Plumb, following along behind, peered over Petra's downy head – she had somehow adhered to his arms – and felt like a man entering a snake pit. In this he was not far wrong since the sibilants spoke of sensational beauty but of change also. This, Sissie Slipper did not suss.

Petra, Plumb and Sissie settled down for a good blow-out, as any English family might on a winter bank holiday. Plumb, still intent on another purpose, fed Petra hugely with the idea that a full baby needs a long sleep after lunch. Meanwhile, Sissie received those admirers who approached her table with a calculated friendly freeze. Stars must not be too amenable. Thus, time passed to Sissie's satisfaction, Plumb's frustration and at his truly enormous expense. It was dark when they found themselves climbing once more into a waiting taxi. Again, Plumb carried Petra who now slept although, regular hiccups suggested, not as soundly as he would have liked.

'Where to?' asked Sissie, the attention she had been receiving from film crew and diners adding hauteur to her manner.

'Where to?' Plumb's dark eyes welled.

'Where are you staying?'

'Where? Where? I have to stay with you. I have brought your tooth in order to be with you. You are my, my—'

'That's all very well but I *hate* chutney.' Sissie looked out at the dark streets through which they moved as if they were lined with chutney.

'Chutney?'

'Chutney.'

Plumb tried to recapitulate. 'I know I used to eat a lot of cheese and chutney sandwiches. They were nutritious and easy to prepare after my wife left me.'

'I loathe and detest chutney.'

'It was only a habit,' pleaded Plumb. 'The moment Mrs Patterson came, she insisted all chutney bottles, full or empty, were put into the bottle bank.'

'Don't you understand?' Sissie became fiercer. 'To me you *are* chutney. And I hate chutney. It makes me feel sick. The very thought of it makes me feel sick. So *you* make me feel sick.'

'But your tooth!'

'Securely Superglued in place, for months, almost certainly, years. You told me so yourself.'

'But I brought it to you . . . I . . .'

'You know what I suggest?' In order to avoid waking Petra, Sissie whispered into Plumb's ear so that he felt the close sweetness of her bodily presence. 'I suggest that you drop me off and then take this taxi directly to the airport and return forthwith to the harridan housewife.'

'Oh, Sissie. Sissie.'

But Sissie was beginning to think that he had taken advantage of her shocked, bruised and broken condition on their first meeting. She had already given him more than he deserved once in a lifetime.

'I loved you toothless. I ran my tongue soothingly along your gum—'

'Your time is up, Plumb. You were lucky to have lunch with us. Now, hand me Petra. I'm leaving.'

They had stopped at Sissie's apartment. The driver opened the door for mother and baby, just for the pleasure of being near such a gargantuan beauty. At the door Sissie turned and waved. 'Don't forget! Stay away from chutney.'

Sissie tripped triumphantly upstairs to her garret. Plumb was already forgotten. What she celebrated was her reception in the restaurant, for it told her that she was groomed and ready for the world. Tomorrow she would look up Bianca.

However, in the slow reaches of the night she woke in very different mood. She felt alone, abandoned and, although she could not think of Howard Howard, her Stetson-hatted husband, with reproach, it seemed cruel of fate to give her the joys of loving protection, or, if not protection, association, before dragging him so speedily away. Nothing about him had suggested he would disappear. His solid frame, his absurd accent, his determined, straightforward love-making had given him a permanence that she had never felt for a second with Sebastien or Plumb. It was what had attracted her to him. It was the same with Janice who had also deserted her. Janice had seemed so secure that Sissie had felt quite confident in being out of touch for years. Janice would always be there. Isn't that what people said about mothers?

Yet now, lying in the not-quite-dark, because a street lamp shone through the cracks in the shutters, she saw a different kind of reality emerge. Howard had been in disguise when she first saw him, strange voices commanded him over his mobile telephone, he had appeared in the Amazon rainforest with a blue spirit hovering over his head. When they married, he had produced no family or background. When he had disappeared, the message had come out of nowhere, as had the envelope with the money, not enough money. She saw now that her act of faith in him had been based on so little that it had made her a fool and she wept disillusioned tears. Perhaps he, too, had been merely using her and she had mistaken their happiness together for love. True, lasting, mature, unselfish love.

Miserably looking on the worst side, Sissie slid into thoughts of her morther and saw that here, too, there was the disquietingly unexplained. Why did she feel that Janice had always treated her differently from Adam and Ruth? Why did Rob treat her as if she were not quite his, with a kind of wariness? Why had she herself been so determined to leave their house as soon as she could earn her living? And then Janice had repaid her doubts by not behaving like a mother at all and dying and leaving her alone.

Sissie tossed off her duvet with her long feet and struggled with a drowning sense of mystery. For hours she tried to formulate questions for which she had no answers and, finally, exhausted, convinced herself that the only reality was this little room in which she and her baby lived and from which they would soon emerge into victory. Let the powers of darkness declare themselves or go away, she thought, and soon after fell asleep. That night the catwalk was a mirror, reflecting Rudolf's face, so distorted as to be unrecognizable.

'Non, Mademoiselle,' the voice was friendly. 'Bianca n'est pas ici. Elle est sur le yacht de la famille. Elle visite les Boobies. C'est complètement fou, n'est-ce pas?'

Crazy, indeed. Sissie put down the telephone's receiver and kicked the post on which it stood. Petra and she were on a windy corner of the Rue Mouffetard and, as usual, it was raining. She was sure it had not rained so much in her glamorous youth.

Over a café au lait and a sugar lump for Petra, Sissie came to the brave conclusion that there was no reason to wait for Bianca's return from her ornithological exotica before entering the welcome embrace of her rich, admiring mother.

Lily Skourou had decided to dye her hair the same colour as her white mink coat. Naturally, the hairdresser, a nervous young refugee from Croatia whom Lily had plucked from the salon, had come to her. Lily liked to patronize the young. She did it with genuine good intentions but was also glad to feel that it distinguished her from the other rich wives who spent fortunes on couture without giving a thought to others less fortunate than themselves.

However, Leni, as the hairdresser was called (or had decided to be called), was taking far too long about the matter of turning black to white, simple enough to Lily who, underneath her glamour, was a no-nonsense practical sort of person, and now she was bored.

The entrance of her maid, a trodden-down girl rescued from a nightclub, was cheering.

'Oui, Delphine, parlez.'

Lily spoke three languages: Greek for her family, American for couture and business and French for the servants. A fourth, Italian, she reserved for love but that had not come her way lately.

'Une amie de votre fille, une femme et son bébé . . .'

'Un enfant?' Lily shook her head free from Leni's potion-ejecting hands – perhaps she had patronized the wrong hairdresser. Lily liked babies. Pregnancy and giving birth to Bianca, a further daughter and finally, deoxa to Theo, a son, or she would not be in such comfort now, had been the happiest times in her life. How her husband had spoilt and petted her! How clever she had felt to be a mother and how much she had adored her children! Even now, Bianca was her closest confidante.

'Elle dit qu'elle s'appelle Sissie,' continued the maid, pleased to have pleased her mistress.

'Sissie!' Lily hadn't felt so excited since she bought Waldo Walenska's opera cloak edged with pink-dyed ostrich feathers. '*Vite*, Delphine.' Just short of maliciously, Lily slapped away Leni's anxious hands, pale they were, and dampish.

Sissie knew about impressing clients. Women like Lily had the genius of Sartre for spotting Style. She had to get it right. But she, too, had her own genius.

Lily's dressing of her hair was taking place in a gothic conservatory that adhered like a glittering jewel to the third floor of her apartment. She sat in her gilded chair, hair plastered close with peroxide, acolytes hesitating around her, like butterflies round a flower, and received Sissie. Would Bianca's mother give Sissie the Paris that lay beyond the glass, at her feet?

'Madame. Je suis ravie d'avoir fait votre connaissance.'

'Please speak English.' So this was business. So far, for Sissie, so good.

Sissie wore black, a safe choice apparently although hardly the way she wore it. Petra, on the other hand, sported a smocked floral dress of the sort worn at children's parties in London. She looked enchanting, pink cheeks glowing, fair curls twisted into tight rosettes all over her head, blue eyes glistening with good humour. Sissie might as well have been a nanny as far as Lily was concerned. If she saw her at all it was only as a statuesque backcloth for this divine creature who had come to enliven a dreary winter's day.

In a few minutes coloured building blocks had been produced, a rug laid down on the floor, other toys and entertainments provided, and Lily, uncaring that she dangerously dripped peroxide, played on the floor with Petra. It was love at first sight. Excluded, Leni, Delphine and Sissie watched with various emotions. Sissie felt pretty certain it would work to her advantage but Leni shuddered at an image of green hair coming out in tufts.

After refreshments, spooned into Petra by Lily's devoted hands, Sissie felt it possible to raise the name of Waldo Walenska. 'But, of course!' Lily spoke without removing her attention from Petra but spoke positively. 'That is why Bianca, my darling daughter, has sent you to me. Delphine, apportez-moi le téléphone.'

Waldo Walenska, at the haute of haute couture, striving over a bias-cut skirt that would not flow, was surprised by this call and yet not surprised. He knew he must demur at once or not at all. He had heard of Sissie's height, her swivel-swinging walk and he pictured his magnificently cut skirts (which they would be, pray to God) swirling about her long thighs. Did he want dainty, one-dimensional waifs? Absolument pas! 'But, Lily, my angel, how have you found her? When can I see her? When can I have her for fittings? My collection will be built upon her. Your protégée, dear Madame.'

This was all very well but Lily had not quite finished. 'And Waldo, maestro, we must not forget the baby.'

'Un enfant?' Waldo's hand, still holding the scissors, clawed convulsively, cutting across the bias in a way from which no skirt could hope to recover.

'Sissie's baby. You will be as entranced as me. Perhaps you could have a cradle swinging from the chandelier.'

'Gug,' responded Waldo, all known languages deserting him.

'She is a very distinguished, English-looking baby,' continued Lily, a touch severely, as if she had not sensed enough enthusiasm down the line. 'She will raise you from the ranks of other designers who lack aristocratic connections.'

'Farg,' said Waldo.

The next two weeks were very satisfactory ones for Sissie. While Petra delighted Lily hour after hour – she dallied her and dangled her and even liked changing her nappies and attending her sleeping hours – Sissie spent the time at Waldo's studio. Although his East European background made her hope and fear for a reincarnation of the late, great Rudolf, she quickly discovered an important difference. Whereas in the past her terms of employment had been so high that, even with beloved Rudolf, she would appear before a show and be more or less fitted into the clothes she was to model with the help of needle, staple gun and Sellotape, plus that top model's plastic capability of modifying her shape as required, now she spent hours performing the function of what Waldo called grandly his muse because the moment he saw this gigantic earth goddess – thinner she might be but in strictly relative terms – he was inspired to a whole new line. Lily was right. Fashion had seen enough of androgynous waifs. He would design for the Real Woman.

The Real Woman had the curves to show off his passion for bias. 'I adore you, Sissie,' he said. He was gay, of course, like almost all great designers, and Sissie basked calmly in approval knowing very well that his serious love was reserved for a dazzling Algerian boy who preferred sniffing coke to anything else in the world, certainly to any other person in the world.

'I think maybe you are earth goddess mixed with warrior,' Waldo explained to Sissie when she arrived one morning to find the studio filled with breast plates and helmets. 'I have as my inspiration a nineteenth-century engraving of Boudicca, that hero of the strong woman.'

'Surely it should be Joan of Arc.'

'Pas du tout. Chérie, where is your education? Jeanne d'Arc had no children. Boadicea or Boudicca, as she is called, justement fought side by side with her daughters. Boudicca represents woman, man and motherhood!' His voice rose to a triumphant flourish.

'I see,' said Sissie, and she did, because Waldo possessed or, rather, was possessed by a mother notorious for her powers of domination. It was said that when Waldo first arrived in Paris, his mother, who was small, dark, sturdy, ageless and sexless, had impersonated her son at any crucial meeting. She would have had no trouble in disposing of a phalanx of ex-patria Romans. Sissie picked up an ancient weapon of war and fingered its not unsharp blade thoughtfully. Would the image of a Celtic warrior queen living in the second century AD really appeal to Lily and Waldo's international clientele – many from Arab lands – who looked to him to clothe them in European sophistication? However, hers not to reason why. She was merely the model.

That afternoon as Sissie walked briskly across the Seine – she was practising her model's glide and glad to feel herself getting back into the swing of it – she had the distinct sensation that she was being followed. A dim mist arose from the river and dusk was turning into darkness with a murky mystery. It was not easy to be sure of your own footstep on the pavement, let alone anything further away. Nevertheless Sissie stopped when she reached the end of the bridge and peered backwards. There were several ghostly hurrying figures but one stood out because of his large size and kind of halo round his head.

Sissie took a step or two forward and saw the gleam of yellow hair. She took a further step and was able to see that the man, now bending over the parapet of the bridge, carried a coil of, perhaps, wire round his shoulder and under his arm a traditional leather toolbag. Un ouvrier, decided Sissie, who enjoyed a rational explanation when possible, a workman about to inspect a screw loose in the bridge. In which case, the yellow top-knot was not hair at all but a shiny protective helmet. At any rate, he would not have the time to follow her. Satisfied, Sissie continued on her way. Frankly, she could not allow herself the indulgence of suspicious thoughts.

Chapter Thirty-Five

In which Death is defeated and Waldo's Mother suggests a Voice would be more Appropriate than Music.

HOWARD HOWARD stumbled out of the forest. His kidnappers had been kind enough to bring him from the centre to the edge. Perhaps that was part of the deal. He did not know. When he saw a sturdy-looking Caboclos Indian blocking his path, he did not hesitate for a minute. The Caboclos had boats and now he could see the soft space of water between the dark trunks.

The retired school-mistress living in the ugly bungalow in the pretty English valley was clearing up after her sister's New Year visit from Canada. Being a conscientious housekeeper, she moved out the spare-room bed from the wall. A small battered book was revealed, with a desolately reproachful air. Since her sister had never been much of a reader, always a source of contention between them, the school-mistress picked up the volume with interest.

Magic and Fate, she read, a most unlikely title and particularly for her sister, who despised anything she could not touch, see or smell. Her final attempt at appreciating fiction had been a copy of *Tess of the d'Urbervilles*, which she had described as 'an unconvincing story of inadequate people', a condemnation which the school-mistress had never quite forgiven.

No. *Magic and Fate* could not possibly belong to the Canadian visitor. It did not take her too long to think of her summer tenant. Glad that she could find a tidy home for a book that had an

309

uncomfortable subversive feel about it, for the first lines read, 'In the unreal lies the art of truth', she hurried away to find the address given to her by Sissie's father. She had less than happy memories of that afternoon since, after their departure, she had found herself dealing with a bag of vomit, but this would not stop her doing her Christian duty. Besides, she had been lucky enough to hold the winning ticket for the Great Orchid Raffle and looking after the orchids had been so demanding as to give her a whole new lease of life. So she did owe Sissie a debt.

The manager of the Hotel Brasilia Lux in Rio de Janeiro had been sacked for financial corruption and for violating the moral code of the hotel's parent company, who were American Baptists. They also had a report that the hotel's lack of morals was matched by its lack of hygiene, especially in areas where guests were not expected. Staff-rooms, corridors, elevators, storerooms, pantries, larders and some areas of the kitchens had not been thoroughly cleaned for years and playful rats could be seen not only at night. A new manager was installed, a Swiss American who wished to close down the hotel while he poured bleach into its every orifice. But the Baptists needed money to convert the world so he was not allowed such an expensive option. Guests continued to arrive while a full-scale clean-up took place.

Mo sat in a strip bar, the only sort he knew, with a very thin, very sunburnt, very scratched, scarred, bruised, exhausted American with a shaven head. Mo was paying for the drinks or, rather, ordering them free from a friend, and they were both very drunk. The live music, loud and far better than the bar's owner deserved, made dialogue impossible even if either of the men had been capable of taking in another's point of view. But now and again each felt moved to air a sentence or phrase outside their heads.

For example, Mo, the Caboclos come to town where he had spent some years as a guide to just such night-life as he was now enjoying, clapped his friend on the back every so often, shouted, 'Pink dolphin!', and followed this with curiously silent laughter. It seemed to be both a matter for congratulation and for mockery. He varied the pink dolphin theme with a sort of dirge about a crocodile, accompanied and illustrated by his white teeth champing up and down.

His companion seemed bewildered by this pantomime but obviously held the Caboclos in high esteem; his few wild-eyed words were about 'the final conclusion of dark nights' and 'the waters of escape' and 'the tread of the barefoot saviour.'

At three or four in the morning the two men struggled back to a large hotel on the sea-front and made their way via a staff entrance to a small airless room, which another friend of Mo's, a cleaner at the hotel, had allowed them to use. There they collapsed into swinish sleep.

They did not wake even when Mo's friend came in from his shift and lay beside them on the floor. It was midday when Howard surfaced, through scenic layers in the countries round the world, to find himself dripping with sweat and in front of his eyes, filling his whole focus, a gigantic white tooth. Since one of his scenic dreams had been in Sri Lanka where he had worked as an agent provocateur in league with the Tamil Tigers, he thought that he was still asleep and had arrived at Kandy's Temple of the Tooth. In reality, he had never seen a Buddha's tooth, merely a gold casket, but by the time he was awake enough to recall reality he had shifted position and seen that it was only the tooth's close proximity to his eyes which had presented it on such a grandiose scale and that it was a perfectly normal size tooth. Indeed an exquisite pearly lady's size tooth, which immediately set up joyful memories.

'Sissie's tooth!' he exclaimed, waking up the hotel worker. Mo, it seemed, had vanished without farewell or thanks.

'My darling, beautiful wondrous Sissie! You are speaking to me, welcoming me in this imaginative way!' After so long in the forest he could be forgiven such flights of fancy. It was a miracle he wasn't right round the twist, given his experiences too awful to relate. He was just about to take up the magic jewel with all reverence when a sinewy hand snatched it from him.

'My tooth! My gold!' growled the semi-naked hotel worker. 'I find. I keep. Have a good day.'

'Gold?' queried Howard, playing for time.

'Gold,' repeated the man, showing a shiny rim where the tooth could be affixed.

The two men stared at each other. One for financial reasons, the other for romantic, neither was willing to give up. There *was* gold. Howard remembered it, but he did not feel seriously attached to it. But was the gold seriously attached to the tooth? His mind, he noticed, was still working slowly but getting there in the end. 'You keep the gold, I take the tooth.'

'You're welcome,' agreed the man, who had swapped his job as a failed miner to become one of the hotel's new brooms.

'Where did you find it?' asked Howard, as the sweeper got out a penknife and began hacking away enthusiastically. But he only looked up to hand over the tooth. 'Have a good day.'

Armed with this talisman, Howard Howard set off to find his beloved. Because he might still be recognizable to his enemies and because he no longer wished to be servant to his disloyal masters who had left him to his death, he adopted a black bristly wig found by the sweeper on cleaning up after a recently departed guest.

Mary showed Ted the book that had come through the post. 'Rob wanted me to have it. You see, it belongs to Sissie.'

'Your daughter,' said Ted, who had a behavioural therapist's talent for making people face up to the truth.

'My daughter,' agreed Mary, blushing.

'I expect he means us to take it to her in Paris,' continued Ted, 'on our honeymoon.'

'Oh, Ted.' Mary put out her hand to the man she was going to marry in a couple of days and looked at the hand without comprehension. She retrieved it and used it to tidy her hair.

'And tomorrow you're coming in with me.'

'Oh dear!' exclaimed Mary in heartfelt tones.

'It was your idea.'

'I know.'

'You'll feel better after.'

'Do you think?' She stared anxiously at the television, which was quietly flickering the six o'clock news.

'They want to meet you.'

'But they'll know. They won't respect you any more. You'll be tarred and feathered.' Unconsciously, she picked up the words of the newscaster who was reporting on an item about Vichy France.

'No, dear. They're nice people and they'll like you.'

The walls were red-brick with some quite elegant cross-brick ornamentation near the top, as if the builder had become bored of placing one brick upon another for such a high stretch. Mary stared upwards to where the winter white sky, even taller, took over from the red. It would be the same sky over her cliffs beyond the sea.

'Come on, now.' Ted took her arm.

'I wasn't in a hurry to get out and I'm not in a hurry to get back in. Even if it was my idea.'

Ted smiled as if she had made a joke and drew her past the straggling line of prisoners, mothers and children, elderly parents. The door through which they entered was big but seemed small. Mary remembered this from before, becoming Alice in Wonderland, changing size, small in the wall, high over your head. Ted's hand held her as firmly as that prison officer who had brought her in, but then she had felt nothing.

'I'm fine.' She shook him off, her right to walk alone, head high.

'This is a very modern prison,' explained Ted, above the noise of doors unlocking. 'An old shell, of course. There's talk of turning it into a resettlement unit. I'd like that.'

He talked as if he were showing any old visitor round his prison, Mary thought.

'Our appointment with the governor and then coffee with the boys.'

If Ted's plan was to include her in his job, make her feel part of his life, Mary thought, as they moved round the prison, meeting, talking, displaying, then exactly the opposite was happening. With every minute that passed – the kind librarian, the enthusiastic education officer, the staff-room politeness – she felt more unreal, less connected. They were looking from the outside in, but she had been inside, so far inside she could hardly see out. There seemed no link between her experience and Ted's.

*

Huddled in their coats after the overheated prison, Ted and Mary walked home. He waited for a comment from her.

'We didn't see any prisoners.'

'It was lunch-time. Our free time. They were locked up.'

'Oh, yes. Yes. Them. *They* were locked up. I should have known that.' They walked on further, the space between them as large as the pavement would allow. When they arrived at the house, Mary put on her walking shoes and set off silently for her caravan. Ted had the good sense not to follow her.

Mary stayed away all that night. Ted thought it was a strange way to spend the twenty-four hours before your marriage, unless that was off. He had known that to happen before. He took down their tickets to Paris from the mantelpiece and then noticed that the book *Magic and Fate*, which had been with them, had gone. So then he decided to go and look for Mary. He had found her once before, after all, when she had needed saving.

Seagulls whirled round and round the cliff edge as Ted followed the coastal path. It was a still, dry day, turf flat and cropped brambles shrunk to their smallest size, nothing dramatic to report except these birds, dark against the light on his right side, white against the grass on his left. He remembered how he had seen them behave in just such a frantic way round the carcass of a fallen sheep and he hurried his step.

Mary, inside her caravan, the last remaining caravan on the headland, saw him coming, his fast anxious walk, the little feather on his hat agitating with his speed. She opened the door to him. She opened her arms.

'I am sorry.' They held each other standing upright but so loving. Fear of loss had made them expressive. Now they were tired and wanted to lie down together but Mary's bunk was far too small. Somehow they had moved aside the table and, two old folk, found themselves clasped together on the thin carpet. But they wanted to be still closer so, looking into each other's eyes, clumsy dancers who hardly know their moves, they took off as many layers as possible till they could reach warm skin and show their love and care with pats and stroking. Their lack of practice, their inefficiency at all this only make them smile with greater affection. They knew it was a miracle they had come together, or however far they managed to get

314

together on this hard, not very clean floor, and they were bursting with love for each other.

Darkness enclosed the little tin caravan, like a forgotten toy in the wide landscape. Cleo, the black cat, came out of the night and jumped up through her three inches of open window. Delicately she trod the route to her bowl, lapped a tongueful of fresh milk (she noted the freshness with pleasure) and then felt her way to a delightful source of warmth. Mary and Ted lay in each other's arms, half dressed and half undressed, and when Cleo jumped on top of them, they hardly stirred.

Waldo Walenska, although in his view a genius, also had a sense of proportion which made him wary of failure. His enthusiasm for Boudicca had not lessened, 'a sexy symbol of an end-of-century armoured woman, motherhood giving her a further fecund majesty' – Waldo always wrote his own press releases – but he was worried about the presentation. The clothes would speak for themselves in one sense, he did not doubt, the Celtic citrine, amethyst and emerald overlaying silver and gold, a colour and texture combination that he was certain would ravish the eye of every beholder and unloose even the tightest purse strings, but he needed something for their ears also and he was fairly certain this was not music. Particularly not 'The Ride of the Valkyrie', which one of his assistants had suggested, causing him to point out that she had obviously missed the import-ance of the motherhood theme.

He did have a short foray into the area of battle cries, experi-menting with the team of workmen who were constructing his special catwalk, which contained rails for a mechanical chariot. But the men's cries, led by a large blond man who wielded his hammer as if it were a mace, had been so harsh and threatening in the enclosed space that he feared his clients would not feel at all comfortable and it is well known that people need to feel comfortable (psychologically not physically speaking – the horrid gilded chairs merely kept them on the edge of their seats) to open their purse-strings.

Waldo could find no answer to his problem so he went to his mother. Madame Walenska, a woman of indeterminate age for as long as her son could remember – although his indetermination had become more pronounced after she celebrated his success in the West by a series of top-notch plastic surgery operations – thought over Waldo's problem. She was confident of finding an answer but first tested the ground a little.

'The authentic instrument for such a period would be a stringed instrument, played by hand, something of a cross between a lyre and a harp, with undertones of a zither.'

Although impressed by the breadth of his mother's knowledge, which was hardly rational since she had always known about everything all his life, Waldo did not look happy at this suggestion. 'Far too prim,' he said. 'No strength. No richness. No help "in rolling back the centuries to the days when life and death, birth and rebirth, the real and unreal have come together in a mystery as fateful as life itself".'

'You can't have "life" twice.' Madame Walenska always corrected her son's press release for repetition and grammar. 'However, I have now solved your problem.'

'Ah, Mama,' breathed Waldo, paying homage ahead of time.

'He is a man who will speak such words for you that people will both hear and not hear and believe and not believe. And some will believe it poetry and some history and some will think it all a load of rubbish but everyone will know you are a genius and that this voice speaks your genius.'

'Ah, Mama,' repeated Waldo. 'A Voice. You are incomparable. But wherever shall we find such a man?'

'A few years ago,' Madame Walenska reached for her pocket computer in which she stored her thousands, even millions of addresses, 'I was in a hospital, undergoing lipo-suction on my inner thighs,' she never hid such self-improvement from her son, 'when a man was introduced to entertain myself and other recuperating patients. He spoke about our operations and healing in a way that made us feel we had taken part in a sacred rite. I recognized him as a supreme master of presenting nothing as if it were the meaning of life and took him aside to note down his address – or, rather, addresses for he seemed to have telephone numbers all over the world.'

'Don't worry, Mamuska, we will track him down in whichever part of the globe he now resides.'

Business over, Madame Walenska allowed herself to become a little nostalgic. 'In this man's mouth "hypodermic lipo-suction" sounded like the line Keats missed out from "Ode to a Grecian Urn". I shall be glad to hear such a maestro speak again.'

'Me too,' said Waldo, filled with filial faith.

Sissie was glad she was to have a commentary or 'a Voice' as Waldo insisted on calling it. Her secret fear of looking ridiculous – no model can afford to worry about that – was allayed by what she hoped would be a background of sober history. She wished Bianca would return from her travels so that she would have someone with whom to share her worries.

Chapter Thirty-Six

In which Paris seems to be a Magnet for most of our Protagonists although Father Pedro and Maureen are naturally too busy Doing Good.

HOWARD SAT in the restaurant of a P & O ferry. Outside the long glass window, the line between blue sea and blue sky tipped up and down like a seesaw. The air was wintry, the wind strong, the sea rough. But the sun shone and that, combined with P & O's efficient air-conditioning, gave the room a summer-time feel. A man at the table next to Howard's had even taken off his jacket, revealing a startlingly white shirt with what appeared to be numbered epaulettes. Howard would have liked to have taken off his wig, which was heavy and itchy and, judging by the odd looks he had been getting, not altogether, if at all, convincing. He had already noticed on the ship several shaven-headed young men – not that he put himself in the category of youth any more – so he assumed that, since his disappearance, baldness, moving to stubble, had become acceptable head fashion. He felt as if he were wearing a thatched roof.

'The man at the table next door is wearing a wig,' Mary whispered to Ted.

'Perhaps he's a spy,' suggested Ted fondly. This wonderful woman he had married that morning had been wonderful enough to overlook his forgetful donning of his prison officer's shirt. It was a wonderful, wonderful day, the best day of his life. At last he had someone to care for and love. Someone who noticed men in wigs and inspired him, good old Ted Mack, into a light-hearted, even witty rejoinder. 'He must be a very bad spy to have such a bad wig,' beamed Ted.

'He looks as if he's suffered.' Mary had noticed the not quite faded scratching, bruising and battering above the yellow complexion.

'Perhaps he's on the run.' Ted's beam spread further. This was companionship, emphasized by their subject of a solitary diner. 'Is your shrimp cocktail as you expected?' he asked solicitously.

'Hardly that,' Mary looked at him, with her new, unafraid eyes, 'because I've never had one before. But the shrimp is tender and the sauce piquante.'

'Tender and piquante,' repeated Ted, words that he might have used to describe Mary herself. 'Well, my soup is – is splendid.' He gave the adjective he wanted for himself for he was determined to be as splendid as possible for his bride.

'I think he's unhappy.'

Mary returned to their neighbour but now Ted wanted her attention all to himself. 'After lunch I think we should take a walk on deck. It looks as wild as a Dorset cliff-top.'

'Quite as wild,' agreed Mary, content to build on their shared experience.

Howard fought his way to the front of the ship. He felt that his constitution, weakened by wet-heat fever, needed the stimulus of northern-latitude sea air and, with every step, he felt the old strong-heart, strong-bone health returning. At the very prow of the ship he found the couple who had been sitting next to him in the restaurant. They hunched close together, holding hands with their faces up to the sun and wind. They did not recognize him because he had substituted for his disagreeable wig a thick hat with ear-flaps.

'Another brave one!' shouted Ted, above the howl of the wind.

'Uh-huh,' agreed Howard, hardly able to keep his footing on the deck.

American, thought Mary and Ted. 'Sit down here, if you like,' shouted Ted, 'before you get knocked down.'

So Howard sat, buffered from the wind by this stalwart couple. They did not make the effort to speak for a while and then Ted found he couldn't resist. 'We're going to Paris for our honeymoon,' he advised.

Given their age, this seemed an unlikely piece of information and Howard assumed he had misheard, at least the second part of the sentence. 'I'm on my way to Paris to look for my wife.' The second part of his sentence, however, disappeared on a gust of wind.

Ted, who was disappointed not to receive congratulations, recovered at the idea that they were all bound for the same great cosmopolitan experience. 'Paris,' he repeated and they all three smiled and nodded at a shared password.

Far away on a hot, flat, blue sea, Sebastien and Bianca pledged their troth. Sebastien, sunburnt and less bony than usual, gazed at Bianca's Greek curves. 'You are everything I've ever dreamed of,' he said. 'Beautiful, rich, unselfish, clever . . .'

'You don't mind I'm a woman?' asked Bianca, who had a practical streak.

'I want you to be my wife,' replied Sebastien, as if that answered the question. 'I want to live in four or five capital cities, excluding Paris and New York which we should take for granted, and winter on this delightful yacht. How old is your benevolent father, incidentally?'

'He's not going to die yet, if that's what you're thinking. In fact, he's just been given a post in the Greek government and married again which has given him two new leases of life.'

'I love you all the same!' cried Sebastien.

Bianca looked smug. This English-French youth, Eton and Oxford educated, so elegant, so brilliant, so well able to appreciate what she had to offer, loved her too. It was the moment to mention Sissie.

Sebastien, drowsing on his top-deck day-bed, skin flushed by the sun and cooled by a mellifluous breeze, waved away a white-coated Filipino offering iced water. His physical being was already perfectly balanced, in temperature terms. Bianca, on the other hand, accepted a chunky glass and took such a large gulp that an ice block hit her strong nose with quite a wallop.

'I've seen Sissie in Paris,' she began, quite testily. She rubbed the nose she had inherited from her father.

'Sissie? Sissie! Oh, God, Sissie.'

'Well, yes, Sissie,' agreed Bianca.

It was not that Sebastien had anything but the fondest feelings for Sissie who, quite apart from anything else, had provided him with a very nice life in Paris for at least eighteen months for which he'd always be grateful, but that he did not want to risk any alteration to his present state of comfort. Sissie represented risk. Suddenly he was in need of that water. 'I last saw her with her daughter,' his tone irritated him by its defensiveness, 'snug in a happy valley. A dull place, actually. I left with . . .' He rethought. 'I left sooner than I intended. But I had the feeling she would stay for ever.'

'She's left too.' Bianca was brief. Sissie was an old idol. Sebastien a new, if ultimately important, acquisition. 'She gave away all her money. She had, has, no money.'

Sebastien sat up. Surely he was not competing with Sissie for Bianca's financial patronage.

'So I have introduced her to my mother. She has become Waldo Walenska's preferred model.'

Sebastien sighed and lay back again. He had never been interested in the details of Sissie's career but appreciated that it solved money problems.

'So she's not important to you?'

He eyed Bianca upside down. He saw that she was serious. He crossed one knee over the other and considered. 'Important? Yes. Once. Real? No. Never. Model was the right name for her. She was a model of a girl, a super-model. Superior plastic, but not real.'

Bianca looked blindly at her toes, painted with a red dark enough to be mistaken for black. 'Not real in Brazil? Not real in her happy valley with the baby?'

'Physically she had the reality of a mountain, big enough to make a contour on the map.'

'You are cruel,' said Bianca, satisfied that Sebastien wanted nothing further from Sissie. 'But we shall attend her magnificent comeback.'

As she finished speaking a faint shadow crossed her face, causing her to look upwards. High above, an aeroplane, black against the sun, traversed the blue sky from one side of the globe to the other.

*

321

Mary and Ted descended the ship's gangplank not far behind a hunched, shaven-headed young man, who had no discernible baggage. They all looked up as an aeroplane came in above them from the direction of the sea.

'One of those big transoceanic jobs, I expect,' said Ted, impressing Mary.

The Author flipped open the window shade in his Super Starlight cabin, three steps up from first class both literally and figuratively – good old Madame Walenska. He had never seen so much sucked out of one woman's thighs. Cold European light illuminated the sheaf of papers on his lap. It had been a long flight, passing in and out of night, but he had used the last few hours to prepare his forthcoming assignment. This was unusual. His more normal practice was to allow the words to flow from him 'as naturally as leaves to a tree', a comment on Keats's poetry with which he'd always aligned his own unique art form. But, on this occasion, he was determined to present a masterpiece since this was to be his swansong, the song of a Trumpet Swan bowing out from the public arena. In short, and to mix musical metaphors, he was planning to pull out all the stops.

'Thank you, my dear.' The Author accepted with relish a glass of Buck's Fizz offered by a stewardess.

The stewardess, as smoothly, blondely young and glamorous as a Super Starlight advertisement, saw a wise old bird with a thinning plumage of white hair and winking black eyes, set in a gnomic wrinkled face. 'You're welcome,' she said kindly. 'I hope the flight has not seemed too long and tiring.'

'Not at all,' replied the Author benignly. 'I always find time flies.'

As the time for the Walenska show drew nearer, Sissie began to have regular nightmares about the evening Rudolf had died. She woke yelping and writhing with the horror of it and often her cries disturbed Petra. Then the two of them would sit in bed together with a calming drink for an hour or more. Sissie told herself that

Rudolf had died from a heart attack, a fatal version of one he'd had a few years earlier, yet in her dream it was the stiletto heel flying off her foot, and which had been found still clasped in his clenched hands, which had sliced through his chest and delivered the coup de grâce.

In her dreams, there was blood and anguished screaming and no doubt at all that a murder had been committed. By the light of day she tried to convince herself that the dream was merely a distortion of her anxieties about returning to the catwalk, but at night, even after she had woken, it seemed to have a much deeper and more vivid reality than mere anxiety could produce.

One of the most frightening features of the dream was that Rudolf was never visible beyond his neck. He was only legs and torso as if seen from a very low eye level. Or as if he had no head. Or as if he had the head of a *monster*. This was the idea that most frightened Sissie so that, although the headlessness was horrible, she dreaded even more seeing whatever grew on top. If anything did.

Mary and Ted were on the fifth course of a set dinner in a Swiss restaurant on the Left Bank. It was not clear to either of them why they were eating in a Swiss restaurant on their first night in Paris but at this point in the evening their feelings about Switzerland had become very positive.

Mary and Ted reeled out of the restaurant in search of the Métro. Instead they found a news-stand, and facing them, in black and white, and very large, was a photograph of Sissie. '*Magic and Fate!*' exclaimed Mary, because it had reminded her she had left the book in the restaurant. She hurried back to retrieve it while Ted bought the newspaper.

He stood under a lamp-post and was glad to see that it was called the *International Herald Tribune*, a paper written in English. Under the photo was written 'Sissie as she was last seen on the night of Rudolf's death. Will the model's come-back Wednesday revive Waldo Walenska's fading fortunes? See page 5.'

Ted was turning to page five when Mary reappeared, breathless and flushed.

'What's the matter?'

'It had gone.'

Ted took a closer look at her face. 'It's only a book.' He stubbed the paper with his finger. 'This is what matters. Now we can find her. Tomorrow. We'll go and see her in all her glory.'

Later that evening Mary lay awake in Ted's arms. This position was still new to her and so was staying in a hotel, being abroad, drinking wine and having the expectation of seeing her daughter the next day. She did not expect to sleep that night. Neither did Ted.

'How do you think we'll get into the show?' she whispered.

'Buy tickets, I suppose.'

'I don't think it's like that. Janice used to bring the newspaper reports. I think it's only for the privileged.'

'Doesn't her mother count as privileged?'

'Yes. But . . .'

'We'll go early, that's what we'll do. We'll put on our wedding clothes and get to the Hôtel du Roi so early no one will be there to stop us.'

'That's all right, then,' agreed Mary, who wasn't much more able than Ted to picture the scene that awaited them at eleven o'clock the following morning.

Bianca took Sebastien for a late-night aperitif with her mother. Lily did not seem pleased to see her, which was unusual. She admonished her daughter for the unfashionably deep tone of her suntan and told Sebastien that she couldn't shake his hand because she had already applied her freckle-removal cream, which cost millions of francs for a one-ounce jar but he could kiss her cheek if he felt that was appropriate.

'Ravissante!' Sebastien performed the kiss enthusiastically, and then stood back to admire her successfully mink-matched hair and the elegance of her at-home velvet and brocade robe.

Lily melted a little. 'The truth is, chérie, I was not expecting visitors because tonight I have a very special person in my charge.' With anyone else this reference must have been to a lover, but Bianca knew that her mother had only tolerated sex as the means to the end of giving birth.

'Darling Maman. You are not usually so coy.'

Lily relented still further. 'Come, I'll show you.'

The cot was swagged and tailed and flounced and frou-froued. Inside Petra, cheeks rosy as a cherub, yellow curls damp, slept with a finger in her mouth. 'I wouldn't have thought she was your sort of baby at all.' Bianca sounded miffed, even though it was she who had set up this whole scenario.

Lily smiled without taking her eyes off the baby. 'What you mean is she doesn't look at all like you.'

Sebastien peered from the end of the cot. 'She doesn't look like Sissie either.'

'She's got the looks of an English aristocrat,' said Lily, in a dignified tone.

'I don't know when you became so keen on the English. Snobbish and uncivilized are your usual epithets.'

'American,' commented Sebastien, turning away. 'Her father was American. From a town called Dime Box.'

Before Lily could become seriously offended, Bianca intervened. 'The point is, will she do her stuff tomorrow?'

'That's why she's here.' Lily pulled up Petra's coverlet lovingly. 'Sissie has nerves. She does not sleep too well. She wakes little Petra. But little Petra must be happy tomorrow, not tired and fretful. So I have her for tonight.'

'Kidnap,' commented Bianca, looking for Sebastien and time to leave.

But he had turned away with a humanitarian pang. 'Poor Sissie,' he murmured. 'I should have warned her never to give in to a charitable impulse.'

Sissie had been given her helmet so that she could get used to wearing it. It felt like a coal scuttle on her head, burnished metal from top to toe, although the top was far taller than any coal scuttle. It was unwieldy, heavy and impaired her vision. Sissie removed the helmet and laid it on the bed where it reflected her anxious face in bulbous distortion. Wearing it now would not help but would just make her dread when she would also be carrying a shield, especially constructed to hold Petra, and plus a spear in the other hand. It was true the chariot would bear her along. She would get out and walk only after this first grand appearance, swing along, the old great Sissie.

Waldo wandered among his wolfskin dresses, twitching a tail here, displaying a silken lining there. They were the triumph, he now believed, the hues of brown and grey fake fur speaking of the mysteries of deep woodland, the jewelled Celtic brooches winking like wolves' eyes in the darkness. He had invited the Voice, whom he had not yet met in person, to see them so that he could be inspired to greater heights of poetic vision. Such a man could not be expected to appreciate his masterly solving of the almost impossible challenge of cutting fur on the bias but he must appreciate the savage beauty of his image, the symbolic significance of featuring the wolf, who had once roamed Europe but now was pushed to fewer and darker corners.

It was one o'clock in the morning but Waldo did not mind waiting among his collection for the Voice. He would not sleep, anyway. At some point he would go to his mother's apartment and snatch a few hours' rest. It was a tradition.

Waldo moved further down the rails. Now he had reached the metallic tunics, the armour and helmets that had been his original inspiration. And yet his face fell. Ever since the wolves had taken hold of his imagination, he had been less happy with his martial material. Boudicca and her followers were fighters for freedom, the enslaved, the underdog, taking on the greater might of the Roman Army, but somehow they seemed intrinsically antagonistic rather than primarily defensive. The chariot, supposedly a romantic image, looked unpleasantly aggressive with its angry knives pointing out in all directions. Waldo sighed and fingered the metallic cloth, which was as mobile and iridescent as a fish tail. The chariot was far too expensive an item to jettison now. Perhaps the baby would soften the impact.

There was a knock at the street door. Ah, the Voice, at last. Waldo hurried downstairs through to his office and picked up his key.

Howard Howard did not expect anyone to be in the Walenska showrooms at two in the morning but when he saw the light he decided to try his luck. He, too, had read the *Herald Tribune*. He, too, knew that the next morning he could see his beloved. But that was not enough for him. He put his hand deep in his pocket and felt his talisman, the pearly little tooth, giving him strength.

'Come in, please.' Waldo held open the door with a welcoming smile. 'Entrez. I am honoured that you are here so late.'

'Ditto,' replied Howard, playing for time. Least said, soonest mended.

'They are upstairs. I will take you up.' As Howard moved further into the light, Waldo was surprised to see he was quite a young man with a convict-like stubble head. Yet his drawn face had an aesthetic character as if he had spent more time in his mind than in the world outside. This was reassuring. 'I will not hover or explain.' He said charmingly, 'You must find your muse in privacy.'

The two men went upstairs. At the top Howard found himself faced by a life-sized photograph of Sissie. She was almost naked and very thin. It must have been taken in her super-model days. He wanted to stop but Waldo drew him into the long room where the racks of clothes hung. 'My collection!' he cried, sweeping his arm proudly. Despite his promise to leave the maestro (as he thought) to his own judgement, he could not resist waiting for a reaction. But Howard's thoughts were elsewhere. Waldo braced himself to produce the modesty necessary for the heartfelt compliment.

At length Howard spoke with deep emotion. 'Where is Sissie?' he asked.

Waldo, dark face flushed, peered and shrugged. 'At home with her baby, I assume.'

'Her baby!' exclaimed Howard, clutching so hard at a wolfskin that Waldo moved involuntarily to rescue it. He recovered himself. He must remember that he was dealing with a fellow genius, although he had to admit he was a little surprised to discover he was an American genius.

'I see that the baby is important to you. Rebirth. A new vision. Regeneration. But I must not put words into your mouth. I shall leave you.'

But before he could go, Howard, pale as a new-born rat, snatched his arm. 'What sex?'

'Female. What else?' Struggling against petulant bitterness, Waldo descended to the office.

Stepping along the ranks of wolves and warriors but seeing neither, Howard faced the fact of fatherhood. It was too much altogether. He sat down on the floor with his head in his hands.

After half an hour, in which he varied from hope to despair to uncontrollable impatience, Waldo could not restrain himself any longer and mounted the stairs. He found Howard still on the floor with his head in his hands. As Waldo watched he saw his visitor's shoulders heave and a sob escape him. Moved to emotion! And now wrapped in creative thought. This was a greater homage than he could have hoped for. Quietly, in order not to disturb the muse, he tiptoed back to his office.

Some time later Howard, eyeballs red, reappeared. 'I must be at the show at least two hours before it starts,' he said.

'I understand.' Waldo was grave. One artist respects the needs of another. 'I will give orders to my staff at the Hôtel. As early as you like.'

Now Howard clasped Waldo's hands together in his and looked deeply with his hot eyes. 'You are a great man,' he said, with heartfelt emotion for this man had made him a father and would bring him together with his wife.

'Thank you,' said Waldo with the simple modesty he had been saving up for such a moment. 'I am sure your contribution will be the collection's crowning glory.'

All night long the Author dipped in and out of his stolen copy of *Magic and Fate*. It did not seem to hold him as it used to and he found himself staring out of the window of his luxurious penthouse suite over the silver grey slate roofs and towards the domes of Le Grand Palais. Now that was artistry of a magnificent sort!

At six he put on a black velvet eye-mask, inserted ear-plugs and lay down on his king-size bed. It's a sad business when a book no longer has any meaning for its author.

Mary and Ted crept along the streets to the magnificent portals of the Hôtel du Roi. They felt insignificant, ignorant but totally determined. Mary carried a large plastic bag in one hand. 'We are the early birds,' she whispered, as they avoided a cleaner hoovering the foyer carpet in long straight sweeps as if he were mowing a lawn. Another cleaner confused the indoor-outdoor issue further by watering the great urns with a hosepipe while the ceiling, painted blue with white clouds sailing, was as domed and high as the sky. But then Ted spotted a man putting up a sign for the Waldo Walenska show and they were on their way.

Sven, outsized and even more filled with vengeance than usual, saw two pale faces peering round the heavy, gilded door. Their noses were sharp, their eyes were round and they were staring directly at him where he lay under the catwalk with a large screwdriver. He had not expected discovery at this early hour. On the other hand, he could see that they were at least as nervous on seeing him as he was on seeing them.

'Ouvrier,' he said, with a workman's flourish of his screwdriver.

But neither Mary's nor Ted's French was equal to that and they assumed he meant 'Ouvrez' so they opened the door and went in. They stood silent, awed by the ornate majesty of the room, the high catwalk that ran down its centre and the huge chariot partially revealed through curtains at one end.

Sven took two giant strides towards them, as if wanting an introduction or explanation.

'Nous sommes les oiseaux du matin!' exclaimed Ted, suddenly inspired.

Sven wondered whether to admit that English was as far up his language tree as French now that it was clear that they did not suspect him of nefarious activity.

'We are waiting to see Sissie,' Mary explained, with dignity.

'Comme moi.' Sven came closer still, his bulk looming hugely. Maybe these innocents could be put to use in his master plan.

In the event, Howard Howard did not arrive early at the Hôtel du Roi. After leaving the Walenska collection, he walked the streets for several hours exuding such an air of manic excitement that two tramps, several prostitutes and a hitman, exiting fast from a job well done, gave him a wide berth. Just before five, he returned to his room where he made the mistake of looking at himself in the communal bathroom mirror. Such a haggard, frantic image looked back at him that he shut his eyes in horror. How could he show himself to Sissie in such a state? How could he introduce himself to his child, who would probably scream with terror and be put off the male sex for life? He decided to take action.

The sky was still dark but the pavements and streets were already filling for the early-morning rush hour when Howard presented himself at a discreet door through which, in the life he now hoped to leave behind, he had often passed. His press on the doorbell was answered by a noise with a questioning note. 'Peanut-butter maker,' whispered Howard, and the door sprang open.

Sissie had fallen asleep enough to have her nightmare. The torso with its bleeding wound had come closer to her, and the screaming, previously anonymous, was now quite clearly issuing from her own mouth. She was also aware that she was hiding under something dark and low and that this whole horrible scene was near the end of a chain of events. Worse still, she was on the edge of remembering the earlier part, which she was quite sure she didn't want to. She stood up to wake herself further and saw, with relief, a grey light coming between the curtains. Soon she would be out of the dark night.

Chapter Thirty-Seven

*In which Sissie is on the Catwalk again and too many Excitements
happen for this or any other Author to deal with.*

N EVER HAD the invitations for a couture show been more highly
prized. Each guest's name was lovingly tied to a gilt chair with
a ribbon of wolfskin. It was already being talked about as the event
of the season. The press, journalists and photographers had been
told by their newspapers to cover the show and cover it well. Beefy
men, pony-tails swinging, duelled with their long lenses for a good
position before they had even been let through the door to the
salon. Sharp-nosed fashion journalists, all dressed in black as if at a
funeral, spiked their pens at each other and used the pointed corners
of their pads to cripple rivals while all the time smiling vivaciously.

The press pressed and so did the clients, the super-rich and the
super-glamorous (not necessarily the same) in their last year's
designer clothes, filled with chatter and gossip, using a bowdlerized
English, like old girls at a school reunion and some of them were
indeed 'old girls' with their wrinkle-removed, taut skin over recently
renovated bodies. Lily Skourou was in the midst of them, mink-dyed
hair coming into its own, the greenish tinge receiving extra
compliments.

Madame B. was there, Sissie's ex-agent, coming to taunt and
defame. Madame Walenska was also there. If Lily carried the aura of
Most Popular Girl in the School, Head Girl and Captain of Lacrosse,
Madame Walenska was High Mistress. People approached her but
circumspectly, no chatter here. She had a role to play, which lent
itself to de haut en bas. Waldo was nowhere to be seen.

As soon as the doors were opened, rich and famous, hacks and photographers alike, shoved their way in. There was a democracy in this crush but the seating plan displayed a rigid hierarchy. The most prestigious position was at the far end of the catwalk where the platform expanded to a bulb and the models were used to doing a special flourish, a twist and turn, even, if the photographers who massed behind these desirable seats bayed loud enough for it, a smile. They had never bayed loud enough for Sissie, although strong men were hoarse at the conclusion of her parade.

Lily sat at the end of the rostrum among a handful of clients whose husbands owned a car company or a bank or a detergent company or sold arms to developing countries for defence purposes. Sometimes there were film stars but not today, as if Sissie were star enough. The fashion writers of the *Herald Tribune*, *Vogue*, the *New York Times*, sat in these seats, as grand as any client and just as important since their words shot approval or disapproval round the world. There were half a dozen important journalists and then Waldo's boyfriend. This was Waldo's boyfriend's day of the year, the cynical might say the number-one reason he wished to be Waldo's boyfriend. He wore a green suit, with a Walenska design label, and his beautiful oval face speared from it like a bud from a stem. How he longed to be interviewed! How the words teetered on the edge of his sensitive tongue! But next to him, elegant, majestic, control-ling, sat Madame Walenska. So he remained silent and consoled himself with the knowledge that he was the most desirable male in the most desirable seating.

But only just. Sebastien and Bianca, she bronze, he golden from their post-Booby party, leant, heads together, just behind Lily. As if touched with the hand of God, thought Mary, gazing at this exciting scene from the hidden spot where she and Ted had been placed by Sven. What a kind man, she thought to herself, taking pity on their urgent need before she had even told him she was Sissie's mother. Then how he had reacted! What emotion. When he had exchanged disbelief for conviction – she had been in tears – he had found them this seat nearer the ceiling than the floor, and assured them they would see everything from there. 'Every last twirl and twiddle and blink,' he'd asserted, grinning enthusiastically. So here they were, hearts pounding, quite ready to do the one little thing he'd requested to help make his job easier.

Heavy curtains hung at the far end of the catwalk, the end where the more humble or, rather, less-privileged guests had been placed. Immediately the other side of the curtains, the chariot waited for its moment of glory. There was a blank then, an emptiness of space before the next room where a scene of frantic hysteria was taking place.

Nor was it the normal frantic hysteria of final preparations before presenting a show to an audience, of models too short, too fat, of seams refusing to lie flat, of shoes that had been made in men's sizes instead of women's. Waldo's collection was always perfectly finished. On time. Before time.

'I need a Voice,' groaned Waldo, as if he had groaned it many times before. He knelt in the middle of the room in a black boiler suit, cut on the bias, as if he was imploring the Almighty, although actually he was checking that Sissie's wolfskin hemline had not been pulled up by her armour.

Sissie stood patiently, wishing that the first part of the show would be over and she could take off her coal scuttle. Behind her, eight other girls, with the pin-heads, broad shoulders and prominent buttocks of top (if not super) models also waited reasonably patiently, considering they had other shows to do afterwards. They were also in wolfskins and armour, Boudicca's sisterhood.

Word was brought to Waldo that everybody in the salon was seated. But still no sign of his Voice. He let fly a scream of reproach. 'Mamuska!' His mother had never let him down. How could she be wrong about this maestro? 'Mamuska!'

'Mama! Mama!' echoed a high-pitched cry.

'Sssh, Petra.' Sissie looked down anxiously at her daughter sitting on a bright shield, sturdy arms and legs spilling over the edge. She was hardly a baby any more and recently over-indulged by Lily.

Another urgent message was brought to Waldo. He made up his mind. 'We will proceed in silence.'

All fashion shows start late but this delay beat the record set in

1994 when a consignment of dyed turkey feathers from Suffolk due to soft-pedal the catwalk had failed to arrive owing to a baggage handlers' strike at Charles de Gaulle. Such was the atmosphere, however, so keen were the audience to view Sissie (Madame B. was keen to see the imposter) plus the Waldo Walenska New Look that nobody left, nobody complained, but the noise of expectancy rose to new heights. When the curtains were slowly drawn back, the whole crowded salon burst into spontaneous applause. So the chariot, Sissie at its helm, slid forward on the catwalk to a rush of enthusiasm – everything Sissie had known before and lost so suddenly.

The lights glared, flared, dazzled. Head up, chin down, keep the coal scuttle at the right angle. *But why this sinking feeling?* Where was the flow, the rapport with her audience? Widen eyes, headlamps beaming forward, part lips, white teeth gleaming, hips forward, buttocks prominent, Petra, eyes amazed, good as gold on the burnished shield she sat upon. Inch by inch the chariot slid along its well-oiled rails, a grand effect, grandly executed, worth the wait, the audience thought, worth the secret.

Sissie enormous, gigantic. Petra in her baby wolfskin. What an image! Motherhood back with a vengeance. Vengeance is mine, saith Sven, crouched at the back of the photographers' bear pit. Why had no one recognized him? Why did no one remember the tragedy of Rudolf's death?

So slowly, hardly moving – hundreds of thousands of francs had gone into this piece of theatre – Boudicca made her stately process amid oohs and aahs and only one grinding of teeth. Sissie felt the triumph of so-far-so-spectacular, but in her head what did she hear but her baby's piping 'Mama! Mama!' and Waldo's wailing 'Mamuska!' These mixed in her head, fragment cries like passing birds, mixing with fragment memories, the memories of nightmare. *Help me, Mother.*

Waldo laid his head on the stiffness of the closed curtain, unable to follow the progress of his brilliant creation. Where was his Voice? He moaned. He groaned. Boudicca's sisterhood would have to push past him, which they would do in just a minute when the chariot reached the turning point, when Sissie descended on her long, long, everlasting long and now stalwart legs. The sisterhood crowded round Waldo, who had his eyes shut. It wasn't every day you saw a mechanical chariot on a catwalk, they thought, and were also glad they didn't have to wear a tin helmet and carry a large baby on a shield in one hand and a spear in another.

Body erect, spear without a quiver at the tip. 'Ssh, Petra,' hissed Sissie, through bared teeth, definitely not a smile. Only a few feet more. At the other end of the room, although Sissie didn't see it, the door handle of the monumental door was cautiously turning. Hardly space to open it against the crush of the audience's back – rapt though they were and therefore more easily pushed. The door was *definitely* opening. But all eyes (apart from Waldo's) were on Sissie and Petra in their chariot.

'Smile! Sissie! Smile!' screamed the photographers, in old-style adulatory demand. 'Sissie est morte!' hissed Madame B. Would the Voice ever have been heard? Waldo could have consoled himself by answering in the negative.

'Mixed military media.' The fashion journalists tried out words before reaching for their lap-top computers. 'Sliding into battle, Waldo Walenska uses Sissie as his spear carrier.' 'Majestic mother-hood, no holds barred . . .' The show was only beginning, of course, but a first line gives a girl confidence.

High above, in their Sven-nest by the lights, Mary and Ted peered down. The scaffolding on which they sat was precarious but the view should have been splendid.

'I wish she wasn't wearing that thing on her head,' whispered Mary. 'I can't see her face.'

'Royalty never make that mistake,' agreed Ted, but then added with sudden urgency, 'Just look at that baby!' Dazed, dazzled, Ted was composed enough nevertheless to work out that the gilded cherub below him was his wife's granddaughter and therefore his step-granddaughter. He could dandle her, give her a piggy-back, buy her a bicycle. It was a miracle, that's all, a bloody miracle. (Despite working in a prison, Ted only swore, even to himself, on special occaions.)

'She must be boiling in that fur,' worried Mary. She didn't say how enormous Sissie's breasts were, simply vast, not at all as they'd been in those photos.

'We mustn't get carried away and forget our duty.'

'No. No.' Ted could see Mary was going to leave it to him. The screwdriver was at the ready, hole identified, light as big as a kettledrum directly over the end of the catwalk. But Sissie had to step out first, that's it, flood her with light, the workman had said, although in these days of remote control, it seemed odd to him. But, then, just look at that chariot! Who was to judge what was odd?

'No, Petra. Sit.' Sissie hung on to Petra's toes with her free thumb, afraid she'd squirm right off her perch . . . Head up! Was it the constriction of her surroundings that made it so difficult to breathe? Surely she wasn't going to have her nightmare here, front stage, in the glare of a hundred per cent public eye. *Just hang on.* One second more and she could get out of the chariot, worst pressure over, twirl and retreat. *Look forward, dare them not to like you.*

The door was open a foot, enough to allow a thin brown-suited figure with American features and discreet fair hair, to slip into the salon. At the same time, Sissie, shield plus baby in hand, reached the end of the catwalk and started, with more enthusiasm than was strictly dignified, to descend from the chariot and Ted pushed the screwdriver in the hole and turned it firmly round and round. Round twirled the screwdriver, and round twirled Sissie, baby and all.

The timing was so perfect that Sven could not resist a bellow of acclaim, lost naturally in all the other bellows of acclaim. (Excluding the jeers of Madame B.) The wolfskin maidens set out on their trail and Waldo was just thinking he dared open his eyes (who needs a Voice?) when there was a wrenching, juddering, falling, crashing, screeching of metallic matter hurtling from the ceiling.

'Mama! Mama!' screamed Petra, or possibly Sissie. Probably both of them together. It was certainly Waldo who, eyes tighter shut than ever, wrenched 'Mamuska!' from his heart. How could she let this happen?

A huge lamp was falling towards Sissie's head, aiming directly at where she and her baby stood as transfixed as cynosures usually are, although in this case it was more because Sissie had entered her nightmare and was screaming, open-mouthed, without a word entering the public domain.

Then the late entrant, not unlike Superman when he was just an unconvincingly suited ordinary chap, leapt through the audience and yelled louder than anything, 'Sugar!' Just once but once was enough, for the model, previously as posed as if she were made of Bakelite in a shop window, snatched her baby off the shield and threw her into safety. (The particular sort of safety to be revealed later.)

Meanwhile, in this same split second, split so many ways, other things were falling as well as the lamp. Two people and a plastic bag, to be exact, a man and a woman, tumbling down from above, too surprised to make a sound. Head over heels and then heels over heads as they heeled for the most prestigious seats. Did Sissie see this upside-down mother? A fleeting glance of scared blue eyes? Not consciously. She felt, however, a shattering clang, as the heavy screwdriver, dropping from Ted's clawing fingers, bounced off her helmeted head. And all the time the lamp descended.

Sissie, baby safe, head ringing, looking as the lamp's huge eye descended. It fitted her vision. Fate, she thought, waiting to get me all these years and in that moment she remembered her father's face, her sister's death and her mother's lunge with the knife. There, in front of her, she saw the awful scene, herself under the table not unlike a helmet, while the Eye of God descended. She would wait for it with relief, resignation, thankfulness. *Why should she survive such a holocaust?*

'Ha! Ha!' trumpeted Sven, still in the same split second. 'Rudolf is remembered! Rudolf is avenged!' Since pandemonium was reigning by now, he could have trumpeted all he liked and no one would have noticed.

But, as it happened, he had spoken too soon, for the man in the brown suit – who was, of course, Howard – suddenly launched himself like a jet-propelled rocket over a couple of lensers who still barred the way to his beloved darling Sissie, and, in a flying rugger tackle which would have brought a cheer from supporters of the All Blacks even when performed by an American, caught Sissie round the waist and pushed her out of danger. Her helmet, released from her head, bounced along the catwalk like a cannonball until it reached the back of Madame B.'s exiting legs and made them exit even faster.

The lamp fell, hitting the grounded shield fair and square and making a reverberating 'dong' as if announcing a giant's dinner-time.

Just behind, the two falling people also hit the ground but, luckily for them, they fell on a pile of minks, discarded in the anticipatory heat of the long delay. They fell together and found, resting there already, their granddaughter, in a very good mood after such an exciting adventure.

And on the catwalk: 'Sissie. Sugar,' said Howard gently. They were crouched together with the wolfskin girls crowded round them and in less than a trice an ever-enlarging circle of photographers. The journalists, however, stayed in or near their seats. Frankly, it was difficult to find words to describe what was going on. What was it about Sissie that produced such drama?

Sissie could have told them. She knew it all now, although she had only been two years old. This stranger with the shock of hair had saved her so that must be Fate too. 'Sissie,' whispered Howard again. But she still did not recognize him partly because she didn't want to be the sort of heroine whose problems are solved in the arms of a young man and partly because his wig and make-up did not fully disguise his forest face of rough handling and deprivation.

While Sissie fell into the most important memory of her life and teetered on the edge of another, Sven, her enemy, who had done more to help her than anyone – that falling lamp had achieved in a second what years of therapy would have needed – stood stupendously alone. His face turned from purple to black, all the more dramatic against his yellow hair. Reverentially, with Samurai calm, he drew a slim object that glittered from his inside pocket, and aimed it at his heart. But before he could press the tip into his Valentino silk shirt, his concentration was broken by an exasperated cry.

'My heel!' cried Bianca. 'However did you get hold of that?'

Sven did not deign to answer that he had picked it up from the floor where it had fallen from Bianca's bag during all the scuffle. The heel that had killed Rudolf should kill him too. Once again he lined it up for self-croak purpose but this time a bony golden hand dashed it to the ground and there, behind the hand, was Sebastien. The two men stared at each other, as people with a shared history.

'Well,' said Bianca, picking up the heel like a tidying housewife and putting it in her pocket. 'You two have obviously got something to say to each other.' She sighed, but not as someone who had accepted defeat. Taking hold of a man on either side, she led them, peering across at each other yet unresistant, towards the door. 'I have a lunch reservation at the Ritz. Doubtless, it can be extended to three.'

At this point the unhappiest person in the whole salon was Waldo Walenska. Even Madame Walenska had been able to appreciate the living theatre for it was the sort of thing that happened in her childhood and, besides, she had the good sense to suspect that her son's name would make the headlines in all the newspapers. Furthermore, she had never been totally convinced by the wolfskins as individual items. But Waldo, poor Waldo, short-sighted Waldo, cried, his tears falling to his clothes where the models had dumped them as they dashed off to the next show.

Life must go on. Soon the press went too, writers and lensers alike. There would almost certainly be nothing as exciting as that for the rest of the day but you could never be sure. After all, no one had died or even been injured. The one thing it had proved was that a mink coat was more than a status symbol.

The clients were less sure. They had liked the look of that slinky fake fur, of that iridescent armour. After a while, they mounted the catwalk themselves and found their way to the room where stood the racks of exquisite clothes. Madame Walenska, wiping her son's tears on the way, followed them. All might be very well indeed. Drama can be bad for business but it can also be stimulating. These women, reunited with their life-saving minks, looked highly stimulated as they whizzed the clothes along the racks with rapacious appreciation. This was at least as much fun as squeezing into uncomfortable chairs and applauding horny-shouldered models. 'Waldo! You're a genius!' cried one, not noticing that the genius wasn't present and very soon he was. Even Lily came, having lost the battle to wrest Petra from a strange woman who'd dropped from the sky and who insisted that she was the baby's grandmother.

'Kyrie eleison, Waldo dear, it is a triumph. But I can't think what possessed you to put that great lumpy ex-model on the catwalk. And the fat baby too. Just not your style, cher Waldo. The young, you must agree, are much more appealing.' So fickle are the rich. 'Moreover, if I may ask,' Lily continued with even more vitality, 'where was the Voice for which we were all so expectant?'

This question Waldo could not answer. At least not till the end of the day.

Chapter Thirty-Eight

In which we may Enjoy an unusually Happy Ending.

S ISSIE STILL sat on the catwalk in Howard's arms. Shocked, alarmed, reborn, it was hardly surprising that she could not recognize her lost husband. Perhaps she needed a blue butterfly as big as a hand fluttering over his head.

The memory of their romantic coming together gave Howard an idea for a form of persuasion that Sissie could not deny. He put his hand into his pocket.

'Oh! Oh!' Sissie sat up with immediate recognition. 'My original pearly tooth!' Tears sprang into her eyes. 'Howard, darling, Howard!' And she clasped him to her.

The force of her embrace was such, such a loving stroking and a hugging and a tugging, that Howard's wig slipped and slid and ended up in Sissie's hand. Between laughing and crying, she dangled it on high. 'Oh, Howard, Howard, the first time we met, you were wearing a wig, too. But then you had some hair under it!'

'I suspect you're a little concussed.' Seeing her rolling, tear-filled eyes, Howard spoke tenderly, smoothed her hand, calmed her brow, which still had a runnel along it where the heavy helmet had pressed.

'I think I am concussed,' said Sissie. 'You see I saw . . .' Words hardly seemed adequate for the vision of hell, followed so quickly by heaven.

'I know. I know.' Howard did not know but he sat her up more comfortably, placed her like a large doll within the hard circlet of his arms. Thus secured, she saw Mary and Ted, with Petra in Mary's arms, negotiate the obsolete chariot and come towards her along the catwalk.

Mary, quite an ordinary middle-aged woman, was remarkable for only one thing: the hat she wore. It came low over her wide blue eyes, layer upon layer of feathers, circling the crown, circling the brim, as if her head had been wrapped in a shimmering rainbow.

'My hat!' exclaimed Sissie.

Howard stared. Did he remember Sissie wearing such a hat? Composed of what were clearly illegally exported feathers?

'The hat I sent to my mother,' continued Sissie.

'Your mother?' questioned Howard, who was becoming aware that he had a lot of catching up to do after his months in the forest.

Petra, scrambling out of Mary's arms, ejected herself onto the floor and began to crawl towards Sissie who was drying her eyes on Howard's wig.

'Mama! Mama!' squealed Petra eagerly.

'US Property,' said Howard, removing the wig, although he did not replace it on his head. Sissie loved him. He had no need of artifice. And now there was this child, the cutest child he'd ever seen. Howard got down on his hands and knees and began to crawl towards his daughter.

'Oh, look.' Ted nudged Mary. 'That's the man on board ship who was wearing a . . . you know.'

'Sshh,' admonished Mary. 'He must be Sissie's husband.'

It was all too much for everybody, this ridiculous coming together, and Mary, just before she reached Sissie, side-stepped off the catwalk to where the helmet had bounced and rolled and lay discarded. She picked it up, slipped the handle over her arm and tried to approach her daughter once more.

'A very useful coal scuttle,' she told Sissie approvingly. 'Ted and I have a little fireplace where it would sit nicely.'

'Take it please!' cried Sissie, and Petra's continuing 'Mama! Mama!' as, avoiding the large man in her path, she crossed the last few yards to her mother's bosom, would have to do for the wild 'Mother! Mother!' Sissie felt somewhere in her heart. Besides, the brutal images in her memory could not be wiped out in a second. Mary was right to pick up the coal scuttle and hold that close rather than to try to touch her daughter.

Petra could do that, snuggling in confidently, staring up, with a challenging expression, at the man in the boots who stood above them. This was not the moment for an introduction there either. They were like actors, who, although sensitive to their roles, had not yet found confidence enough to tackle the dialogue.

Mary knew that at some point she would need to cry out, 'I am your mother,' but for now the coal scuttle would have to do. Ted might have spoken about his place in the matter too. 'I am her husband as of the day before yesterday.' But he hardly liked to intrude.

Howard, resurrected, also could have provided a point of information. 'I was kidnapped in the forest and might have died except that I lived and when I walked out I was saved by Mo, who sort of tried to rape you, Sissie, honey.' But that seemed inappropriate and he didn't have the energy left over from supporting Sissie to separate the wheat from the chaff.

'I guess my super-model days are over,' said Sissie, quite calmly.

'I'll say.' Howard frowned at the chariot disapprovingly.

Sissie stood up, her huge height putting her well out of reach. Petra sat at her shoulder like a bird in a tree.

'Just like her father,' murmured Mary for Ted's benefit, because she could tell him such things without the world turning black.

'Such memories! Such memories!' cried Sissie suddenly, so perhaps she had overheard Mary's remark. 'How can I live with such memories!' Her mode was rhetorical but Howard took a firm stand in front of her.

'You've been looking for those memories your whole life, sugar. So don't go denying them now.' It was clear enough to all of them that now she could go forward with her own story.

'Fortunata,' murmured Sissie.

The maid to the Grand Luxe Suite in the Hôtel des Artistes tried yet again to get in to make the bed. It had been the same all day. Locked. Occupied. It seemed time to get the housekeeper. These days you never knew what might be going on the other side of a locked door.

The housekeeper had just taken off her shoes and was examining her misshapen feet. She was a conscientious woman but it seemed hard to have to put them on again so quickly. On the other hand, permanently locked doors tended to reveal dramas for which she had a taste.

'J'arrive, Fleur,' she said, valiantly cramming in her toes.

The two women opened the door very carefully and were not surprised to find the bedroom only lit by one small lamp: it was often the case on such occasions. They tiptoed, metaphorically speaking since the housekeeper's feet hurt far too much for such an exercise, towards the bed, fearful of the dark spread of blood, of a knife fallen on the floor.

They were not to be totally disappointed. A corpse did lie silently on the bed but this was no victim, no murderee. He was an old man, hair sparsely white, skin as thin as parchment and speckled as a thrush's egg. His black eyes were open in their wriggle of aged skin but a film of tissue veiled their gaze. In general, the wasted body was straight enough for a coffin except that one arm hung off the bed, its fingers open and a bony forefinger pointing downwards.

Fleur crouched down in the gloom while the housekeeper watched with interest. A knife could indicate a suicide at least. Or perhaps there would be a tragic note.

'Eh bien, Madame.' Fleur sat back disappointedly on her heels. 'It's only a book.'